Prepositions in English Grammars
until 1801 – with a Survey
of the Western European Background

For Jean

Tom Lundskær-Nielsen

Prepositions in English Grammars until 1801 – with a Survey of the Western European Background

University Press of Southern Denmark
Modern Humanities Research Association
2011

© The author and University Press of Southern Denmark
and Modern Humanities Research Association 2011
RASK Supplement Vol. 19
RASK is an international scholarly journal which publishes articles and reviews pertaining to the field of language and communication. RASK is edited by members of the Institute of Language and Communication at the University of Southern Denmark in collaboration with an international Advisory Board.

Printed by Specialtrykkeriet Viborg A/S
Cover Design by Donald Jensen

ISSN 1395-7236
ISBN 978 87 7674 565 3

Printed with grant support from:
University of Southern Denmark
Moth-Lunds Fond
Modern Humanities Research Association

University Press of Southern Denmark
Campusvej 55
DK-5230 Odense M
Phone: +45 6615 7999
Fax: +45 6615 8126
www.universitypress.dk

Modern Humanities Research Association
1 Carlton House Terrace
London
SW1Y 5AF
U.K.
www.mhra.org.uk

Distribution in the United States and Canada:
International Specialized Book Services
5804 NE Hassalo Street
Portland, OR 97213-3644 USA
www.isbs.com

Distribution in the United Kingdom:
Gazelle
White Cross Mills
Hightown
Lancaster
LA1 4XS
U.K.
www.gazellebooks.co.uk

Contents

Preface	9
Introduction	11
Chapter I – Antiquity	25
1. The Greeks	25
2. The Romans	36
Chapter II – The Middle Ages	59
Chapter III – The Renaissance	87
Chapter IV – English Grammars 1586-1801	97
Introduction	97
Individual grammatical works	103
(i) The Sixteenth Century	103
William Bullokar	103
Paul Greaves	106
(ii) The Seventeenth Century	107
Alexander Gill	107
John Hewes	109
Charles Butler	111
Ben Jonson	113
Joshua Poole	116
Francis Lodowyck	119
John Wallis	122
Jeremiah Wharton	127
William Walker	128
George Dalgarno	130
John Wilkins	134
Thomas Lye	139

Mark Lewis	141
Christopher Cooper	145
Guy Miege	147
John Locke	150
William Clare	152
Joseph Aickin	155
A. Lane	157
(iii) The Eighteenth Century	161
Richard Johnson	161
Charles Gildon & John Brightland	164
James Greenwood	170
Michael Maittaire	173
Thomas Sheridan	177
Hugh Jones	178
Daniel Duncan	179
John Collyer	182
Thomas Dilworth	185
John Kirkby	186
Benjamin Martin	188
James Harris	190
Anne Fisher	195
James and John Gough	200
Samuel Johnson	202
Anselm Bayly	204
Joseph Priestley	208
James Buchanan	212
Robert Lowth	214
John Ash	219
James Elphinston	221
William Ward	228
Daniel Fenning	235
John Fell	238
George Neville Ussher	243
John Horne Tooke	245
J. Wilson	252
Lindley Murray	255

(iv) One Nineteenth-century Grammar	261
John Dalton	261
Chapter V – Summary	267
Notes	279
Bibliography	289
Index of Names	303

Preface

The inspiration for this book stems from my previous study of prepositions, *Prepositions in Old and Middle English* (1993). Although that specifically centred on the syntax and semantics of a small group of English prepositions up to 1400 and far less on prepositions as a word class, it kindled my interest in exploring the latter aspect in greater detail, but this time with an initial survey of the Western European background and with particular focus on the presentation of this word class in the first two centuries or so of English grammar writing. So where the first book may be said to deal with historical linguistics, the present one is a contribution to the history of linguistics.

The period of germination was admittedly a long one, interrupted by a wide range of other tasks, but the topic was somewhere at the back of my mind throughout this period and the work on it gathered momentum in recent years when a few periods of research leave allowed me to concentrate on both the background research and the writing process.

I would like to pay tribute, in particular, to my former supervisor and long-time friend Hans Frede Nielsen who, in his capacity as Chair of the Committee for Research Publications at the Institute of Language and Communication at the University of Southern Denmark, has over the years given me much encouragement and displayed angelic patience in his wait for the finished product, for which I am deeply grateful to him and to the rest of the Committee. He has also read and copy-edited the typescript and suggested various changes, which I have almost invariably complied with. I owe a great debt to Knud Sørensen, who was kind enough to read two versions of the entire book and saved me from a number of errors. Further thanks are due to Dilwyn Knox and Anna Wegener for help with some of the translations of the Italian quotations in Chapter III.

I am obliged to the University Press of Southern Denmark and its director Martin Lindø Westergaard for publishing the book. The sections on John Wallis, John Wilkins, John Locke, James Harris, William Ward and John Horne Tooke are based on a much shorter publication *Some Views of Prepositions in 17th and 18th Century England*, which appeared as part of the series 'Pre-Publications of the English Department of Odense University' in 2000. I was glad to be allowed to integrate some amended sections from that early version into the book.

I am indebted to the Moth-Lund Fund in Copenhagen for a generous grant towards the publication costs; to Claire Thomson, Head of the Department of Scandinavian Studies, UCL, for a departmental contribution to the same end; and especially to The Modern Humanities Research Association who not only agreed to cover half the production costs but also offered to make this a joint publication with them.

The major part of the book has been written at, or with frequent loans from, Cambridge University Library, and I would like to take this opportunity to thank the staff of that wonderful institution for their unfailingly friendly assistance.

Finally, I owe my greatest debt and gratitude – as well as my heartfelt apologies for all the time taken up with this project – to my wife, Jean. Not only has she read through the whole typescript and made some helpful comments, but her support and endurance during the process of writing – with only very occasional expressions of exasperation – have made it possible at last to bring it to its conclusion. For that reason, the book is dedicated to her. Whether it has been worth the effort is, as always in these cases, for others to judge, and all remaining errors are mine alone.

Tom Lundskær-Nielsen
Cambridge, June 2011

Introduction

It may seem odd to some to choose what is generally regarded as a 'minor' word class (or 'part of speech') as the subject for a study in a historical perspective. Such a feeling may be exacerbated by the fact that the study does not go beyond 1801, well before the time when prepositions began to attract closer attention from language scholars.

Indeed, as late as three decades ago, a prominent linguist saw fit to complain, in a ground-breaking article, that '[p]eople seem never to have taken prepositions seriously ... They deny that the category "preposition" has any real intrinsic syntactic interest other than as an annoying little surface peculiarity' (Jackendoff 1973:345). If this sounds like an exasperated outburst, it was in part justified at the time. Until then, prepositions had overwhelmingly been treated as a class that was clearly 'inferior' to, and hence far less important than, the 'major' or 'open' classes of noun, verb, adjective and adverb, and others if we go further back in the grammatical tradition. Within the generative framework obsessed with 'deep structure', which dominated linguistic analysis in the days of Jackendoff's grievance, prepositions were often taken to be mere 'case markers', again following a long tradition. This was particularly so in Fillmore's (1968) starting signal for what became known as 'case grammar', where prepositions are put on a par with case affixes in the following passage:

> The 'universal' character of the base rules is kept intact by the assumption that prepositions, postpositions, and case affixes – semantically relevant or not – are all in fact realizations of the same underlying element, say K (for *Kasus*). We may regard all of the case categories as therefore rewritten as K + NP. (Fillmore 1968:33)

Even if this was an 'assumption', it informed the whole article, in which the 'node' representing prepositions in the tree diagrams is 'K', as well as much of the general linguistic climate at the time. But this view was soon to be challenged, mainly due to Jackendoff's (1977) full-scale presentation of X-bar syntax (building on Chomsky's (1970) earlier suggestions for dealing with headed constructions), where prepositions (P) are treated as a major syntactic category, parallel with nouns (N), verbs (V) and adjectives (A). This analysis soon caught on and influenced a whole generation. It also entered into textbook treatments of syntax, particularly but not exclusively those dealing with English (cf. Jaworska 1999). However, the question of heads is not uncontroversial, and this applies especially to prepositions as heads of prepositional phrases (PPs), which in many ways is a reversal of the long-held view that the prepositional complement, rather than the preposition, was the central and dominant part of a PP. The notion of heads is further discussed in a seminal article by Zwicky (1985), and there is a useful critical survey of these aspects of syntax in Matthews (2007, for prepositions especially pp. 49-55). For these reasons alone, it would be difficult to echo Jackendoff's former complaint nowadays.

If we go a step further back, it could be argued that some of the germs for the expansion of the role of prepositions in modern times are rooted in Jespersen's treatment of 'particles', though in many ways he summarised a view that was quite frequent in English grammars of the preceding centuries. The classic exposition of Jespersen's position on this is in *The Philosophy of Grammar* (1924:87-90) – and this is the site always referred to – but it is found in embryo already in the second volume of *A Modern English Grammar* (1965:II:10-11) from 1914 and appears later as a short textbook overview in Jespersen (1933:68-9). In *The Philosophy of Grammar*, Jespersen argues that adverbs, prepositions, conjunctions and interjections should not be treated as separate classes on a par with 'substantives, adjectives, pronouns and verbs', as they are in 'nearly all grammars' (by which he must mean modern grammars) since this 'grossly exaggerate[s]' the 'dissimilarities between these words' and therefore obscures their 'evident similarities'. For this reason he wants to 'revert to the old terminology by which these four classes are treated as one called "particles"' (1924:87). It should be said that Jespersen is keenly aware that he is not saying anything new, but is harking back to (one line of) an older tradition within English grammar writing.

Jespersen's argument runs through a few phases. First he compares 'adverbs' and 'prepositions' in examples such as 'put your cap on' and 'put your cap on your head'. In the first one, *on* is usually said to be an adverb as it lacks a complement, while it is a preposition in the second by virtue of having a complement ('your head'). This, Jespersen contends (and he provides other similar examples), is parallel to intransitive and transitive verbs, respectively, cf. 'he plays' versus 'he plays the piano', with a direct object in the second version, but in both instances the lexeme PLAY is classified as a verb. Secondly, he compares *after* in 'after his arrival' with its use in 'after he had arrived'. Here Jespersen thinks that there is no reason to call the first *after* a preposition and the second one an adverb, since the only difference between them is that the first has 'a substantive' (or rather, a noun phrase) and the second one 'a sentence (or a clause)' as its complement. He therefore claims that the 'so-called conjunction is really … a sentence preposition' and that consequently there is no need to 'recognize conjunctions as "a part of speech"'. In fact, he postulates 'the essential identity of prepositions and conjunctions' (1924:89). He brings it all together by comparing three kinds of verb complementation with three different uses of *since*, which belong together in vertical sequence:

(1) I *believe* in God.   They have lived happily ever *since*.
(2) I *believe* your words.   They have lived happily *since* their marriage.
(3) I *believe* (that) you are right.   They have lived happily *since* they were married.

In (1) *believe* is (used as) an intransitive verb, in (2) a transitive verb with a noun phrase as its complement (= direct object), and in (3) ditto with a whole clause as its complement (= direct object). In the right-hand column *since* (in traditional terms) is an adverb in (1), a preposition in (2) and a conjunction in (3), so if *believe* can be a verb in all three examples, why not claim that all three examples of *since* belong to the same class, i.e. 'particle'?

On the surface, this reasoning may seem intriguing – and it has certainly influenced other linguists – but does it stand up to scrutiny, and what has actually been gained? We may have become more aware of certain common features between some of the traditional classes, but it is not difficult to spot a number of problems. First, the parallel with verbs is not very fortunate. The possibility of taking an object or not is not the only criterion for 'verbness'. In general, verbs have certain features in common, such as conjugation, being tense markers and having syntactic relations to other elements in a clause. By comparison, adverbs, prepositions and conjunctions have few things in common and apart from the adverbs derived from adjectives, often marked by the *-ly* suffix, the form of these word classes is invariable (though adverbs can have comparison). An appeal to transitivity of verbs as a parallel is therefore not a strong argument for treating the three classes as one.

Secondly, Jespersen seems to apply his examples to the postulated classes without considering the possibility of exceptions, but in actual fact it is only some items in each class that can be compared in this way. For example, among the adverbs the argument is only relevant for those that in form can 'double' as prepositions (*at, in, on, with*, etc.), but not for all those with the *-ly* suffix (e.g. *slowly*) or many of the others (e.g. *here, now, soon*, etc.) – though we shall shortly see an attempt to treat the latter type as prepositions. What have they got in common with prepositions and conjunctions? Adverbs are a particular problem since they have to be defined in this context in a purely negative way as items that *cannot* take a complement, whether a noun (phrase) or a clause, just as intransitive verbs cannot (normally) take an object. Furthermore, very few words allow a three-way comparison like *since* above. To make sense, the superordinate class of 'particles' must be based on a two-step process: a comparison of adverbs and prepositions, and of prepositions and conjunctions (in whichever order). A straight comparison between adverbs and conjunctions could not possibly show enough common ground to justify conflating these two classes. Jespersen therefore appears to say that if A (adverbs) equals B (prepositions) and B equals C (conjunctions), then A equals C. This may hold in mathematics and logic, but as soon as we are dealing with word classes that are notoriously heterogeneous, we run into trouble. There is simply too much dissimilarity between any two of these classes – let alone all three – for a conflation of them to yield any obvious advantage and, as we have seen, it is difficult to justify it in terms of definitions.

It was mentioned above that in setting up the class of particles Jespersen reverted to a much older tradition, but he in turn inspired later linguists to adopt some of his proposals. Let us briefly look at the two most comprehensive grammars of (British) English since Jespersen's *A Modern English Grammar*. The first one is *A Grammar of Contemporary English* (1972) by Quirk et al.,[1] later expanded into the even larger *A Comprehensive Grammar of the English Language* (1985) by the same four authors (henceforth Quirk et al.). In the first version (1972:44-50), the authors distinguish ten parts of speech (also called 'form classes' or 'word-classes'),[2] viz. (a) the 'open classes' noun, adjective, adverb, verb, and (b) the 'closed system items' article, demonstrative, pronoun, preposition, conjunction, interjection. The names of these classes are said to be 'traditional' (1972:49), but one class stands out: demonstrative (*that, this*). This is not usually granted separate status, and if that is curious, it is even stranger that this fact is not further commented on or justified. Indeed, the later section on 'Pronouns' (1972:203-25) has a sub-section on 'Demonstrative pronouns' (1972:217-18), where the items (*this, that, these, those*) are referred to as precisely that, with no indication that they constitute a separate class. One can only wonder if the term appears under parts of speech purely by mistake. It is also noteworthy that there is no general section on 'conjunctions', which are clearly recognised as a word class. Instead, they are divided into 'coordinating conjunctions' (or 'coordinators') (1972:550) and 'subordinators' ('or more fully subordinating conjunctions') (1972:727) and dealt with separately under coordination and subordination, respectively.

Compared with this, the chapter on 'Prepositions and prepositional phrases' (1972:297-337) presents a fairly traditional treatment of this class, but one aspect in particular deserves to be mentioned. One of the sub-sections is entitled 'Prepositions and prepositional adverbs', and a 'prepositional adverb' is defined as 'a particle which shares the form, but not the syntactic status, of a preposition', i.e. it can appear 'without the addition of a prepositional complement' (1972:305). This is exemplified by the following two sentences:

(4) A car drove past the door (where *past* is a preposition)
(5) A car drove past (where *past* is a prepositional adverb – without a complement)

It should be emphasised that other factors play a part in this distinction, e.g. the presence or absence of stress, and that in some cases a complement cannot be added, or as the authors put it, 'there is no equivalent preposition for the adverbs *over* and *off* in the examples: 'At last the war's *over*' and 'He's going *off* on his travels again'. But as far as terminology is concerned, that is not all. In the section on 'Phrasal and prepositional verbs' (1972:811-19), the terms 'adverbial particle' and 'prepositional particle' both occur, respectively, in the examples 'John called *up* the man' and 'John called *on* the man', and we are told that with 'phrasal and prepositional verbs' it is 'convenient to refer to both the adverbial and prepositional element as "particle"' (1972:812), So 'particle' is apparently the preferred term when the item is closely attached to the verb. We shall see in Chapter IV below that this problem is of some concern to many of the English grammarians before 1800 and practice varies as to whether they regard *past* in (5) above as a preposition or an adverb, or indeed a particle. For Quirk et al. it is clearly an adverb, albeit of a particular kind, but with the introduction of 'particle' they appear to muddy the waters somewhat.

Thirteen years later, in *A Comprehensive Grammar of the English Language* (1985), Quirk et al. have had a rethink about the word classes and now use this term as their heading rather than 'parts of speech' as found in (1972). The 'open classes' remain the same with one exception: the category of 'verb' is here confined to 'full verb', but the 'closed classes' have changed significantly. Three of them have survived (preposition, pronoun, conjunction), but two new verbal classes ('modal verb' and 'primary verb', the latter denoting what is often called 'auxiliary verb') have been added and the former class of 'demonstrative' (which, as we saw, was problematic) has been replaced by 'determiner', under which term the 'article' is now included as well as some former demonstrative and indefinite pronouns, such as *that, every, some* (1985:67). As a matter of fact, these items apparently remain 'pronouns', too, for this is indeed what they are called in the chapter dealing with pronouns (1985:333-92). Thus there seems to be some confusion between classes and functions. Finally, there are in addition 'two lesser categories', viz. numerals (consisting of cardinal and ordinal numbers) and interjections, which no longer have the same status as the main classes.

There are also alterations to the treatment of prepositions in (1985). In (1972) there is no discussion of items that can function as – and, in word class terms, belong to – both prepositions and conjunctions, other than the paragraph on 'Adjunct and conjunction' (1972:272-4), but the adjuncts in question are mostly prepositional phrases (PPs) and not prepositions. In (1985) we find a paragraph on 'Prepositions, conjunctions, and verbs' (1985:659-61) where items such as *after*, *as*, *since* and *until* are discussed together with present and past participles. Quirk et al. are careful to separate the three functions that these items may have and use the following three sets of examples as illustration (1985:660; their emphasis):

(6a) *Considering his age*, he has made excellent progress in his studies.
(6b) *Given the present conditions*, I think she's done rather well.

(7a) *Considering the conditions in the office*, she thought it wise not to apply for the job.
(7b) *Given the chance*, I'd do it again.

(8a) *Considering that he is rather young*, his parents have advised him not to apply.
(8b) *Given that this work was produced under particularly difficult circumstances*, the result is better than could be expected.

Here the authors state categorically that the participles function as (and presumably *are*) prepositions in (6), participles, i.e. verbs, in (7) and conjunctions in (8). In the same place they also distinguish between *when* (conjunction only), *after* (conjunction *or* preposition) and *by* (preposition only), as in 'when speaking', 'after speaking' and 'by speaking', respectively, but you cannot have *by* in front of a finite clause (*by she spoke; cp. *when/after* she spoke) or *when* before a noun phrase (*when her speech; cp. *after/by* her speech).

The distinction between prepositions and prepositional adverbs in (1972) has changed slightly in (1985). Items like *across* in 'She walked *across*' (cf. the previous example 'A car drove *past*') are still 'prepositional adverbs', but *up* in 'She looked *up* the word' is now an 'adverb particle' (cp. 'adverbial particle' earlier, which – given the general distinction between 'adverb' (a category) and 'adverbial' (a function) – was admittedly an unfortunate term). The term 'particle' is thus preserved from (1972) and under the heading 'Multi-word verbs' (a term that the authors find it necessary to justify) we are informed that the 'words which follow the lexical verb in expressions like *drink up, dispose of,* and *get away with* are morphologically invariable, and will be given the neutral designation *particles*' (1985:1150). So in a way 'particle' neutralises the choice between adverb and preposition in such cases. We may finally note that 'postposed prepositions' in (1972:300), e.g. in 'Which house did you leave the car *at*' or 'He's impossible to work *with*', are called 'deferred prepositions' in (1985:663).

When Quirk et al.'s *A Comprehensive Grammar of the English Language* appeared in 1985 (1779 pages long, whereas (1972) is a 'mere' 1120 pages), it was hard to imagine that it would be matched, let alone surpassed, for either length or detailed argument and exemplification within two decades, but this in fact happened with the publication of Huddleston & Pullum's *The Cambridge Grammar of the English Language* (2002) (1842 pages, henceforth H&P).[3] In many ways this work marks more of a break with the established grammatical tradition, for which the parts of speech (or 'lexical categories') will serve as a good example. To be sure, H&P (2002:22) have nine classes like the more influential grammars towards the end of the eighteenth century, such as Murray's *English Grammar* from 1795 (see Chapter IV), but some of them are radically different from earlier presentations. Only six of the time-honoured parts of speech survive (noun, verb, adjective, adverb, preposition, interjection), and to these are added 'determinative', 'subordinator' and 'coordinator'. The traditional class of pronouns is here relegated to 'a subclass of nouns', and the previous category of 'conjunctions' is split up into the two separate categories of 'subordinators' and 'coordinators'. However, the membership of the two latter classes is very limited; coordinators basically comprise *and, or, but, nor*, while the group of 'subordinators' is much reduced from the traditional 'subordinating conjunctions' and only seem to include *that, for, to, whether, if,* and of these *for* just in the '*for* X to + inf.' construction, *to* in the role of the traditional infinitive marker, and *if* when it is 'equivalent to *whether*' (2002:22, 600, 951-6, 1181ff.). The class of adverbs is also greatly reduced in number and consists largely of the items that have the *-ly* inflection plus a few others such as *soon, so, too*, etc., and articles are no longer a part of speech, but members of the new category called 'determinatives' along with some items that used to be called, for example, demonstrative and indefinite pronouns, such as *this, that, some, all, every, each*.

So what has happened to all the 'discarded' adverbs and conjunctions in this extensive re-categorisation? Broadly speaking, they have 'become' prepositions in what is a vastly extended category. As the authors say, '[m]any of traditional grammar's adverbs and most of its subordinating conjunctions ... are here *analysed as prepositions*' (2002:58; my emphasis). However, like other attempts to redistribute lexical items, this one is not unproblematic either. The authors concede that the term 'preposition' for such an expanded category is not only 'ambiguous'; it is also said to be 'by no means ideal for our purposes' (2002:602). It is obvious that the conflation of most of the traditional adverbs and (subordinating) conjunctions with prepositions, as well as some of the arguments for this category shift, owes much to Jespersen (1924), though this is not overtly acknowledged.[4] It should be said at once, though, that the discussion of category assignment is far more detailed and sophisticated than Jespersen's and that the perceived problems are not swept under the carpet. Nevertheless, many readers (including the present writer) will no doubt regard some of the conclusions with a certain degree of unease. However, this is not the place to enter into a full discussion of the meticulous arguments put forward, so I shall confine myself to presenting a flavour of them.

Many of the step-by-step arguments in the preposition chapter (2002:597-661) seem quite persuasive and there are comparisons with several other word classes, for example with transitive versus intransitive verbs *à la* Jespersen. The overall conclusion is therefore not as easy to dismiss as Jespersen's much more superficial analysis, but for the readers it is a question of how far they are prepared to follow H&P. For instance, it is one thing to accept items that can potentially take a (prepositional) complement – whether they do so or not in concrete examples – as prepositions, as in 'The owner is not *in* (the house)', and there is a long list of such words (2002:613). It is another also to want to include items that can *never* take such a complement, but this is precisely what H&P propose. One group of these consists of compounds composed of *here/there/where* + a preposition (*at, by, from, in, of, on, to, with*), such as *herewith, thereby, whereof*, etc., and in some cases with *-abouts* as the second element, e.g. *thereabouts* (note the *-s* ending). They are claimed to be prepositions for no other apparent reason than the purely negative one that they *cannot* occur with an 'NP complement', for *not* doing so, we are told, 'is not a property found just occasionally with one or two prepositions, or only with marginal terms', but one 'found systematically throughout a wide range of the most central and typical prepositions in the language' (*ibid.*).

Also included among prepositions are some words 'belonging to the spatial domain that occur as goal complement with such verbs as *come* and *go*, and also, in most cases, as locative complement to *be*', e.g. go/be *ashore*; take X/be *downstairs*; come/be *home*; put X/be *indoors*. It is argued that '*be* does not licence adverbs in *-ly* as complement' and that the italicised words 'cannot reasonably be said to "modify" the verb' (2002:614), but even so, are they therefore prepositions? Again, this can only be postulated by means of a negative definition. The same applies to a number of words divided into seven subgroups, e.g. (to take a representative from each) *away, hence, east, back, downhill, underground, upwards*. It is not possible here to go into the details of all seven subgroups, but it is notable that H&P rely heavily on a combination of historical, morphological and semantic arguments where syntactic ones are harder to employ. Thus, for instance, we are informed that the words in subgroup (i) (*abroad, abreast, adrift, away*, etc.) 'contain the prefix *a-*, which originates historically in a form of the preposition *on*' (*ibid.*). This is true, but how relevant is it for their new-found status as prepositions in a synchronic description? Similarly, how important is it that the words in the last three subgroups morphologically are compounds? Semantic considerations include the division of 'prepositions' into spatial and non-spatial terms. While most of the items we have examined belong to the former group, a few 'belong to the temporal domain', viz. the simple words *now, then, when* and the compounds *afterwards, beforehand, henceforth* and the rare *thenceforth*.[5] Although it is mentioned that the first three are the 'temporal counterparts of spatial *here, there,* and *where*', the authors admit that the 'case for analysing single-word temporal terms as prepositions *is weaker than with spatial* *ones*, since they occur predominantly as adjunct rather than complement' (2002:616; my emphasis).

H&P's analysis of prepositions as a category is certainly one of the most detailed and scrupulous to date and it provides much food for thought about the criteria for assigning words to this or other classes. It is also true to say that, as we have seen, they do not always seem happy with their own conclusions, be that the general term 'prepositions' or the membership of certain items. Readers have to decide for themselves how far they are prepared to 'swallow' the arguments put forward. The history of linguistics has demonstrated again and again that what you gain in economy in one area, you are likely to lose in, for example, clarity of definitions, and I believe that this charge can brought against H&P when it comes to their concept of prepositions. It is very difficult to come up with a meaningful definition of prepositions that will allow the inclusion of a number of the words that are labelled as such in the chapter, and in my view H&P fail to do so. This is particularly true of the words that, unlike the central prepositions, are incapable of combining with an NP complement. Despite a variety of arguments of different kinds, the assignment of these to the class of prepositions is not very convincing and is at times done mainly on negative rather than on positive grounds.

It would perhaps be unfair to claim that this treatment is tantamount to devising a syllogism with a negation in each of the two premises, for the argumentation is much more subtle than that, but it is nevertheless a comparison that readers could be forgiven for contemplating. Let us say that prepositions, at least as understood in 'traditional grammar', proto-typically govern, or *can* govern, a complement of whatever nature (e.g. noun (phrase), pronoun, gerund, adjective, adverb or clause). We shall then maintain that such prepositions have the property x when they govern a complement and the property y when they do not on certain occasions (but may do so in some contexts), e.g. (a) 'they went *through* the tunnel' (here x), and (b) 'they went *through*' (here y). Traditional grammarians would usually assign *through* to the class of prepositions in (a) and to the class of adverbs in (b), but many others (especially in modern times) would classify both as prepositions. In my view there are valid arguments for both positions. But H&P go an important step further. They also include words that lack both property *x* and property *y* and only possess what we will call property *z*, viz. that they can *never* govern a complement, as is the case with words like – to take a few examples from above – *afterwards, downstairs, here, now, thereby*. It is this (very heterogeneous) group that causes the real controversy and may persuade many that H&P's class of prepositions has become so inclusive and diffuse that it is close to being meaningless.

Whatever else this brief survey of the treatment of prepositions in recent grammars of English shows, it is clear from it that there is as little consensus among grammarians nowadays regarding the number and constitution of word classes, and the definition of prepositions, as there was during the more than two centuries of English grammars that will form the core of the present book. Whether this is seen as worrying or reassuring is a matter for individual judgement.

Another matter that must be touched on briefly at this point relates to the term 'preposition' as used throughout the book. Since this study deals with prepositions in English grammars and prior to that the early development of this class in the Western European tradition, it is less important (but not completely irrelevant) to distinguish between 'prepositions' in a strict sense (i.e. items that are 'preposed' or positioned *before* their complement) and 'postpositions' (i.e. similar elements that are 'postposed' or placed *after* their complement), as is generally the case in some languages, e.g. Turkish, Japanese and Hindi. Although 'prepositions' sometimes occur *after* a pronoun or adverb complement in, for example, Old English, and are therefore described by some writers as 'postpositions', there are arguments for treating them as 'postposed prepositions' (cp. 'stranded prepositions' in English) rather than as 'postpositions', which would imply a more fixed word order system (cf. my own discussion in Lundskær-Nielsen 1993:37-44). I shall therefore use 'preposition' as the general term through this work.

A study of this nature can never lay claim to being complete, and the present one certainly does not do so. After tracing the broad lines in the establishment, development and successive definitions of prepositions as a word class in Ancient Greece and Rome, I shall deal with a few expositions of Speculative Grammar in the High Middle Ages and look at some samples of the vernacular grammars that began to appear during the Renaissance, but the main focus of this study will be on a selection of fifty treatments of prepositions in English grammars (in a broad sense) up to the beginning of the nineteenth century.

I. Antiquity

1. The Greeks

Like so many other academic disciplines, linguistics – at least as it developed in Western Europe – has its origins in ancient Greece. The Greeks were the first to address a number of fundamental questions and issues in grammatical theory, including the establishment of the parts of speech (or word classes), which grammarians from the Romans onwards built on and which are of crucial importance to any historical view of the subject. Sadly, most of the Greek primary sources have been lost, and with them our knowledge of the detailed development of many aspects of grammatical studies in the ancient world, but from what has survived, including fragments and a number of secondary sources, it is possible to piece together an overall sketch of how the notion of word classes began to evolve, including the class of prepositions which is the focus of the present study.

It was among the Greek philosophers that awareness of language as an object of study arose. We can date this interest back to the second half of the fifth century BC, the time of the city states, between the successful wars with Persia and the Macedonian expansion and colonisation of the near Orient and Egypt that were a result of the conquests of Alexander the Great (356-323 BC). And since the earliest surviving attempts to devise anything like grammatical categories for natural language were made by Greek philosophers, their language of reference was invariably Greek.[1] The Greeks themselves were, at first, above all interested in philosophical matters and therefore chiefly concerned with logic rather than 'grammar' as we know it, so it is not surprising that the early divisions into what we may call 'sentence elements' (Gr. *meros tou logou*, Lat. *partes orationis*) tended to make use of logical rather than grammatical criteria.

From at least the fifth century BC onwards, Greek men of learning operated with the terms *grammatiké* (originally merely in the sense of the understanding of letters) and the much broader *philosophía* (roughly, the sum of human knowledge), but it was only with the Stoics that a kind of linguistic studies was distinguished as a genuine sub-field of *philosophía*.

Plato (427-347 BC)
As far as we know, Plato was the first to make the basic distinction between the noun or subject (*ónoma*) and the verb or predicate (*rhēma*) in a sentence. However, it should be borne in mind that terminology can be treacherous and the Greek terms rarely, if ever, have the meanings that we now associate with them. This, of course, constitutes a serious problem for translations of Ancient Greek texts, and any rendering of them can only suggest an approximate meaning. Plato's initial division into a 'nominal' and a 'verbal' element, which both have to be present to form a sentence, or, strictly speaking, a proposition (*lógos*), is a clear case in point. His was certainly a philosophical approach, not a linguistic one, so the logical terms 'subject' and 'predicate' may be more accurate than the grammatical counterparts 'noun' and 'verb' found in some modern translations and presentations, but even the former terms may be misleading when applied specifically to language since a strict grammatical terminology did not come into existence until many centuries later. In fact, Law (2003:168) claims that it was 'not until the late eighteenth century' that 'the terms subject and predicate [were] assimilated into the mainstream grammatical tradition', as opposed to their use in logic. This somewhat loose terminology should therefore be borne in mind in the following passages and quotations.

One example of this fundamental distinction is found in the dialogue *Cratylus*, where Plato has Socrates say, '… and so we shall form syllables, as they are called, and from a compound of syllables make nouns and verbs; and thus, at last, from the combinations of nouns and verbs arrive at language, large and fair and whole' (Plato 1964:424e-425a).

Another example comes from *Sophist*, where the Stranger states that 'there are two sorts of intimation of being which are given by the voice', one of which 'is called nouns, and the other verbs'. He defines them notionally by saying that 'that which denotes action we call a verb … And the other, which is an articulate mark set on those who do the actions, we call a noun' (Plato 1964:261e-262c).

The point that Plato apparently wants to make is that neither nouns nor verbs alone can make up a sentence (*lógos*). Only when 'verbs are mingled with nouns' do 'the words fit, and the smallest combination of them form a sentence, and is the simplest and least form of discourse' (*ibid.*). Here, then, we seem to have the earliest division of sentences into what also posterity came to regard as their two main constituents, but there is nothing about any other sentence elements.

Aristotle (384-322 BC)

It has been argued that Aristotle turned Plato's twofold division into a tripartite system by bringing in a third class: *sýndesmos* (plur. *sýndesmoi*). This term has been variously translated as conjunction, particle, ligature, conjunctive particle (cf. Michael 1970:61) or connecting word / connective (cf. Aristotle 1984, *Rhetoric* Book III.5; 1407^{a}20-30, 1407^{b}13, p. 2244).[2] Matthews (1994:29) renders *sýndesmos* (or, in his version, *súndesmos*) as a 'binder together' and notes that 'such elements are said to "make many things one"'. According to Robins (1997:32-3), *sýndesmoi* as a class comprise 'conjunctions (and probably prepositions …), the article and pronouns'. However, Aristotle does not grant this class of 'grammatical words' the same status as the two primary parts of speech: the noun and the verb, so there is clearly a lot of uncertainty about the precise meaning of the term.

Some of our information comes from *Poetics*, Chapter 20, which begins like this: 'The diction viewed as a whole is made up of the following parts: the letter, the syllable, the conjunction [i.e. *sýndesmos*], the article, the noun, the verb, the case, and the speech' (Aristotle 1984:1456^{b}20-22, p. 2331). From our point of view, it is of significance that not only *sýndesmos* but also *árthron* (here translated as the article) is mentioned, as both terms are used widely in the later Stoic tradition, but it is a problem that the latter term (*árthron*) does not occur elsewhere in Aristotle's treatment. So whereas it cannot be ruled out completely that Aristotle meant to distinguish the article as an independent part of speech, the evidence for this is flimsy, to say the least, and the Stoic tradition seems to be unaware of it.

Shortly afterwards, in a notoriously problematic passage that is far from clear and of which the authorship is doubtful, the text seems to say approximately: 'A conjunction [again, the translator's term for *sýndesmos*] is a non-significant sound which, when one significant sound is formable out of several, neither hinders nor aids the union, and which naturally stands both at the end and in the middle but must not be inserted at the beginning; e.g. *mén*, or *dé* ('on the one hand', 'on the other hand') (Aristotle 1984:1457^{a}1-4, p. 2331). This is, at best, a kind of conglomerate definition of *sýndesmos*, a mixture of phonetic, morphological, syntactic and orthographical components, and one should be wary of attaching too much importance to it.

The Stoics and their tradition (*c.* 300-100 BC)[3]
Whether Aristotle intended a threefold, or even a fourfold, division of the parts of speech or not, his exposition formed a basis that the Stoics built on, though it should be emphasised that our extant sources for the Stoic development of the parts of speech are secondary ones.[4]

Nevertheless, we know that much of the groundbreaking work in the foundation of language studies took place in the centuries following the death of Aristotle. Although *philosophía* continued to be an umbrella term for different strands of intellectual pursuits, various sub-fields gradually developed, such as rhetoric, dialectic, etymology and grammar (cf. e.g. Robins 1997:20ff.; Law 2003:Chs. 3-4), as did a crucial distinction between the perspective on language analysis between philosophers and grammarians which had repercussions for their respective presentations well beyond late antiquity (see Luhtala 2005).

One should not forget either that one of the effects of Alexander's colonisation of Egypt and vast areas of Asia was the dissemination of Greek language and culture in these regions in the following centuries – the so-called Hellenistic Age – during which new intellectual centres emerged, such as Pergamum and, in particular, Alexandria. The latter was founded by, and named after, Alexander himself, and in due course it attracted some of the greatest scholars of the time and boasted the largest and best equipped library in the antique world before it burned down. For centuries the whole of this large empire was dominated by Greek thought, by the Greek way of life and not least by the Greek language. The impressive strides that Greek scholars (in a wide sense) made in language studies up to the time of the Roman Empire were exclusively based on studies of Greek. No other language seems to have been of interest to the Greeks, so it was left to the Romans – with their general reverence for everything Greek – to be the first to study language matters with reference to more than one language since, for generations, Greek texts constituted the basis for their work, and Greek scholars continued to be among the foremost practitioners in the field of language studies.

Different centres represented different interests and specialities in the enlarged Greek world, and emphasis on this or that sub-field therefore varied a great deal. Alexandria, for instance, became famous for its concern with literary studies and commentaries on literary texts (especially Homer), but that did not preclude scholars in this area from carrying out important work on grammar as well. It would be wrong for our specialised age to view studies in any field in the ancient world in isolation. Such a separation from related areas was generally unknown at that time. For example, the Alexandrian scholar and head of the famous library Aristarchus (first half of the second century BC) and his pupil Dionysius Thrax (see below) were both eminent Homeric scholars as well as authors of influential works on language.

Our most important secondary sources for the Stoic views on language issues include works by Dionysius of Halicarnassus, Quintilian and Diogenes Laertius. We shall briefly look at them in chronological order.

Some secondary sources for the early period including the Stoics:

(a) **Dionysius of Halicarnassus** (first century BC)
Dionysius of Halicarnassus's (see Dionysius of Halicarnassus 1974/1985)[5] remarks about the primary parts of speech in the section 'On the style of Demosthenes' in *The Critical Essays* (in two volumes) (see Dionysius 1974/85, I:421) are greatly expanded in a later passage 'On Literary Composition'. The latter is worth quoting at length:

> Composition is, as the name itself indicates, a certain process of arranging the parts of speech, or the elements of diction, as some call them. These were restrict-

ed to three only in number by Theodectes[6] and Aristotle and the philosophers of their day, who made nouns, verbs and conjunctions [i.e. *sýndesmoi*] the primary parts of speech. Their successors, and in particular the leaders of the Stoic school, raised the number to four, separating the articles from the conjunctions. Subsequent grammarians distinguished appellatives from the other substantives, and represented the primary parts as five. Others detached the pronouns from the nouns, and thus introduced a sixth element. Yet others divided the adverbs from the verbs, the prepositions from the conjunctions and the participles from the appellatives; while others introduced still further divisions and so made the primary parts of speech many in number. (Dionysius 1974/85, 2:21)

To the extent that this is a reliable account, it presents an interesting outline of the development since the time of Aristotle and thus of the gradual establishment of most of the parts of speech that the Romans inherited from the Greek tradition.

If we look at Dionysius's statement in more detail, we notice that he attributes three (not four) primary parts of speech (viz. nouns, verbs and *sýndesmos*) to Aristotle and his immediate followers and then mentions the expansion of these classes in the Stoic tradition. To begin with, the articles (he does not mention Aristotle's *árthron*) are separated from conjunctions (*sýndesmoi*). The Greeks also, as indicated by Dionysius and later sources, came to distinguish common nouns (or appellatives) from proper nouns, and pronouns from nouns, and Dionysius himself is familiar with a system of nine classes, including the two classes of noun. But for the purposes of the present study the most significant fact is the separation of prepositions from conjunctions and thus the establishment of prepositions as a class in their own right. Until that time, prepositions seem to have been subsumed under the general term *sýndesmos*, which in the later schemes became restricted to denote conjunctions, so modern translations of *sýndesmos* from the previous period should be treated with caution as 'conjunction' may be too narrow a term.

(b) **Marcus Fabius Quintilian** (*c.* 35-*c.* 100 AD)
Dionysius's statement is generally corroborated by Marcus Fabius Quintilian, whose father, himself a distinguished rhetorician of Spanish origin but working in Rome, ensured that his son had a proper

Roman education with, among others, the grammarian Palaemon and the rhetorician Domitius Afer as his teachers (cf. Butler's Introduction in Quintilian 1921:vii). Quintilian's comprehensive and wide-ranging *Institutio Oratoria* in twelve Books (see Quintilian 1921) is one of our best secondary sources on earlier grammatical works as well as a fascinating account of many aspects of language in the first century AD. In his discussion of the parts of speech, Quintilian notes that 'there is some dispute as to their number' (Quintilian 1921:70-71). Like Dionysius of Halicarnassus, he cites Aristotle and Theodectes for claiming that there are three parts of speech, viz. verbs, nouns and convinctions (Lat. *convinctiones*), the latter being Quintilian's preferred translation of *sýndesmos*, though he admits that 'conjunction' is 'the term in general use' (*ibid.*). He then goes on to say that '[g]radually the number was increased by the philosophers, more especially by the Stoics' in the following way: '*articles* were first added to the *convinctions*, then *prepositions*: to nouns *appellations* [i.e. appellatives] were added, then the *pronoun* and finally the *participle*, which holds a middle position between the verb and the noun. To the verb itself was added the *adverb*.' He also mentions that since Latin 'dispenses with' articles, these are 'distributed among the other parts of speech', but he then adds '*interjections*' (Quintilian 1921:70-73; his emphasis). As Quintilian noted earlier, not everybody recognises the same number of parts of speech. For example, he informs us that the Alexandrian scholar Aristarchus and his own teacher Palaemon accept only eight parts, classifying the *appellation* (or *vocable*, as he also calls it) under the noun. Yet others make a distinction between the 'vocable' (concrete nouns) and the 'appellation' ('something imperceptible … to sight or touch'; that is, abstract nouns, in modern terminology). Some of these people also included 'the *asseveration*' (e.g. *alas*, Lat. *eheu*, though it is not clear why this is not an interjection) and 'the *derivative*', usually taken to mean 'collective'. In a rare judgemental remark, Quintilian distances himself from these last additions: 'But of these classifications I do not approve' (Lat. *quae mihi non approbantur*) (Quintilian 1921:72-3). However, his flexibility soon returns and he leaves it to others to decide whether *prosygoria* should be translated as 'vocable' or 'appellation' and even whether it should be regarded as a subgroup of the noun; for him it is ultimately 'a matter of no importance' (*ibid.*).

(c) **Diogenes Laertius** (third century AD)
According to Diogenes Laertius, Chrysippus (third century BC) and Diogenes of Babylon (third-to-second century BC) both operated with a scheme consisting of five parts of speech, viz. proper noun, common noun, verb, conjunction and article. He briefly summarises Diogenes of Babylon's definitions of these five and says of the conjunction (as before, the term is *sýndesmos*) that it is defined as 'an indeclinable part of speech, binding the various parts of a statement together' (Diogenes Laertius 1925, I:57, II:166-7). This definition is sufficiently vague to cover both conjunctions and prepositions, so it is reasonable to suppose that at this stage *sýndesmos* may well have included prepositions.

Based on the evidence from these sources, it is therefore reasonable to conclude that the recognition of prepositions as an independent part of speech began around the second century BC, and by the first century BC the later dominant scheme of eight word classes must in the main have been established though, as we saw, some grammarians operate with a nine-part division or even more. The eight sentence elements were: the noun (*ónoma*), the verb (*rhēma*), the participle (*metokhē*), the article (*árthron*), the pronoun (*antōnumía*), the preposition (*próthesis*), the adverb (*epírrhēma*) and the conjunction (*sýndesmos*) (cf. Matthews 1994:38). It was a scheme that would be modified only slightly by the Romans.

Dionysius Thrax (c. 170-90 BC)
Half a century ago, we seemed to be on even firmer ground in our assessment of the kind of word class scheme that was developed by the Greeks. Until then, Dionysius Thrax was considered not only a primary source but also the author of the oldest surviving Greek grammar, and his scheme of the parts of speech was taken as proof of the achievements of the Alexandrian school in this area. The first part of Thrax's text is almost certainly genuine, but since a seminal article by Di Benedetto (1958) first raised serious doubts about the authenticity of the section of Thrax's *Tekhnē grammatikē* that includes the parts of speech, scholars in the field have become increasingly reluctant to attribute it to Thrax.[7] It has therefore become common practice to use the expression '(pseudo-) Dionysius Thrax', when referring to this

section of the *Tekhnē*. It should be noted, however, that Thrax is supposed to have been the pupil of Aristarchus, who (as we saw) is himself credited with a division into eight parts of speech, so a word-class division of the kind found in Thrax was almost certainly 'in the air' at the time of Thrax.

In any case, eight parts of speech are set out in the *Tekhnē* (cf. Kemp 1987:176-85), some of them with subdivisions and comments. The section on prepositions is very short and reads as follows in its entirety:

> A preposition is a word which is placed before other parts of the sentence both in compound forms and in grammatical constructions.
> There are eighteen prepositions in all, including six monosyllables – *en, eis, eks, sun, pro, pros* – which are not capable of anastrophe, and twelve dissyllables – *ana, kata, dia, meta, para, anti, epi, amphi, apo, hupo, huper*. (Kemp 1987:XVII,183)

Beyond the listing of these eighteen prepositions, there is very little information about the syntactic constructions that they may enter into, and what we are told is not particularly helpful. It was certainly common in the Latin tradition to regard what we now call prefixes of nouns and verbs as prepositions, just like their homographic independent counterparts. In this way, the first element of words like *indoctus* (untaught) and *proclamo* (I proclaim), i.e. *in-* and *pro-* respectively, are as much prepositions as *in* and *pro* are when they occur independently in what is here called 'grammatical constructions' such as *in partes tres* (in(to) three parts) and *pro patria* (for the fatherland), and a similar analysis was used by the Greeks with, for example, *pro(-)* and *anti(-)*. What is surprising, if this part of the *Tekhnē* is really as late as 400 AD or even later as is now widely believed, is that so little is said about the syntax of prepositions considering that by this time the Romans had proceeded much further in their analysis.

The only other piece of information about prepositional syntax is the distinction between the monosyllabic and the dissyllabic members of the class, since the monosyllabic prepositions in Greek could not appear after the noun that they governed (this is what is meant by 'not capable of anastrophe' in the quotation above), whereas dissyllabic prepositions could be preposed as well as postposed in relation to their noun complement (cf. Kemp 1987:188). Note, though, that whereas the point about prefixes as prepositions can hold equally well for a range of languages, this one is specific to Greek.

In the same tradition is an anonymous grammatical fragment in Greek, written on papyrus and dating from the first century AD, and thus one of the earliest primary sources so far discovered.[8] In it we are told that

> A meaningful utterance (*logos*) is a prose collocation of word forms (*lexis*) revealing a complete thought. Its parts are nine: proper noun, common noun, participle, pronoun, article, verb, preposition, adverb, conjunction.

This seems to be a good reflection of the standard Greek view in the early days of the Roman Empire. Whether eight or nine parts were recognised mainly depended on whether the noun was divided (as here) or not. After this follows a brief definition of each part of speech, and this is what is said about the preposition:

> The preposition is an uninflected word form which stands before the word classes in composition. These are the prepositions: *ana* 'up to', *kata* 'down to', *dia* 'through', *meta* 'after', *para* 'besides', *anti* 'against', *amphi* 'around', *huper* 'over', *apo* 'from', *peri* 'about', *en* 'in', *eis* 'into', *pro* 'before', *pros* 'towards'.

This definition uses both morphological and syntactic criteria. Morphologically, prepositions are characterised as uninflected, and syntactically, they appear before other word classes 'in composition', i.e. in a sentence. It is not clear, though, if 'before the word classes in composition' means both as 'prefixes' of nouns or verbs and as separate words (in prepositional phrases). Both functions appear in (pseudo-) Dionysius Thrax and in the Roman tradition.

The fact that our sources are so sparse and mostly second-hand, written long after the events, has not surprisingly resulted in some disagreement about how to interpret the information that we do possess. An example of this is the alleged debate about *analogy* versus *anomaly* in the Greek tradition. Robins (1967 and later editions) makes a lot of this 'controversy' and (still in 1997:25) calls it 'the second linguistic controversy of Antiquity', the first being that of *phýsis* (nature) versus *nómos* or *thésis* (convention). He states, among other things, that Aristotle favoured analogy and the Stoics anomaly. Basically, the disagreement is claimed to be between those who saw language (i.e. Greek) as being typified by 'orderliness and … proportional regularity' (analogy) or by irregularities (anomaly), cf. Robins (1997:26).

This account has been contested by a number of scholars from the 1970s onwards, in particular Robins's statement that

> It is generally accepted that the controversy between Analogy and Anomaly … was a significant part of the theoretical context with which grammatical theory and the descriptive grammar of Greek and Latin developed in western antiquity. (1976:333, also cited in Taylor 1987:7)

The issues are summed up by Taylor (1987:1-8), who refers to Robins's presentation as the 'traditional model' (1987:2). For our purposes, and as an illustration of the uncertain ground that we move on in dealing with grammar in antiquity, a flavour of these objections to Robins's 'model' will suffice. One key objection relates to the use of evidence in the light of the paucity of extant primary sources and the over-interpretation of presentations and remarks in some secondary sources. Thus the chief source of the analogy/anomaly 'controversy' is Varro's *De Lingua Latina* (see below), but Fehling (1956-57) and others after him have argued that the 'traditional' account of the 'debate' is a smokescreen invented by Varro, and Blank (1982:4) confidently asserts that it 'never took place'.

Furthermore, Taylor (1987:6), citing Frede (1977) and Blank (1982), suggests that there have been serious misrepresentations of other important issues. For example, the traditional distinction between 'technical' and 'philosophical' grammar is seen as a 'false dichotomy' since it is impossible to maintain the received version of the Stoic philosophy versus Alexandrian philology. Both sets of practitioners – the Stoa in Athens and the Library in Alexandria – we are told, were concerned with technical grammar. We should therefore acknowledge that the two schools had overlapping interests in linguistic matters because they were 'asking many of the same questions' (*ibid.*).

Even more fundamentally, Frede (1978:28) attacks the traditional overview of the Greek tradition by claiming that 'to treat Plato and Aristotle as part of a continuous tradition along with later grammarians is to invite neglect of important questions'. In fact, he adds, 'some of those questions concern the doctrine of parts of speech and the nature of syntax, both of which figure prominently in early Stoic linguistics and which seem to be more closely related to each other than has heretofore been thought'. In other words, Robins and others are accused of trying to create an artificial unified development of linguistic analysis based on the very sparse evidence available. This did not, however, stop Robins saying essentially the same in the third (1990) and fourth (1997) editions of his textbook from 1967, both of which list Taylor (1987) in the bibliography to the section on Greek, though not any of the other writers that Taylor refers to and to some extent bases his argument on.

More recently, Luhtala (2005:6-8) essentially supports Taylor's version of events, but objects to the perceived 'autonomy' of grammar, as distinct from disciplines such as rhetoric, philosophy and philology from approximately the works of Varro onwards. It is her contention that grammar continued to interact with philosophy, in particular, 'during the first three Christian centuries' and she claims that 'philosophical influences adopted into grammar during this time are substantial rather than sporadic' (Luhtala 2005:8). Where Taylor in another article argues that the canonisation of grammar took place 'during the first two centuries of the Christian era' (Taylor 1995:87), Luhtala moves the culmination of this process 'to the third and fourth centuries', during which time philosophy, in her view, continued to exert a significant influence on grammar.

2. The Romans

The transition from Greek to Roman grammatical descriptions is far from clear-cut. The Greeks had established colonies on the Roman mainland as well as on some of the surrounding islands. Many Greek scholars lived and worked in Rome and in the areas south of it which gradually came under Roman jurisdiction, and Romans went to study in Greek centres of learning, such as Athens and Alexandria. There is therefore considerable overlap between the work of Greek and Roman grammarians and between descriptions of Greek and Latin.

Generally speaking, the Romans followed the Greek and in particular the Alexandrian grammatical tradition, but grammarians such as Varro

(1st century AD), Sacerdos (3rd century AD), Charisius, Diomedes and Donatus (all 4th century AD) and Priscian (early 6th century AD) all added their individual, and in some cases substantial, touches. Thus, for the most part, the Romans preserved the parts of speech established by Greek scholars, but with at least one important change: since Latin had no articles, the class of article was dropped, but on the other hand the interjection was given word-class status. Furthermore, the distinction that some Greek grammarians had made between proper nouns and common nouns was on the whole not transferred to Latin.

In the following sections we shall briefly look at the relevant works of the four most prominent grammarians, from our perspective, during the centuries that roughly coincide with the heyday of the Roman Empire.

Marcus Terentius Varro (116-27 BC)

The first important Roman writer on language is Marcus Terentius Varro, who is a fascinating and somewhat controversial figure. His long life spanned the period when Rome was in the process of becoming the dominant European power. Thus he witnessed the civil wars, the rise and fall of Caesar, and the end of the Roman Republic, and he received lavish praise from Cicero, to whom he dedicated his main work, *De Lingua Latina* (On the Latin Tongue), before falling out with Marc Antony, being forced into hiding and having his impressive library destroyed. Quintilian called him *vir Romanorum eruditissimus* (the most erudite of Romans) (Quintilian 1921:X,1,95).

Varro was a prolific writer, but from a linguistic point of view it is *De Lingua Latina*, written between 47-45 BC, that he is remembered for. It was originally in 25 (XXV) books, which – after the dedication and introduction in Book I – were divided into three principal parts (cf. Law 2003:43):

1. Imposition of names upon things:
   (a) Books II-IV: principles of etymology, with arguments for and against.
   (b) Books V-VII: examples of etymology in different areas of the Latin vocabulary.

2. Modifications in the form of the original words, i.e. *declinatio* (approx. 'inflection').
   (a) Books VIII-X: the role of analogy and anomaly in language.
   (b) Books XI-XIII: examples of analogy.

3. Bringing words together to express a meaning:
   Books XIV-XXV: the 'conjoining' of words, apparently along the lines of the Stoic analysis of different types of propositions.

Of these, only Books V-X have survived, and that is thanks to a single copy from the eleventh century found at the monastery of Monte Cassino in southern Italy. Furthermore, this copy is damaged, has several lacunae and presents a textual challenge to modern scholars. Varro discusses the parts of speech twice in the extant Books. The first mention is in Book VIII (XXIII, 44), where he says:

> I shall speak of what concerns the individual parts of speech. Since there are several methods of division thereof, I shall now take by preference that by which speech is according to its nature divided into four parts: that which has case-forms, that which has time-forms, that which has neither, that in which both case and time are indicated. Some grammarians call these the parts respectively of naming, saying, supporting, joining. (Varro 1977, 2:405)[9]

Varro's division into parts of speech is highly original and differs radically from the previous attempts we have looked at, in that he uses exclusively *formal* principles and makes no appeal to semantics. After acknowledging that there are 'several methods' of dividing the vocabulary, he goes on to define the parts of speech according to their interaction (or not) with the 'accidental' categories of case[10] and time (or tense, as we would say). Logically, this results in four classes (note that Classes 3 and 4 are reversed below for clarity):

1. those that show case, but not tense
2. those that show tense, but not case
3. those that show both case and tense
4. those that show neither case nor tense

Compared with the 'traditional' scheme, i.e. the scheme worked out by the Alexandrian grammarians, Class 1 (here also called 'naming') includes nouns (both kinds if a distinction is made), pronouns, articles and adjectives. Class 2 consists of verbs only (here also called 'saying'), Class 3 of participles only (here also called 'joining'), while Class 4 (here also called 'supporting') contains the uninflected classes: adverbs, prepositions and conjunctions. Further distinctions are made in Group 1, which need not concern us here. Prepositions are not mentioned directly by name, but they clearly constitute a sub-class of Class 4 by not inflecting for either case or tense.

Apollonius Dyscolus (middle to late second century AD)
Apollonius Dyscolus proves the point made earlier about the difficulty of making any sharp division between Greek and Roman linguistic writings. Apollonius Dyscolus was a Greek who lived and worked in Alexandria in the middle of the second century AD. It is therefore no surprise that his analysis is based on the Greek language. His (nick) name 'Dyscolus' means the 'difficult' or 'grumpy'; it is unknown why he was given it, but Householder (1981:5) lists several possibilities from perhaps less than reliable sources. As with Varro, most of his writings have been lost. What has survived comprises three sections on some of the parts of speech: 'On the Pronoun' and two shorter ones 'On Adverbs' and 'On Conjunctions', which – or so Householder speculates – may have been 'three parts of a long treatise *On the Classification of the Parts of Speech*', plus the four books that make up his Syntax as well as some fragments. The four books on syntax deal with the following parts of speech (ignoring other aspects found in them):

Book I: The Definite Article and The Relative Pronoun
Book II: Pronouns
Book III: Verbs (and their arguments) and Participles
Book IV: Prepositions and Adverbs (not complete)

In Householder (1981), which includes an English translation of Apollonius, there is a further section (Book IVa) on 'Adverbs (continued)'. This is the first (extant) detailed treatment of syntax (Gr. *sun-*

taxis 'setting out together', i.e. structural ordering; Lat. *construction*), but whether it really is the first such study is uncertain. Apollonius himself (IV, 36)[11] refers to one by Tryphon (first century BC) called 'On Prepositions' and generally mentions Tryphon as someone who 'got it wrong'.

Apollonius's division is exactly the same as in (pseudo-) Dionysius Thrax, i.e. noun, verb, participle, article, pronoun, preposition, adverb, conjunction. The order is important and Apollonius goes to considerable lengths to justify it since, according to him, this is the order in which the parts of speech should be discussed in a grammatical treatise, but at the same time there is an appeal to chronology. He begins, quite traditionally, with the noun and the verb, on the grounds established by Plato that 'any sentence which lacks (either of) these is not complete' (I, 14), and he defends it in the following, slightly tortuous way:

> The noun necessarily precedes the verb, since influencing and being influenced are properties of physical things, and things are what nouns apply to, and to things belong the special features of verbs, namely doing and experiencing. (I, 16)

In other words, the primacy of the noun is due to the fact that the things or physical objects that nouns refer to are prior to any actions or events that they experience or undergo, as expressed by verbs. But what about pronouns? he asks. Since pronouns can replace nouns syntactically, shouldn't they be given the place after nouns? His main answer to this seems a little unconvincing as he states that 'pronouns were invented for the purpose of accompanying verbs' (I, 19), thus verbs must have existed before pronouns. This puts pronouns on a different footing to nouns, which is syntactically unjustified, but strange arguments are often used when people try to come up with a chronology for the establishment of different parts of speech. The very idea that such a chronology exists, or can be rationalised, is dubious.

When it comes to the preposition, we are told that 'it is clear that the preposition also [i.e. like the pronoun] does not rank first or ahead of any of the parts of speech we've already discussed [noun, verb, participle, article, pronoun], and hence is placed here' (I, 26). In fact, he continues, it gets its name from its syntactic position, being placed before one of these five classes, which means (apparently) that 'if they were not preestablished, it could not be combined with them' (*ibid.*). Apollonius adds later (IV, 5) that for the Stoics the position of the preposition was the most important aspect and that this explains why they sometimes called it 'prepositive conjunction', its 'force' being of secondary consideration.

On the other hand, the preposition comes before the adverb in the established order, which is justified in the following way:

> And since the adverb (ad-verb) has a structural position added to [i.e., after] the verb, just as the placement inherent in its name testifies, and since the verb is second to the noun, so the adverb is second to the preposition, which in composition and construction is placed before [e.g.] nouns. (I, 27)

Hence the preposition comes in sixth place out of the eight parts of speech, and whatever one thinks of the individual arguments (which, as regards most of the classes, have been left out here), Apollonius is painstaking in his application of them.

He even makes a secondary division, which cuts across the order shown above. This is done by comparing the various parts with vowels and consonants, respectively. Vowels are 'complete sounds even in isolation', while the pronunciation of consonants 'is not possible without vowels' (I, 12). Similarly, some words (e.g. verbs, nouns, pronouns, adverbs) are 'independently speakable', like vowels, while others (prepositions, articles, conjunctions) 'resemble consonants, and just as they [i.e. consonants] require vowels, so these require the presence of some of the aforesaid parts of speech' (*ibid.*). Or, to put it more succinctly, some classes are syntactically more independent than others.

If we move on to consider Apollonius's treatment of prepositional syntax, there are some terminological problems, as pointed out by Householder (1981:2-4). The most important of these is the lack of a word for 'phrase', which is obviously significant when dealing with 'prepositional phrases'. The closest equivalent, according to Householder (1981:2), is *parathesis*, which is generally used when two words forming a construction are placed next to each other as separate words, whereas the phenomenon where two words are 'put together' into one is referred to as *sunthesis* ('compound'). But Householder also considers that *suntaxis* may, at least at times, have the meaning of 'phrase' since it signifies 'a grammatical relation between two words'. Thus in a prepositional phrase, where the preposition 'governs' the noun (or another type of complement) in an oblique case, we have *parathesis*, but when it precedes a nominative, it must be a compound and consequently it is an example of *sunthesis* (composition).

This issue is addressed head on at the beginning of Book IV, where Apollonius devises a series of tests in order to determine when prepositions are part of a compound and when they can be considered independent words and thus part of a prepositional construction (or phrase).

One such test is phonological and concerns word stress. In general, there is only one accent in a compound, as there normally is on non-compounded words. This works in the majority of cases, but there are (for Apollonius) a worrying number of exceptions of a type that he exemplifies with the verb *katagraphō* ('I write down'; IV, 3). Here there is no indication whether we have one word *katagrápho* or two words *katà grápho* (the grave accent being the equivalent of there being no accent) as they are pronounced the same way. And there are further complications surrounding the use of accents, for example when the position of a preposition (despite its name) shifts to being *behind* its complement (a so-called 'postposition'), in which case the accent in two-syllable prepositions moves from the last to the penultimate (in effect, the first) syllable. The existence of 'postpositions' (Apollonius does not actually use such a term, but instead refers to 'the rule of anastrophe'; IV, 4), or perhaps more correctly 'postposed prepositions', might have given rise to the establishment of particular 'movement rules', but he confines himself to talking about 'transposition' (IV, 7) and finds it futile to speculate on whether this is a case of right-movement of the preposition or left-movement of its complement (IV, 8). Nor are prepositions the only part of speech to have 'two accentuations'; the same can be found, for example, in personal pronouns and in adverbs.

Another test, which can be used in conjunction with the first one, is based on the fact that prepositions cannot case-govern a nominative or a vocative, but only an oblique case (i.e. accusative, genitive or dative; Greek had no ablative case). It therefore follows that if a preposition is combined with a nominative or a vocative form it must be a compound, whereas if it combines with an oblique case it will be a phrasal construction (IV, 12). Between them, Greek prepositions can appear with all oblique cases, some governing one, some two, and five of them (*epi* 'on', *para* 'by', *peri* 'around', *pros* 'towards' and *hupo* 'by/under') all three cases. So even when the accent is not a reliable guide, the case form can determine the difference between a compound and a phrase. Thus the nominative form *hupérdoulos* ('super-slave') must be a compound, which can furthermore be declined in the other cases, given the right syntactic environment, without affecting the syntactic status, while *huper Aristarchon* (acc. 'beyond Aristarchus) and *huper Aristarchou* (gen. 'on behalf of Aristarchus') can only occur in the respective case, depending on meaning, which shows that they are (prepositional) phrases.

The possibility that a preposition plus an oblique form can be said to establish a compound is refuted (IV, 19) on the grounds that although such forms exist, they are not actually compounded in the oblique form, but are merely inflections of the nominative, with which the preposition *originally* compounded. An example of this is *peribolou* (gen. 'of an enclosure'), a combination of the preposition *peri* and the nominative *bolos* ('casting').

A third point is that prepositions can enter into compounds with nouns or verbs, but not with pronouns or articles (IV, 53-4). However, as with nouns, they can enter into phrasal constructions with pronouns, governing these in an oblique case. They can also, we are informed, 'combine with each other [i.e. with other prepositions] both in composition and in construction [phrases]' (IV, 55). Thus an example of compounding is *parakatathēkē* ('a deposit'), derived from the verb form *parakatatithēmi*, which has the constituents *para* (prep., 'with someone') + *kata* (prep. 'down') + *tithēmi* (verb, 'I put'). But, as Householder points out, in all Apollonius's examples the first preposition interacts not only with the second preposition but with the whole construction (PP) that the latter forms part of.

The fact that prepositions cannot form compounds with the definite article allows Apollonius to use the article for yet another test of whether we are dealing with a compound or a phrase (bearing in mind the comments on the notion of phrase above). The articles are described as 'phrasally bound but never compounded' and they 'always occur in phrases with nominals in the same phrase-construction' (IV, 54); or, to put it differently, when the definite article enters into a construction with a nominal element (e.g. noun or adjective), the result is a phrase, not a compound. Therefore, if the definite article is added to a preposition + noun construction, 'it yields first position to the preposition if the construction is a phrase … But if the expression is a compound, this does not happen, since the preposition here is part of the [compound] noun and so will have before it the so-called prepositive article' (IV, 13). Cast in modern terminology, this means that when the article precedes a word consisting of a prepositional prefix plus a noun, that word is a compound, but when the article occurs between a preposition and a noun, we have a prepositional phrase. Among Apollonius's examples we have the following: *peri Aristarchou* ('about Aristarchus') is indeterminate on its own, but with the article added, *peri tou Aristarchou* (same meaning), it is clear that it is a phrase, as opposed to *ho periklutos* ('the renowned man'), which cannot be the ungrammatical **peri ho klutos*. Even more obvious is the juxtaposition of the phrase *para tou nomou* ('from the law', as written on a stone) and the compound noun *tou paranomou* ('of the illegality').

Apollonius also appeals to semantic phenomena, for example when considering how a preposition interacts with the elements of a sentence consisting of a noun and a verb (in practice, as subject and predicate). He starts with the simple sentence *Platōn bainei* ('Plato is coming'). 'Nominatives and vocatives', he states, 'always refer to the same persons as the verbs which go with them' (i.e. that they are the subject of), 'whereas the other [oblique] cases all presuppose an additional person'; e.g. in *Truphōni legei* ('he is speaking to Tryphon') the referent of Tryphon is different from the one represented by the verb (and hence the implied subject), i.e. the one who carries out the act of speaking (or the agent) (IV, 15), though as Householder points out (IV, 46), Apollonius does not allow for reflexives, here or elsewhere. When a preposition is added to this initial sentence, it can only enter into composition with the verb 'because the implicit … verbal relation accepts the associated meaning of the preposition', which apparently the noun does not. Hence by adding the preposition *en* ('in') we can get *Platōn embainei* ('Plato comes in'), but not *emPlatōn bainei, or by adding *sun* ('together') *Platōn sumbainei* ('Plato comes along') is possible, but *sumPlatōn bainei is not. This is summed up by the statement that in a 'one-place predication ... when a preposition is brought in from outside, it will gravitate ... to [the] position before the verb, since it's a prepositive element and the verb is postpositive' (IV, 15).

However, this raises two questions:

(a) what is the nature of verb compounds with prepositions as the first element?
(b) what interaction is there between independent prepositions and those that are compounded with verbs?

For (a), there are two possibilities: either all verbal forms are generated from the same basic (i.e. present) form or they are all compounded separately. Apollonius chooses the second option on the grounds that not all past forms (aorists and perfects) have a corresponding present form, so such a rule could not apply generally (IV, 40-41). The opposite solution would mean postulating some 'underlying' forms where none exist. As Householder points out, Apollonius does in fact do this in another context (III, 146), but he apparently rejects this option here. Moreover, it seems to be the opposite of his argument for compound nouns, where the nominative compound form is inflected in the other cases.

As far as (b) is concerned, Apollonius considers the possibility that independent prepositions may have been transposed to their (surface) position before a noun in an oblique case from their position in a compound verb (IV, 20). He refers to this as *hyperbaton* (word order change). If such a rule applies, an example like *sun Apollōniōi ēmēn* ('I was with Apollonius') would be derived from *sunēmēn Apollōniōi* ('I met Apollonius'). A (slight) change of meaning is not in itself an obstacle, but in order to be accepted it must apply in all cases, since, as Apollonius says, 'in genuine cases of transposition' the grammatical construction remains the same. However, this is not so, which is why Apollonius rejects that option. For example, there can be differences in the use of case; in *pros Apollōnion erchomai* the noun is in the accusative, but in *proserchomai Apollōniōi* it is in the dative. Hence the grammatical construction does *not* remain the same.

Finally, Apollonius turns to the relationship between prepositions and adverbs. In doing so, he sums up his earlier findings by reiterating that prepositions proper, i.e. used independently as part of a prepositional phrase, only occur with oblique cases (of nouns or nominal elements). With 'caseless words' (which for him include nominatives and presumably vocatives) 'they are all only compounding elements' (IV, 65). The same is true of adverbs, for 'it is absolutely necessary that the same principle apply to adverbs, which have no oblique cases by which they could be recognised as governed by a preposition'. The argument is therefore that since they have no oblique form(s), adverbs cannot form phrases with prepositions, only compounds with a 'prefixed' preposition (*ibid.*).

This is emphasised in the relationship between verbs and adverbs:

> Since adverbs depend upon verbs and the pattern of verbs with prepositions is always the same [i.e. compounding], naturally adverbs should follow the same pattern as that upon which they depend. (IV, 66)

In temporal expressions, such as *apo tou nun* ('from the present'), *apo tēs sēmeron* ('from today') and *apo tēs aurion* ('from tomorrow'), *nun* ('now'), *sēmeron* ('today') and *aurion* ('tomorrow') are thus adverbs (IV, 67). His own solution to these potentially uncomfortable examples is to assert that 'some adverbs [clearly including the ones found here] contain an implicit nominal, semantically, and this is what controls the prepositional syntax' (IV, 68). For instance, the word *hēmera* ('day') is implicit in the word *sēmeron* ('today') but not vice versa. However, this explanation seems less than convincing and one cannot help wondering whether Apollonius himself finds it satisfactory to resolve a syntactic difficulty by making this appeal to semantics, but apparently he could not see his way to proposing a functional explanation by claiming that the adverbs in the examples *function* as nouns, as in the modern English phrase 'until now/tomorrow' (etc.).

From a modern perspective, it is easy to find shortcomings in Apollonius's analysis. Adverbs may 'depend on' (or modify) verbs, but that is no guarantee that they behave in the same way vis-à-vis prepositions. As it happens, there are some awkward examples which

Apollonius needs to 'explain away'. Earlier he used the 'definite article test' to decide if a construction of preposition plus noun was a compound or a phrase; for example, the intervening article in *para tou nomou* ('from the law') shows that here we have a prepositional phrase. But what then, he asks, is the difference between that and examples with an adverb in a similar construction (IV, 67)? Such examples do exist, and sometimes he appears to reject explanations which are very tempting to draw based on his own data. A case in point is when he makes someone else (a real or imagined opponent) speculate that a preposition as part of a verbal compound 'is no longer a preposition, but merely the first syllable of a verb' (IV, 39). If he had taken this suggestion seriously and generalised it to apply to all examples and classes when a preposition forms the initial part of a compound, he might well have developed the idea of a difference between (bound) prefixes and independent prepositions/words. That might of course have made some of his detailed arguments redundant, but the notion of a functional level between letters/syllables and words was not one that was entertained in antiquity or for many centuries to come (the term 'morpheme' does not appear until the late nineteenth century), just as the notion of 'phrases' only emerged at a much later time.

On the other hand, one should be careful not to assess writers anachronistically, and there is no doubt that Apollonius's treatment of syntax, not least prepositional syntax, is far more detailed and advanced than any expositions that preceded it, certainly anything that has survived. He is extraordinarily inquisitive and does not shy away from tackling awkward issues and examples, nor from addressing other views and presenting arguments against them. His mind is one of the most original among the grammarians of the ancient world and he may even be the first to use 'underlying forms' as part of his arguments, though it is doubtful if he can be said to be the originator of 'deep structure', as Householder (1981) will have us believe. One can therefore only deplore the fact that his writings faded into the background in the early Middle Ages, apart from the considerable influence that they exerted on Priscian, for they truly formed a basis which medieval grammarians could with advantage have built on.

Donatus Aelius (mid 4th century AD)
One of the two most influential grammarians in the whole of antiquity, Donatus (Aelius), was a teacher of rhetoric in Rome. He wrote commentaries on Roman authors such as Vergil and Terence, but is most famous for his two grammatical treatises: *Ars Minor* and the larger *Ars grammatica*, better known as *Ars Maior*.

Ars Minor (see Donatus 1926) is the most famous example of the so-called *Schulgrammatik* genre (cf. Law 2003:65-80) and is exclusively concerned with the parts of speech. The first sentences simply read:

> *Partes orationis quot sunt? Octo. Quae? Nomen pronomen verbum adverbium participium coniunctio praepositio interiectio.* (Donatus 1926:28-9)
> (How many parts of speech are there? Eight. Which? Noun, pronoun, verb, adverb, participle, conjunction, preposition, interjection.)

One notices that the order differs somewhat from earlier treatments we have looked at. Instead of starting with the two original parts, the noun and the verb, Donatus lets the pronoun and the adverb follow the class (noun and verb, respectively) which they are most closely linked to. Then comes the participle, which has both nominal and verbal features, and at the end we have the three indeclinable classes, of which the preposition is one. After this briefest of introductions, Donatus goes on to deal with each part of speech in this order. The section on prepositions, which takes up just over a page (though here with parallel Latin and English versions, the best part of four pages; 1926:52-5), begins as follows:

> *Praepositio quid est? Pars orationis quae praeposita aliis partibus orationis significationem earum aut mutat aut complet aut minuit.* (Donatus 1926:52-3)
> (What is a preposition? A part of speech which, placed before other parts of speech, either completes their meaning or alters it or diminishes it.)

This is *not* a formal definition, and rather a minimalist one. Apart from a mention of the typical position of prepositions, it only appeals to meaning; not the meaning of prepositions, though, but how they affect the meaning of the words they enter into construction with (one assumes). In fact, it is not entirely clear whether Donatus attaches independent meaning to the preposition itself, as opposed to the whole construction (i.e. the prepositional phrase) or, in the case of 'prefixes', the whole word. But at least a preposition is claimed to *affect* the meaning of the word(s) it relates to, which indirectly invests it with meaning of a kind. In any case, it seems to be the first explicit suggestion that the definition of prepositions should be, at least in part, semantic; not to be confused with their earlier (and also sometimes later) alleged property of 'binding words together', which was partly based on a logical framework rather than a grammatical one.

We are then informed that prepositions have one 'attribute', viz. case, and can combine with two cases: the accusative and the ablative. After this, there is a list of those prepositions that govern the accusative (28) and an example of each of them with a case-inflected noun, followed by a list of those that govern the ablative (15, but that includes variants such as *a, ab, abs* and *e, ex*), again with an example of each.

As a third group, Donatus mentions the four prepositions that can govern both cases (i.e. *in* 'in(to)', *sub* 'under', *super* 'over' and *subter* 'under(neath)'), and in each case explains under what circumstances they take the accusative and the ablative, respectively. Thus we are told that *in* and *sub* are 'used with the accusative case … whenever we mean that either we or someone else are going, have gone, are about to go *into* a place', whereas they combine with the ablative 'when we mean that either we or someone else are, have been, are about to be, *in* a place' (1926:52-5; the translator's emphasis), and both uses are exemplified for the two prepositions. Of *super* we hear that 'when it means place, it more often governs the accusative case than the ablative', but 'when we make mention of anyone, in the ablative only', and with *subter*, too, there is a distinction between 'to a place and in a place'. This is clear instruction in the difference of case assignment between instances of spatial motion and non-motion.

Finally, Donatus briefly addresses the question of which prepositions can be used in compounds and which independently. He states that *di, dis, re, se, am, con* can only be used in compounds, while *apud* 'with' (cf. French *chez*) and *penes* 'in someone's power' are the only two prepositions that cannot appear in compounds. All the others have both functions.

It is unclear why Donatus regards *di, dis, re, se, am, con* as prepositions as he does not discuss it at all. They do not appear in his earlier lists, since those contain prepositions that can govern their complements in an oblique case and as such are used as independent words. As we have seen, Donatus is not the first (nor is he by any means the last) grammarian to state that prepositions occur in both compounds and in prepositional phrases and to try to distinguish between them. Modern terminology was of course not available to him, but it is nevertheless surprising that he does not seem to see these forms as a problem and conclude that they have a different status to 'independent' prepositions. So although he does not come up with a solution in terms of prefixes versus prepositions, let alone of 'bound' versus 'free' morphemes, it would have been helpful to know the reason why Donatus thought that the five items should be called prepositions at all. His examples might have given him a clue, e.g. *diduco* 'I spread', *distraho* 'I tear/pull (to pieces)', *recipio* 'I receive/get back'. A more inquisitive mind, such as that of Apollonius Dyscolus, might well have speculated whether *di* and *dis* were somehow related, or have wondered that if *distraho* is related to *traho* 'I tear/pull', what then is *recipio* related to, if anything? He might also have discussed the nature of any relationship between the *con* of *congredior* 'meet, encounter' and the forms (i.e. allomorphs) *col(-)*, *com(-)* and *cor(-)* on the one hand, and the preposition *cum* 'with' on the other.

On this issue, one suspects that Donatus may be a victim of his own mainly semantic definition of prepositions, for the 'prefixes' in question do roughly what we were told that a preposition does to the other parts of speech, viz. 'completes their meaning or alters it or diminishes it'. This is in fact a fairly accurate description of the semantic role of prefixes, but much less informative about that of prepositions in constructions with nouns or pronouns, i.e. in prepositional phrases.

The chapter on prepositions in the *Ars Maior* does not add anything substantial to this presentation, but the two works (particularly *Ars Minor* as the quintessential Latin primer), together with the grammatical works of Priscian, were copied and reworked, and were the objects of numerous commentaries in the Middle Ages and even well beyond the Renaissance.

It should be mentioned at this point that **Diomedes** (late 4th century AD) makes the important observation that prepositions become adverbs if they are not followed by case-inflected forms (*adverbia faciunt, si quando illas non subsecuntur casus*; cf. *Ars grammatica*, Book I; Keil:I.409). This concerns the question whether words which are classed as prepositions when occurring in a prepositional phrase (i.e., prototypically, when governing a following noun) should be regarded as prepositions even when they are not followed by a complement, or whether, alternatively, they should in such cases be classed as adverbs. This is a problem that has challenged grammarians ever since as part of the definition of prepositions and which is, arguably, still unresolved.

Priscian (early 6th century AD)
Together with Donatus, Priscian was *the* authority on grammar in Western Europe for more than a thousand years. He hailed from the area of Mauretania in North Africa, but became a highly respected teacher in Constantinople in the early sixth century. The three works on which his fame rests cover different aspects of Latin grammar, although in Constantinople he would probably have taught in Greek, the language of the Eastern Roman (later Byzantine) Empire.

One of these works is *Partitiones duodecimo versuum Aeneidos principalium* (Analyses of the Twelve First Lines of the *Aeneid*). This later gave the name to a specific, and very influential, type of grammar: the parsing grammar. The name refers to Priscian's approach in this work, where he 'parses' every single word in the first line of each of the books of Vergil's *Aeneid*, the only Roman epic poem that could emulate Homer's *Iliad* and *Odyssey*.

The second work is the short *Institutio de nomine et pronomine et verbo* (Instruction on the Noun, Pronoun and Verb), of only fourteen full pages, in which Priscian basically deals with inflectional morphology in Latin from a formal perspective, but without going into too much detail. This became a very important source for later grammarians, but given its self-imposed limitations, it is of little relevance to an examination of prepositions.

If *Institutio* is rather short, that cannot be said about the third title by Priscian; his masterpiece, *Institutiones grammaticae* (Grammatical Instruction). It is a monumental work in eighteen Books, covering close to 1,000 pages (note that unlike his *Institutio*, this title is in the plural). It is in parts strongly influenced by Apollonius Dyscolus and Donatus, in particular, but differs from them in other respects and became the reference work *par excellence* throughout the Middle Ages and even in the post-Renaissance period. Where Donatus has been associated with the *Schulgrammatik* genre, Priscian is generally thought to represent another type: the *regulae* grammars (Gr. *kantones*), which promote 'paradigms' though in practice these different approaches to grammar writing were often found within the same work, e.g. in *Institutiones grammaticae*.[12]

In *Partitiones* (see Priscian 1999), as mentioned above, Priscian examines the first line in each of the twelve Books of *The Aeneid*, and in each line he parses every single word with as much commentary as he finds necessary. These lines are copied below (the numbers refer to the Book):

I. Arma virumque cano, Troiae qui primus ab oris
II. Conticuere omnes intentique ora tenebant
III. Postquam res Asiae Priamique evertere gentem
IV. At regina gravi iam dudum saucia cura
V. Interea medium Aeneas iam classe tenebat
VI. Sic fatur lacrimans classique immittit habenas
VII. Tu quoque litoribus nostris Aeneia nutrix
VIII. Ut belli signum Laurenti Turnus ab arce
IX. Atque ea diversa penitus dum parte geruntur
X. Panditur interea domus omnipotentis Olympi
XI. Oceanum interea surgens Aurora reliquit
XII. Turnus ut infractos adverso Marte Latinos

(A translation of these lines is not offered since it would involve looking at the larger context, i.e. the following line(s), in each case, and few of them contain prepositions anyway.)

These lines are not rich in prepositions; in fact, there are only two instances of the same preposition *ab* (Book I and VIII) plus the 'prefix' *im-* (< *in-*) in *immittit* (Book VI). It should also be mentioned that in *interea* (in Book V) *inter-* does not seem to be considered a preposition though it is shown to be the first element of the word.

Each part of speech is defined the first time that a member of it occurs so that this part of the analysis can be omitted in subsequent examples. Thus *ab* in Book I is given the most comprehensive analysis, which begins as follows:

> *Ab quae pars orationis? Praepositio. Quid est praepositio? Pars orationis quae praeposita aliis partibus orationis significationem earum aut mutat aut complet aut minuit; complet ut facio perficio, mutat ut doctus indoctus, minuit ut rideo subrideo.* (1999:60)
> (*Ab* is what part of speech? A preposition. What is a preposition? A part of speech which, placed before other parts of speech, either completes their meaning or alters it or diminishes it; completes it as in *facio* (I make) vs. *perficio* (I complete), alters it as in *doctus* (learned) vs. *indoctus* (ignorant), diminishes it as in *rideo* (I laugh) vs. *subrideo* (I smile).)

Priscian often, where possible, bases his definitions on formal criteria without appeal to meaning (cf. Michael 1970:65; Law 2003:87), but on some occasions meaning plays a part. This definition certainly refers to meaning ('completes, alters, diminishes'), and there is a reason for that: in *Partitiones* Priscian simply copies Donatus's definition from *Ars Minor* verbatim (see above).

We further learn that *ab* governs the ablative case both in 'composition' (i.e. in phrases like the one in the example *ab oris* (from the coasts) and in apposition as in *abduco* (I lead (X) away). He also explains that *ab* has the alternative forms *a* and *abs* under certain conditions which we need not go into. Nor are the subsequent stress patterns of much relevance here (Priscian 1999:60).

In his comments on *ab* in the first line of Book VIII, Priscian (as in other repetitions of the same word class) dispenses with the definition of a preposition and merely states that it is a preposition that takes the ablative, though he does repeat in some detail the uses of *a*, *ab* and *abs*, respectively (Priscian 1999:105).

In the first line of Book VI, Priscian explains that the first element of the verb *immittit* is the preposition *in* and that *in-* changes to *im-* because the verb begins with the letter <m> and adds that this is also the case in front of <p> and <b> (Priscian 1999:91). Like Donatus, Priscian thus regards the elements used as prefixes in nouns, verbs, etc., as prepositions, and this double endorsement had a profound influence on Western grammarians for more than a thousand years, and not only when analysing Latin.

The treatment of the parts of speech is on a much larger scale in Priscian's main work, *Institutiones grammaticae*. Priscian is well aware that a division into parts of speech could be seen from two different points of view: a logical one and a grammatical one, as had been demonstrated in the past centuries. Without providing anything like a full overview of former positions, he informs the reader that the number of recognised parts of speech have varied through the ages and mentions that according to the dialecticians (*dialecticos*) – in effect, logicians – there are two primary parts: the noun and the verb, because they express a complete sense both on their own and when they are joined together. This sets them off from the rest of the classes which can only carry meaning when they are combined with other words and are therefore known by the term *consignificantia* (Priscian's latinisation of the Greek term *syncategoremata*) (cf. *Institutiones grammaticae*, II.IV.15-6; Keil 1855:II:54); a system that can essentially be traced back to Aristotle. In the same place he also states that the Stoics had established five parts: noun, appellative, verb, pronoun or article, and conjunction, and that with later additions some grammarians claimed the existence of nine, ten and even eleven classes. This is reminiscent of the information provided by Quintilian, who may be one of Priscian's sources here, though the former is much more explicit in his summary.

However, this is only a presentation of earlier views. Priscian himself proposes the eight parts of speech that had become common currency in the late Roman age. He defines them briefly before going on to deal with each one in much greater detail. They are: the noun, the verb, the participle, the pronoun, the adverb, the preposition, the conjunction and the interjection (*Institutiones grammaticae*, II.IV.18-21; Keil 1855:II:54), though the interjection is not defined until later (*Institutiones grammaticae*, XV.VII.18-21; Keil 1859:III:90), where it is said that the Greeks categorised it under adverbs. So in fact, these parts are precisely the same ones that Donatus sets out, though the order differs, but they probably owe much to Apollonius as well, not least in the definitions. Compared with the Alexandrians' late Greek system, the only change is the replacement of the (for Latin) irrelevant article with the interjection. Much has been made of the order in which the classes appear, but we should probably treat it with some care since Priscian deals with them individually in a slightly different order. Nevertheless, that latter order, which is inspired by the Greeks rather than by previous Roman writers such as Donatus (see above), achieved nothing less than canonical status and was reproduced again and again for many centuries to come.

As for the criteria used in establishing the parts of speech, Priscian makes it clear that recourse to meaning plays an important part: 'The parts of speech cannot be separated from each other unless we consider their individual properties for expressing meaning' (*Institutiones grammaticae*, II.IV.17; Keil 1855:II:55).

However, when it comes to prepositions, Priscian changes the definition that he uses in *Partitiones* to one which makes no reference to meaning. He first defines this class in Book II (together with the other classes) where he says of the preposition:

> *Praepositionis autem proprium est separatim quidem per appositionem casualibus praeponi, ut 'de rege', 'apud amicum', coniunctim vero per compositionem tam cum habentibus casus quam cum non habentibus, ut 'indoctus', 'interritus', 'intercurro', 'proconsul', 'induco', 'inspiciens'.* (*Institutiones grammaticae*, II.IV.20; Keil 1855:II:56)
> (The property of the preposition is to be used as a separate word before case-inflected words, such as … and in composition before both case-inflected and non-case-inflected words, such as …)

Here prepositions have two main roles: as separate elements governing a noun (note that both his examples are with nouns) in the appropriate case (*de* takes the ablative and *apud* the accusative) or in compounds (*per compositionem*), here in the examples with nouns, verbs, adjectives and participles. It is clear from these that while 'independent' prepositions can only precede nominal elements since they determine case inflection, 'prepositions' functioning as part of other words can easily be attached to other parts of speech. But it also shows that Priscian – following on from his comments in *Partitiones* – still considers the compounded elements to be prepositions just as much as their separate counterparts that govern case-inflected words.

Later, in the section 'De praepositione' (*Institutiones grammaticae*, XIV.I-VI.1-54; Keil 1859:III:24-59), we find the following definition:

Est igitur praepositio pars orationis indeclinabilis, quae praeponitur aliis partibus vel appositione vel compositione. (Priscian XIV.I.1, see Keil 1859:III.24)
(The preposition is an indeclinable part of speech, which is placed before other parts either independently or in composition.)

This is clearly a shortened version of the one that appears in Book II, but it now adds the morphological information that prepositions are indeclinable. It is also the definition that is usually cited and, more importantly, the one which, together with that of Donatus, was repeated over and over again.

In this section Priscian gives a detailed account of the use of Latin prepositions and especially of their case relations, but he also makes reference to Greek usage and quotes many examples from well-known Roman writers, in particular from Vergil's *Aeneid*. In addition, he deals with the form of prepositions, such as the variant spellings of some of them, e.g. *a*, *ab*, *abs* and *e*, *ex*, and explains when each form is normally used (Priscian XIV.V.42, see Keil 1859:III.47).

Further, Priscian distinguishes between natural order (*ordo naturalis*) and (conventional) usage in the order that pertains between the different parts of speech. Thus he says of the preposition that it normally precedes the inflected classes in constructions but is subordinate to them in the natural order of things. This is summed up in the neat conclusion: 'Ergo natura quidem posterior est, constructione vero principalis' (Hence it [the preposition] is subsequent by nature but the first in the construction) (Priscian XVII.20, see Keil 1859:III.121).

In conclusion, it is difficult to overestimate the influence of Donatus and Priscian, the two giants of the late Roman age, on linguistic studies during the following thousand years or so. Their successors tended to follow or write commentaries on one or the other, but they differed on a number of points, thus giving rise to two different types of grammar: *Schulgrammatik* and *regulae* grammars, respectively. Even something so apparently innocuous as the order of the parts of speech became a bone of contention among later grammarians; some preferred Donatus's sequence (noun, pronoun, verb, adverb, participle, conjunction, preposition, interjection), others Priscian's (eventual) order: noun, verb, participle, pronoun, preposition, adverb, conjunction, interjection. On the other hand, it could be argued that the enormous veneration in which they were both held for so long was in the long run detrimental to the emergence of more independent work in this area. It may have been a quirk of fate that Latin became the language of the intellectual elite in Western Europe after the demise of the Roman Empire, but it certainly helped to maintain the status of Donatus and Priscian as the great authorities on grammar and hence models to be revered and emulated by later generations.

II. The Middle Ages

'The Middle Ages' is a loose term covering approximately the thousand-year period between c. 500-1500, from the end of the classical age to the Renaissance. Some date it more precisely from the fall of Rome and the dissolution of the Roman Empire in 476 – the year when the last Roman Emperor, Romulus Augustulus, was deposed – until the fall of Constantinople in 1453. This is both a very long and an extremely heterogeneous epoch, so it is convenient and conventional to divide it into smaller (though still quite broad) sections, which are also of relevance to linguistic studies. In this I follow Law (2003:112-5):

1. The *early* Middle Ages (c. 500-800), the earliest descriptive non-native grammars of Latin
2. The *central* Middle Ages (c. 800-1100), the Carolingian Renaissance
3. The *later* Middle Ages (c. 1100-1350), the Scholastic era and speculative grammar
4. The *end* of the Middle Ages (c. 1350-1500), the rise of vernacular grammars

However, due to the paucity of new information about the parts of speech, and certainly about prepositions, I shall very briefly treat the first two periods as one and consider the Scholastic era in more detail.

In the centuries following the collapse of the Roman Empire, Latin grammars continued to appear, but most of them were derivative and mainly copied the basic tenets of the Roman writers. In particular, they concentrated on adapting the grammars of Donatus and Priscian and presenting these results to a world where the Latin of the classical period was slowly developing into a number of different vernaculars and hence was no longer the native tongue of people anywhere, even in the central parts of the former Empire. In the same era a new institution, the Christian Church, started to gain political as well as religious power and began expanding northwards. In doing so, it gradually came to exert an all-pervading cultural influence over the countries that had embraced Christianity and to dominate the life and thoughts of their peoples.

So in addition to devising new descriptive grammars of Latin for non-native speakers, the grammar writers had to adjust their views of language to the authority and doctrines of the Church. Ironically, just as Latin was disintegrating as a 'living' language with its own native speakers, it was adopted as the official language of the Church. This elevated status of Latin had a profound effect in many areas of the societies of the time, including language studies, and the fact that it was no longer used as a language of general communication among ordinary people only strengthened its position as an almost ideal, unchangeable linguistic system that was not exposed to the natural development that languages in current use undergo. For this reason its importance increased and, in part for lack of any practical opposition, it became the international, intellectual language *par excellence*, a scholarly meta-language, and this was a position that in many respects it maintained almost until the rise of Romanticism in the late eighteenth century.

But this new status created its own problems. In their day, the likes of Cicero, Horace, Virgil and Ovid may have been masters of expressing themselves in the most elegant Latin of the day in their speeches or writings, but it was still something that ordinary literate citizens of Rome could both understand and, one suspects, appreciate. Now the situation was different. The linguistic link between the rulers, in particular the new 'rulers' within the Church, and the general public no longer existed and Latin became a language reserved for a cultural elite in society. The Middle Ages was certainly an era where the adage that 'language is power' is an accurate reflection of the prevailing conditions. As basic education in most places came under the auspices of the Church through the monasteries, the ability to read and write Latin became the single most important skill of an educated person. Without knowledge of Latin, almost any written communication was impossible, and so was any hope of advancement within the Church or acceptance in intellectual circles generally.

This *conditio sine qua non* naturally had consequences for the role of Latin as a language, for it now became necessary to *teach* it to certain chosen individuals, as a foreign language. But who could teach it? Obviously those who had themselves acquired it and who were familiar with the previous grammars of Latin. Indeed, they might even produce some teaching material of their own, but above all they used what was there already, and that meant building on the Roman grammatical tradition, in particular on the works of Donatus and Priscian, who in this way came to dominate language studies of and in Latin. This meant that contributions to linguistic analysis were geared to pedagogical needs, but they were almost purely derivative and consisted largely of commentaries and adaptations of the Roman grammarians. One reason for that is undoubtedly the strong influence of the Church since its effective stranglehold on cultural life ensured the virtual absence of innovative ideas within grammatical theory (and many other areas), as grammarians and commentators attempted, and felt obliged, to 'Christianise' the subject in ways that seem bizarre to us, but may not have done so to people at the time. However one views the circumstances, there is no doubt that Christian dogma was something that also grammarians ignored at their peril. Such dogmatic considerations are known from other subjects, such as the ecclesiastical endorsement of (and insistence on) the Ptolemaic geocentric model of the universe, to take one of the most famous examples, but we have clear evidence that Christian thoughts also affected grammatical theory.

One such instance is provided by Smaragdus (*c.* 800), a Carolingian grammarian in France, in his *Liber in partibus Donati* (Book about Donatus's Parts of Speech; see Smaragdus 1986),[1] namely where he comments on Donatus's observation that according to some people (though not him) there may be more or fewer than eight parts of speech. Smaragdus counters such a possibility with the terse statement that '[t]he Latin language is totally comprehended and brought to fulfilment in its eight parts'. The reason for this certainty lies not in an assessment of the linguistic evidence, but in the Bible and the teaching of the Church, for he continues his argument as follows:

> However, the universal Church sometimes observes the number eight, which I am sure is divinely inspired. Because the elect tend to come to knowledge of the

Trinity through knowing Latin, and with it as their guide on their blessed heavenly homeland, it was inevitable that the Latin language should be contained within the number eight. That number often turns out to be sacred in the Holy Scriptures. For example, eight souls were saved from the waters of the Flood by the wooden ark, and similarly those who are saved by the water of baptism and the wood of the Cross in this world will enjoy the eight Beatitudes of the gospel in the kingdom that is to come. (Smaragdus 1986:6-7)[2]

Michael (1970:51) translates the first clause of the long quotation above (*Modo autem octo universalis tenet ecclesia*) as 'The whole Church, however, holds that there are only eight', which seems more accurate and gives a sharper edge to Smaragdus's statement. In any case, the important point is that Smaragdus is quite prepared to use doctrinal arguments and biblical references as support for Donatus's view that there are eight, and only eight, parts of speech.[3] If this kind of reasoning seems fairly innocuous, it is nevertheless possible to see, with the benefit of hindsight, the obvious dangers that it represents. As soon as religious dogma or state censorship starts to play a part in linguistic analysis, we are intellectually on a slippery slope, and the seeds have been sown that may ultimately culminate in the intervention, threats and reprisals of an Inquisition. This did not happen in the field of language studies as spectacularly as it did in others, but there is little doubt that the stranglehold that the Church exerted over the medieval societies can to a large extent account for the relative absence of innovative ideas in grammatical theory over a very long time.

On the other hand, we should not exaggerate this view of the Middle Ages as a time of stagnation and purely backwards-looking activities. Much research has been carried out in the last three decades or so which has unearthed hitherto unknown authors and texts and altered many of our former perceptions of this long, historical era.[4] However, even this ground-breaking work cannot disguise the conclusion that very little of interest was written (or has survived) about prepositions that had not been said in the classical period. For most of the time a state of diglossia existed in Western European societies, with Latin as the 'high' version and the various vernaculars as the 'low' counterpart, though technically this applies more precisely to the countries with a Latin-derived Romance language as their everyday tongue. The situation was, if anything, exacerbated when the new university institutions began to emerge in the course of the twelfth and thirteenth centuries, and the educational gulf increased between on the one hand Latin, both as a means of communication and a subject worthy of serious study in its own right, and on the other hand the lowly 'vulgar' linguistic medium of ordinary people, which was not thought to be worthy of serious investigation. It was not until near the end of the Middle Ages that scholars began to take a real interest in the vernacular languages, not to mention employing them for general academic communication. There were a couple of exceptions to this in the early part of the second millennium, such as Aelfric (*c.* 1000) in England, the First Grammarian (in the middle of the twelfth century) in Iceland and Molinier (in the 1330s) on Occitan in the *Leys d'Amors*, but they were few and far between.

What was perceived to constitute 'grammar' changed considerably over the centuries. Early Greek and Roman definitions were rather loose, and by the second century AD it had, by different writers, been associated with a wide range of topics, ranging from phonetics and etymology via the mechanics of reading and correctness of use to clarity of interpretation and literary judgement. During the Middle Ages three main types of grammar may be distinguished: literary, logical and speculative. For sheer number, the literary grammars far outstripped the two other types for centuries, but after *c.* 1100 the emphasis began to shift away from the study of literature to that of usage and correctness of language. Accordingly, the term 'grammar' became more narrowly defined as linguistic studies, in many cases to the exclusion of literature, but there was still widespread disagreement about what could, and should, be included under grammar in this more restricted sense.

An important impetus to this aspect of grammatical studies came in the eleventh and twelfth centuries with the rediscovery of the logic of Greek philosophers, in particular Aristotle as mediated by the Christian philosopher Boethius (*c.* 480-*c.* 525), and some commentaries carried out by Jewish and Arab philosophers.[5] Grammar became the first and central element of the *trivium* – ahead of the disciplines of rhetoric and dialectic (or logic) – which was taught widely in the new educational institutions, the universities, that started to proliferate in Western Europe from the middle of the twelfth century. Among the foremost people instrumental in this shift towards a more logical approach to grammar are Anselm (mid eleventh century-1117), Peter Abelard (1079-1142), William of Conches (*c.* 1090-*c.* 1154) and Peter Helias (*c.* 1100-after 1166). Between them they were dissatisfied with the inadequacy of previous grammatical definitions (including those by Priscian) and provided the foundation for a 'new' type of grammar, with more stringency in the wording, that reached its climax with the Modistae (see below).

For example, in a well-known extract from his *Philosophia*, William of Conches (1980:116) attacks Priscian for his treatment of the parts of speech: '... *quoniam etsi Prisciamus inde satis dicat, tamen obscuras dat definitiones nec exponit, causas vero inventionis diversarum partium et diversorum accidentium in unaquaque praetermittit*' (although he says enough about grammar, Priscian gives unclear definitions and does not explain them, and he fails to give the reason for the existence of the different word classes and all their related properties). To repair this deficiency, Peter Helias created a single criterion for the parts of speech – the *modus significandi* of each class – instead of the wealth of criteria used by Priscian. He also set up purely linguistic divisions of grammar and identified the following four parts: letters, syllables, words/parts of speech, speech/discourse (*Partes huius artis sunt quatuor: ... prima pars scientia de litteris, secunda de syllabis, tertia de dictionibus, quarta de oratione*; cited in Michael 1970:35-6). However, from about the beginning of the thirteenth century, the following fourfold division was commonly found:

1. Orthographia (comprising the letters of the alphabet, syllables and spelling)
2. Etymologia (comprising the parts of speech and other classifications of words, but not usually etymology in the modern sense)
3. Oratio/Diasynthetica/Sintasis (covering discourse, syntax and the sentence)
4. Prosodia (i.e. pronunciation)

But such divisions could take different forms. Some writers confined themselves to a threefold (or even a twofold) division, while others expanded the number of distinctions to five or more. Of the four parts mentioned above, orthographia appears to have been the most elastic one. The speculative grammarians generally observed a strict twofold division into etymology and syntax, but – at the risk of pre-empting the next Chapter – at the beginning of the English grammatical tradition William Lily, in his influential Latin grammar *A Short Introduction of Grammar* from 1548/49, restored the fourfold arrangement of orthography, etymology, syntax and prosody, and for many English grammarians – and innumerable schoolchildren, as we shall see in Chapter IV – this remained the standard division for the next few centuries. But there were alternative proposals in the Renaissance. The Frenchman Peter Ramus (or Pierre de la Ramée)[6] agreed with the speculative grammarians that orthography and prosody should be excluded as being somehow 'different' from etymology and syntax, while the Spaniard Sanctius introduced the most radical scheme of all by rejecting all divisions, on the grounds that syntax comprises the whole of grammar (*finis grammaticae*; Sanctius 1795:I,17-18).[7]

Going back to the pre-Modistae period and the contemporary importance of philosophy and logic, not to mention Aristotelian metaphysics, grammatical theory was often compared or contrasted with logical description. Thus, according to Albertus Magnus (*c.* 1200-80), the real subject matter of grammar is the mode of construction (*modus construendi*) whereas that of logic is the mode of knowledge (*modus sciendi*) (cf. Michael 1970:31), and the logical analysis of grammatical structure is usually given a high priority in these grammars.

Another consequence of the strong influence of philosophy is the extended scope of grammar. To be sure, the grammars are all written in Latin and the often very few examples provided in them are nearly always taken from Latin, but the declared aim (if not always the actual practice) of most of the writers is nevertheless to describe language in general, not just a particular language such as Latin. This decisive shift of emphasis away from the grammar of one language (i.e. Latin) towards universal grammar took place around the thirteenth century, presumably in part due to unawareness that different languages could have different structures. In the mid twelfth century, Peter Helias maintained that 'there were as many grammars as there were languages',[8] but Pinborg (1967:24) disputes that he meant precisely that. However, to take a few examples, Robert Kilwardby (*c.* 1215-79) stated as a requirement that 'grammar ... should be the same for all languages and that rules peculiar to any one language were only accidentally a concern of grammatical science' (cf. Bursill-Hall 1976:169-70), and at roughly the same time, by the middle of the thirteenth century, Roger Bacon (*c.* 1214-92) was able to claim that grammar is one and the same in all languages for substance and only shows accidental variations (*Grammatica una et eadem est secundum substantiam in omnibus linguis, licet accidentaliter varietur*) (Bacon 1902:27), but it is only the former aspect (of universality) that is open to scientific enquiry.[9] This set the tone for the following generations of scholars and it is basically the view taken by the speculative grammarians. Admittedly, Albertus Magnus explicitly denies grammar the status of 'a science' by pointing to the distinction between grammar and logic in terms of different modes (cf. Michael 1970:30-31), but this was an exception. The acceptance of 'universal grammar' as the basis for the scientific status of linguistic studies is significant and in accordance with Aristotle's view that a subject can only qualify as a true 'science' if it has universal application.

Another aspect emphasised by these grammarians is the importance of syntax, which had often previously been treated as secondary to morphology and the grammatical categories, and even been considered to be chiefly concerned with speech and communication rather than with written texts, so this may be seen as yet another legacy of the new logical foundations.

The ground had thus been prepared for the most fruitful and interesting medieval period in terms of original contributions to linguistic studies, namely the roughly hundred years from the middle of the thirteenth to the middle of the fourteenth century dominated by the so-called Speculative Grammarians or Modistae (Modists), who represent the culmination of the development towards purely linguistic studies.

Speculative Grammar[10]

In the thirteenth and fourteenth centuries, a number of scholars in different countries began to write grammars which they themselves referred to as speculative grammars (*Grammaticae Speculativae*). Despite the considerable geographical diversity and their divergent views on many details, they did on the whole subscribe to essentially the same basic theoretical framework of grammatical theory, and some of them, centred in Paris, worked together as a group. It is not within the scope of the present study to give a detailed account of speculative grammar, but it is necessary briefly to introduce a few of its most fundamental concepts, before turning to the treatment of prepositions in two of the most important works from this period, by Boethius of Dacia and Thomas of Erfurt, respectively.

The work of the Modistae may be seen as an attempt to integrate the bulk of traditional Latin grammar, including Donatus's and Priscian's eight parts of speech, into the larger framework of scholastic logic and philosophy. This attempt, ingenious though it was in many respects, was only temporarily successful, and the whole concept, permeated by the thought and outlook of the late Middle Ages, did not survive the advent of the Renaissance, which 'revoked' the definition of grammar in favour of literary studies, and after a while it collapsed. But the speculative 'school' generated a lot of linguistic activity for a century or so and provided some interesting insights into language structure, for example in terms of definitions of, and relations between, the established grammatical categories. Its approach to the subject was one that placed the emphasis on language in general ('universal grammar')[11] by establishing several interconnected layers of *modi* (modes).

It is for their conception of language in terms of different modes that this group of scholars have become most famous. In fact, so closely have they been linked with it that they are usually known simply as 'the Modistae', and many of their works are entitled *modi significandi*. Stated briefly, the modistic model[12] is a tripartite system, which takes the real world ('things') as its point of departure. These 'things' are said to have certain properties, or *modi essendi*, and constitute the first level. The second step is that the mind perceives these properties by means of the active modes of understanding, or *modi intelligendi activi*, so that these active modes apply to the mind, whereas their passive counterparts at the same level (*modi intelligendi passivi*) relate to the property of things. The third and final step occurs when the mind imposes the active modes of signifying (*modi significandi activi*) on sounds or expression elements to turn them into words and parts of speech, or as Thomas of Erfurt says, 'The active mode of signifying is the mode or property of the expression vouchsafed by the intellect to itself by means of which the expression signifies the property of the thing.'[13] At this level, too, there are corresponding passive modes (*modi significandi passivi*) relating to the qualities of things as signified by words.

This is often represented in the following schematic way (modified from Covington 1984:31-2):

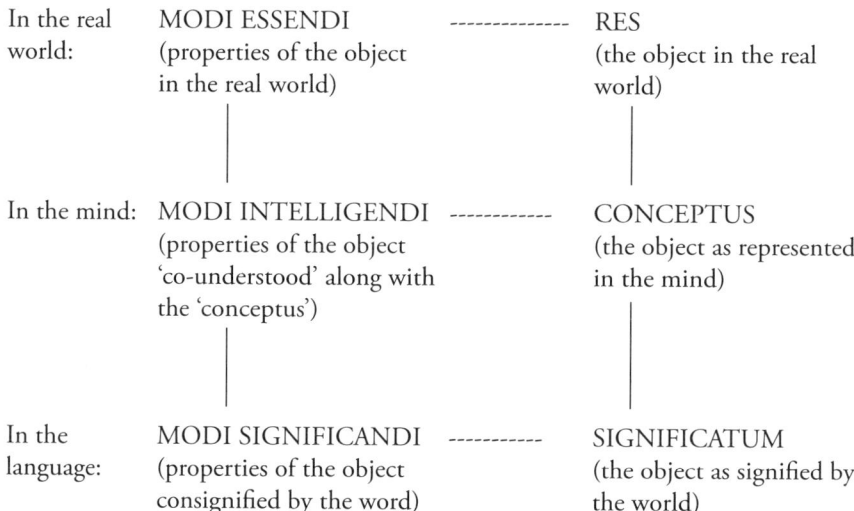

In the real world:	MODI ESSENDI (properties of the object in the real world)	-----------	RES (the object in the real world)
In the mind:	MODI INTELLIGENDI (properties of the object 'co-understood' along with the 'conceptus')	-----------	CONCEPTUS (the object as represented in the mind)
In the language:	MODI SIGNIFICANDI (properties of the object consignified by the word)	-----------	SIGNIFICATUM (the object as signified by the world)

It is fundamental to the theory that there are correlations between the 'things' of the real world, on the one hand, and their representations in language as mediated by the mind, on the other. From a language point of view, the crucial terms are the modes of signifying, since they determine the grammatical categories of words. Consequently these modes of signifying feature prominently in the modistic accounts by Boethius of Dacia and Thomas of Erfurt below, but it is worth remembering that a similar relationship between the known things (*res*), the knowing subject (*intellectus*) and language (*sermo*) is present in Aristotelian thinking as interpreted by Boethius, the philosopher, and 'rediscovered' in the early Middle Ages (cf. Maierù 1994:279).

As far as the parts of speech are concerned, the Modistae in general adopted Priscian's eight-part division, unlike some of their predecessors. For example, Boethius (sometimes called the 'last of the Romans') and Roger Bacon (many centuries later) maintain that there are two parts of speech in logic (noun and verb), but eight in grammar (cf. Michael 1970:51). These eight, however, do not coincide with Priscian's categories; first because, according to Bacon, the grammatical parts can all be subsumed under one or the other of the logical parts; secondly, because conjunctions and prepositions are given almost logical status, and since they cannot be accommodated under either noun or verb, they are excluded from the parts of speech altogether. As justification for this exclusion Bacon quotes Boethius, who uses the image of a chariot:

> Just as the reins and the bridle are not part of the chariot but as it were ligatures and accessories, so the preposition and conjunction are not parts of speech but connectives. (Michael 1970:52)

In other words, they have an 'adhesive' function, binding together words and sentences without having status of word classes themselves.

Overall, the Modistae were not specifically interested in the parts of speech *per se*, but rather in what use was made of them in the analysis of language structure, i.e. in syntax. It is therefore chiefly in order to investigate this aspect of modistic grammar and the views of prepositions presented in it that we now turn to two of the most prominent linguistic contributions in this era.

Boethius of Dacia (early to late 13th century)
Boethius[14] was born in Denmark (hence the epithet 'of Dacia') in the first half of the thirteenth century. We do not know much about his early life, but at some point after 1262 he came to live in Paris and was a teacher at the university in the 1270s. As a leading figure in the radical Aristotelian philosophical movement there, known as 'Latin Averroism' (cf. Boethius 1980:2), he was one of the main targets for Bishop Étienne Tempier's notorious condemnation of 219 philosophical propositions in 1277.

Boethius is arguably the most important of the early Modistae from the Paris 'school',[15] but others include his three compatriots – Martin,

Johannes and Simon, all 'of Dacia'[16] – and Michel de Marbais. Around 1270 Boethius published the comprehensive *Modi Significandi sive Quaestiones Super Priscianum Maiorem* (Modes of Signifying or Questions on Priscian Major) and this work was soon afterwards abridged by Godfrey of Fontaine, which is why the work can be dated with some confidence. It contains Boethius's essential views on grammar in the early modistic period.[17]

In this abridged version Boethius asks and answers 134 questions on the study of language. Questions 1-28 address grammar and the various *modi* in general, while the rest deal with the individual parts of speech. The first four of these are the declinable parts (noun, verb, participle and pronoun), which cover Questions 29-107, followed by the indeclinable parts (preposition, adverb, interjection and conjunction) in Questions 108-34. It should be said, though, that this order seems more a matter of convention than principle. Not only does Boethius not justify it but, unlike some of his predecessors for whom particularly the order of the first two (noun and verb) is of fundamental importance and based on logic (i.e. things or substances precede the acts that they perform or states that they display), Boethius goes out of his way to argue that the noun does *not* take precedence over the verb. Although he does not rule out that the noun *may* be the 'first part of speech' (1980:86-7), he rejects any notion that there is a logical explanation for this and refutes some of the traditional arguments for this assertion.

Among the issues that he tackles under the general part of his Syntax are the questions of the status and scope of the subject of grammar. As regards the first one, Boethius attempts to prove that grammar is a science, for, in his view, in order to be a science the subject matter must have 'determinate causes standing in an essential order' (as opposed to 'accidental causes', such as 'chance and fortune') and it must be 'comprehensible by the intellect', and since both of these apply to grammar, it is by definition a science (1980:30-31).[18] He even talks about 'the unity of the science of grammar' (1980:32-3) and shortly afterwards about grammar as 'a science of discourse' (*scientia sermocinalis*) (1980:36-7). A little later we hear that grammar is not a 'common' [i.e. general] science (*scientia communis*), but a 'special science' (*scientia specialis*); on the other hand, it is a 'common art' (*ars com-*

munis) since 'it teaches a manner of expressing an intended concept which is used in science' (1980:40-41). This shows that the subject matter of grammar consists in 'the modes of expressing an intended mental concept through congruous discourse in every field' since the subject matter of a science is its *cognitive* focus (1980:38-9).

However, we are told that although the grammarian is quite naturally concerned with grammar, he did not 'discover' grammar. That was the achievement of the philosopher, more specifically the 'metaphysician' (1980:24-5). The reason for this hinges on the different nature of the *modi*. Recall that the modes of being (*modi essendi*) are of primary importance and from them the modes of understanding (*modi intelligendi*) are derived, but these two types of modes are the subject matter for the philosopher, not for the 'mere' grammarian. The latter can only deal with the modes of signifying (*modi significandi*), which in turn are derived from, and mediated by, the *modi intelligendi*.

It is not the grammarian's task to consider the essence of the *vox* but 'the *vox* qua sign of an object' (cf. Law 2003:131), which means the word-form and not the meaning/reference (*significatum*), since 'something can function quite well as a noun [*nomen*], which signifies no particular object' (1980:42-3). This is how Boethius explains the existence of abstract nouns, using *nihil* (nothing) as an illustration, and it appears to suggest that the basic modistic link between words, concepts and things in the world is not universal.[19] Or at least it does not apply both ways, for he practically turns the argument on its head by claiming that 'a grammar attains to completeness only when no concept can be fashioned in the mind without there [being?] corresponding to it some similar mode of expression propounded in the grammar' (1980:50-51). Thus words without 'objects' or references are possible, but anything conceived by the mind must have an equivalent expression. However, such references are very specific; the (Aristotelian) 'categories, such as action, passion, substance and accident' are said not to be the business of the grammarian (1980:62-3).

On the other hand, it *is* the grammarian's duty 'to consider the word [here in the sense of *dictio*, not *vox*; cf. again Law 2003:131] and the part of it, which is its *per se significatum*' (1980:46-7). It is clearly Boethius's view that the study of language *per se* should be concerned with form rather than meaning, and mental concepts can be expressed by different parts of speech (1980:50-51).

In Boethius's treatment of prepositions (1980:198-213) it is at first established that the preposition, which is one of the indeclinable parts, *is* a part of speech, on the grounds that it can enter into the composition of a sentence; admittedly, it is not a part that all sentences depend on, like *suppositum* (the subject) or *appositum* (the verb or, strictly speaking, the predicate), but still it 'links something declined with cases [viz., the nominal element] to an act, signified by means of the *appositum*' (1980:198-9). This function combined with the fact that prepositions are not subsumed under any of the other classes makes them distinct from these.

That prepositions can enter into composition with other words, i.e. as 'prefixes', was a commonplace in the description of them by the Roman grammarians. However, Boethius is more detailed in his analysis than most of his predecessors, though he is woefully reticent in providing examples. First, he states that 'the *significatum* of the preposition' may or may not be 'contrary to the *significatum* of the word [*dictio*] to which that preposition is added via composition', that is, in compounds. If it is added, it will change the *significatum* of the word in question; if it is not, it may bring about 'a certain completion or diminution in that *significatum*' (1980:200-201) since it may change its basic meaning. Such compounds can even be ambiguous, as in the one example mentioned, viz. *impius*, which may mean either 'not pious' or 'very pious', i.e. *in* (> *im*) may, depending on the context, act as a negative element or an uptoner, resulting in very different meanings.

Boethius goes on to observe that the compound thus created is a single word with a single mode of signifying as well as being a member of a different word class. The preposition therefore no longer has its specific mode of signifying (only the *vox* is left) but rather 'assumes the species of that part with which it enters into composition' (1980:202-3), and its main contribution is to render the *significatum* of the 'new' word complete or to change or diminish it.[20] The conclusion must be that these 'prefixes' are simply not 'proper' prepositions. Boethius says as much when he states that 'a preposition remaining in the prepositional species *never* enters into composition with another part' and that 'that part which has retained for itself the specific prepositional mode of signifying, *never* loses it ...' (1980:204-5; my emphasis). So words that become (subordinate) components of compounds may contribute their *vox* and *significatum* to the compound, but not their specific mode of signifying. Neither 'type' (*species*) nor 'number' as modes of signifying is inconsistent with prepositions, we are told, and the preposition is an indeclinable part of speech 'because it does not have accidental modes of signifying', not 'because such modes of signifying are inconsistent with it' as a class (1980:206-7). Nor is 'degree' (*comparatio*) inconsistent with prepositions on the basis of the preposition's *significatum* since the latter can be understood to signify increase or diminution, as in *magis/minus clam custodibus* (more/less unknown to the guards) or *magis/minus prope pariete* (more/less close to the wall).

On the other hand, 'case' is *not* a prepositional mode of signifying. Instead, as we were told earlier, 'it signifies a case relationship of an element to an act' (i.e. a noun to a verb) where this element functions as *terminus* or *principium* of this act and is declined in case (accusative or ablative) (1980:210-11). This is because the preposition does not, from its own mode of signifying, 'convey the aspect of the element declined with cases' (*ibid.*). Even so, it is mentioned that a preposition can indeed enter into constructions where no case relationship obtains. For example, in *venio de super parvum pontem* (I come from above a/the small bridge), where the preposition *super* 'is construed with' another preposition (*de*), as in the English translation *above* is with *from*. (One could of course argue that the prepositional complement of *de* (and hence of *from*) is the whole of the following PP, but this is a much more recent analysis.) In the rest of this paragraph – the last in the section on prepositions – Boethius modifies his stance on case and the prepositional modes of signifying, and brings in the relationship between the (prior) *modus intelligendi* and the (derived) *modus significandi*. In dealing with this relationship, and thus appealing to a 'higher' level, he even hints at the possibility of prepositions having the mode of signifying case, since it is possible that a particular part of speech (such as prepositions) just by accident does not possess a certain mode of signifying, though it may logically be present 'in the intellect'. It may therefore in principle be possible for that class to have it, 'provided that some other mode of signifying existing in that part is not inconsistent with such a construction' (1980:212-13). It was essentially for this reason, he informs us, that Donatus took case to be 'an accident of the preposition', since 'it construed with parts declined with cases' (*ibid.*).

Boethius's analysis is not always easy to follow and it seems ironic that the most interesting aspects of his examination of prepositions relate not to their syntactic properties, but to their function 'in composition', i.e. as nominal or verbal 'prefixes'. However, as we saw, his distinction between having a noun or a preposition as the prepositional complement is also significant. In general, it must be said that the early Modistae, building on the substantial work carried out in the previous couple of centuries, took linguistic analysis in a new direction and stimulated interest in this subject for the next few generations of scholars, and the best example of this is seen in the works of Thomas of Erfurt.

Thomas of Erfurt

To many people, Thomas of Erfurt represents the culmination and the summation of modistic grammar. Not much is known about Thomas's life, but he presumably studied in Paris around 1300 and taught there subsequently before moving to Erfurt where he was a teacher at two of the schools that came to form a central part of the University of Erfurt when it was founded later in the fourteenth century (in 1392) as the third university in present-day Germany (after Heidelberg and Cologne). Thomas wrote some commentaries on Aristotle's works and a metrical treatise on syntax for schoolboys, *Fundamentum puerorum*, but the work for which he is still known and admired is his *Grammatica Speculativa* (see Thomas of Erfurt 1972),[21] previously also known as *Novi modi significandi* and believed to have been written in the first decade of the fourteenth century (cf. Pinborg 1967:131-5; Thomas of Erfurt 1972:26-8).[22]

For Thomas a part of speech 'exists formally by means of the active mode of signifying superimposed upon the word, because a part of speech is a word inasmuch as it possesses an active mode of signifying' (1972:148-9). Like Boethius, Thomas keeps the traditional eight parts of speech and deals with them one by one, without first listing them.

In the section called 'On the grammatical case of the noun' (Ch. XIX, pp. 186-95), he defines case as 'the accidental mode of signifying of the noun by means of which the noun connotes [*consignificat*] the property of principium [first member] or terminus [second member]' and mentions the six well-known Latin nominal cases (or 'species') (1972:186-7). Prepositions are referred to under the two cases accusative and ablative, but just as an alternative construction. For instance, Thomas states that the terminus *quem* (whom) may be 'derived simply, that is, without government' in *lego librum* (I read the book) or 'with government, as when it is derived by means of the preposition governing the accusative', though his examples *vado ad plateam* (I go to the street) and *curro ad campum* (I run to the field (etc.)) say little about *quem* (1972:190-91). However, the key term here is 'government'.[23] Under the ablative the information is very similar, with the addition that 'the mode of signifying corresponding and complementary in itself is in this way to be governed' (1972:192-3).

Thomas offers several almost identical definitions of the preposition, so let us choose the one he gives in his summing-up: 'The preposition is therefore the part of speech signifying by means of the mode of adjacency to some case form, linking it and referring it back to the act' (*Est ergo praepositio pars orationis, significans per modum adiacentis alteri casuali, ipsum contrahens, et ad actum reducens*) (1972:264-5). In itself, this formulation is quite similar to other modistic definitions. For example, according to Michel de Marbais, 'The preposition is ... a part of speech signifying through the mode of relating substance to action' (*Praepositio ... est pars orationis significans per modum retorquentis substantiam ad actum*) (cf. Michael:1970:66). Even closer to Thomas's wording is that of Siger de Courtrai, who says that 'prepositions refer a case form back to the act' (*Praepositiones sunt ad retorquendum casualem ad actum*; Siger de Courtrai 1977:62). This is strikingly similar to another version of Thomas's definition, where he pronounces the 'essential mode of signifying of the preposition' to be 'the mode of signifying by means of the mode of adjacency to some case form, linking it and turning it back to the act' (*modus significandi per modum adiacentis alteri casuali ipsum contrahens, et ad actum retorquens*; 1972:262-3). Nevertheless, Thomas's definition is more detailed than the two others and quite close to that of Boethius. This raises several interesting questions, some of which he deals with in the two chapters devoted to the preposition (XLI-XLII, 1972:262-9), which we shall now examine in some detail.

First, one notices the semantic overtones of the definition in his use of 'act' rather than 'verb', and it is certainly for semantic reasons that he dismisses Priscian's definition (see Ch. I) by making a clear distinction between 'prepositions in composition' and separate, independent prepositions. The former 'are not true prepositions' because 'they signify nothing by themselves since they are not words by themselves, nor do they have modes of signifying by themselves' (1972:268-9). This distinction is in accordance with the general modistic claim that each word has its own meaning, which is apparently not true of 'prefixes' (cf. 'they signify nothing by themselves'). They are not completely devoid of meaning, though, in so far as they 'complete, change or reduce' (*complet, aut mutat, aut minuit*; 1972:266-9) the meaning of the whole word. Word order apart, this is a verbatim citation of Donatus's definition of the preposition (see again Ch. I) which, as we noticed above, Boethius too made use of.

Secondly, the definition also makes use of syntactic criteria. The preposition is adjacent to a noun (it usually precedes it), which it case-governs, thereby forging a construction between the noun and the verb ('the act'). In other words, the preposition functions as an intermediary (a connecting word), linking a nominal element (through case) to a verbal element.

There are, however, further complexities in the relationship between the preposition and the following noun (or pronoun) which again are of a semantic nature. As we saw above, it is fundamental to modistic grammatical thought that there is a close relationship between linguistic signs (the *modi significandi*) and the world of reality (i.e. 'things', the *modi essendi*). This is also true of prepositions, as Thomas's addition to one of his definitions makes clear: 'This mode of the preposition is derived from the property of determination and limitation in *things*' (... *in rebus*) (1972:262-3; my emphasis). Just as things are determined and delimited in the real world, so nouns are determined and delimited by prepositions, and '[t]his limitation of the case form is effected by means of prepositions governing the accusative and ablative case' (1972:262-5).

In 'linking' a noun through case-government, the preposition thus delimits its complement (the 'case form'). For example, the accusative, being the mode of signifying *quem* (whom), may be delimited by a mode to yield *ad quem* (to whom), *in quem* (into whom), *prope quem* (near whom), etc., and equally the ablative *quo* may be delimited by a mode to produce *a quo* (from whom), *in quo* (in whom), *sine quo* (without whom), etc. (1972:262-3). 'To link and limit the case mode', we are told, is the first stage for which 'the preposition was invented'. The second stage is to 'refer the case form back to the act' (1972:264-5). But before examining the syntactic relationship between the prepositional (noun) complement and the verb, we need first to take a look at Thomas's general view of sentence structure.

Thomas's analysis is founded on a binary principle and takes its starting-point in the 'construction' (*constructio*). Every construction, he argues, consists of two (and only two) 'constructibles' (*constructibilia*), one of which is, by definition, the 'dependent' (*dependens*) and the other the 'terminant' (*terminans*) (1972:274-5, 280-81), or the 'terminus' (*terminus*) (e.g. 1972:190-91), of the dependency. However, in defining these two parts of any construction, Thomas relies on very vague notional impressions, such as the terminant being an 'entity in action' with the function of 'terminating the dependence' (1972:280-81) or 'terminating the act' (1972:190-91). The following passage is worth quoting in full, since it demonstrates both the imprecision of Thomas's definitions and the close interrelationship between language and the real world in modistic thought:

> Just as from matter and form, of which one is the act and the other the potentiality, create by themselves a composite in nature, so by reason of dependence and termination, a construction is created by itself in the sentence. The dependent constructible is that which only requires various dependences by means of some mode of signifying, but the terminant constructible is that which functions, by means of some mode of signifying, only as a dependence generator. (1972:280-83)

The analysis of a complex construction (in the ultimate case, a sentence) therefore involves integrating (or, conversely, separating) more and more units in a binary process. For instance (to take a couple of Thomas's very few and highly construed examples), when the two fundamental sentence elements, *suppositum* and *appositum*, occur alone, as in *Socrates currit* (Socrates runs), the first constructible (*Socrates*) is the terminant and the second constructible (*currit*) the dependent, i.e. the verb depends on the subject. On the other hand, in *lego librum* (I read the book) the first constructible (*lego*) is now the dependent and the second constructible (*librum*) the terminant, i.e. the verb (also) depends on the object.[24]

This may be illustrated in the following way if we let the arrow point from the 'dependent' to the 'terminant':

If we move one step further to a construction consisting of (overt) subject + verb + object, 'this', Thomas says, 'on account of several dependencies of the verb on the pre-posed suppositum and the post-posed oblique, cannot be one construction' (1972:274-5). Consequently, a two-stage analysis must apply, but although he provides as an example *Socrates percutit Platonem* (Socrates hits Plato), he does not discuss this particular type of example. It is reasonably clear, though, that the analysis must be something like this:

This type of analysis underlies Thomas's concept of transitive and intransitive constructions.[25] A transitive construction is defined as a construction where the first constructible depends on the second, and an intransitive construction, by contrast, as one in which the second constructible depends on the first (1972:282-3). From this definition it follows that *Socrates currit* is an intransitive and *lego librum* a transitive construction.

Both intransitive and transitive constructions are subdivided into *actuum* and *personarum* types.[26] Among the intransitive constructions the (major) *actuum* type is defined as always having the verb as the dependent member (i.e., prototypically, the subject-verb type), whereas the (minor) *personarum* type constitutes an 'expansion' of a nominal or verbal element by means of a 'determinant' (not to be confused with a 'terminant'). For instance, *Socrates currit* represents the *actuum* type, but *Socrates albus* ((the) white Socrates), which is an expansion of the noun, and *currit bene* (runs well), which is an expansion of the verb, are both examples of the *personarum* type. Presumably, then, Thomas would accept the following analysis of a two-tier intransitive construction,

    Socrates albus   currit bene
        ←   ←
     (stage 1)   (stage 2)

though he does not make this entirely clear (cf. 1972:99, 110).

At this point we may return to the question of how prepositional constructions fit into Thomas's scheme. By definition, they belong to the *personarum* types of construction, since they do not have a verb as the dependent element, but the only transitive *personarum* type is the expansion of a noun by another noun in an oblique case, i.e. an NN structure as, for example, in *filius Socratis* (Socrates's son), where, interestingly, *filius* is the dependent and the genitive form *Socratis* the terminant. This may be illustrated in the following way:

    filius Socratis
      →

But Thomas does not merely imply that a prepositional phrase is an intransitive construction; he states it explicitly. Thus he lists conjunction, adverb, preposition and interjection as the 'four modes' that may function as indeclinable determination 'added to the suppositum', and the example he gives for prepositions is *a Socrate legitur* (it is read by Socrates; 1972:294-7).

We should now be in a position to address two crucial problems inherent in Thomas's treatment of prepositions. The first one concerns the constructional relationship between the preposition and its (noun) complement (the 'case form'). The second one involves the relationship between the prepositional complement and the verb.

As far as the first problem is concerned, it is repeatedly stated that the preposition governs its adjacent complement in a case (either the accusative or the ablative) or, as he often expresses it, links and limits (or contracts) its case form (1972:264-5), but apparently that does not mean that Thomas sees the preposition as 'head' or, to use his term, 'terminant' of the prepositional phrase, as it is common to do in modern linguistic theories. (As we have seen, the notion of 'a phrase' was introduced much later.) On the contrary, a preposition + noun construction, being an intransitive *personarum* type of construction, has the noun as the terminant and the preposition as its dependent element, since the latter is said to expand, or modify, the noun, or act as a determinant added to the *suppositum*, Thomas's usual term for the (logical) subject. We may illustrate that as follows:

> a Socrate
> →

In this role of determining the *suppositum*, the preposition is described as equivalent to the three other indeclinable parts of speech: the adverb, the conjunction and the interjection (1972:294-7), but unlike these three, the preposition cannot determine the *appositum* (the verb) (1972:298-9). Thomas makes a further parallel between the preposition, the adverb and the conjunction, when he says that 'case in the preposition is similar to what signification in the adverb and power in the conjunction are' (1972:264-5). This parallel is elaborated in the sentence that follows:

> Just as signification in the adverb consists in a special mode of determining and power in the conjunction in a special mode of relating, so case in the preposition consists in a special mode of contracting and linking. (1972:264-5)

Governing case, then, is an essential function of the preposition. Indeed, for Thomas 'the preposition was in fact invented on behalf of case forms' (1972:262-3), and he talks about 'the general mode' of the preposition (cf. the definition above) being divided into 'three subaltern modes', according to whether a preposition can govern the accusative only, the ablative only, or either, and he calls these three modes 'the case of the preposition' (1972:264-5).

But if the answer to the first problem is relatively straightforward, the answer to the second one (the relationship of the 'case form' to the verb) is less so. In this connection it is important to recall that Thomas does not appear to see a preposition + noun construction as a syntactic unit in the sense in which we are used to talking of a prepositional phrase. As a result, it is possible for him to describe the relation between the prepositional complement and the verb as a more direct one than we might be inclined to do. Nor should we forget that in Thomas's definition it is the function of the preposition not only to 'link and limit the case form' but also to refer it 'back to the act' (*ibid.*). As a matter of fact, the function of a noun seems in no way confined when it occurs as a prepositional complement, as may be seen from the following two examples.

From a previous example (*lego librum*) we learnt that in a transitive construction consisting of verb + direct object, the verb is the dependent element and the direct object the terminus. But, equally, in examples like *vado ad plateam* (I go into the street) and *curro ad campum* (I run to the field) with prepositional constructions, both *plateam* and *campum* are said to be the terminus in relation to the dependent verb. As we saw above, Thomas's explanation for this analysis is that 'the function of the terminus "whom" (*quem*) is sometimes derived simply, that is, without government, as in: *lego librum*; sometimes with government, as when it is derived by means of the preposition governing the accusative' (1972:190-91). Given the ultimate semantic commitment of modistic grammar, the identical analysis of a direct object and a prepositional complement should perhaps not surprise us, but it is difficult to defend on purely syntactic grounds.

The other type of example to be mentioned may be illustrated by the previous *a Socrate legitur*. Here *Socrate*, a prepositional complement in the ablative case governed by the preposition *a(b)*, is said to have the function of 'subject' (1972:288-9).[27] Clearly, the term 'subject' must, in this example, refer to what we would call logical, or underlying, subject rather than grammatical subject, but the important point is that by relying on (vague) notional definitions Thomas does not distinguish between the two. Hence the function of a noun need not be constrained by a governing preposition.

We may thus illustrate the two types of example as follows:

    →
vado ad plateam
    →

    ←
a Socrate legitur
    →

One consequence of this analysis is that the term 'transitivity' must be understood in a wide sense, for to analyse examples like *vado in plateam* and *curro ad campum* as parallel with *lego librum* only makes sense if they are also seen as transitive constructions. Similarly, *a Socrate legitur* must, irrespective of the preposition, be an intransitive construction on a par with *Socrates currit*. Such use of the terms 'transitive' and 'intransitive' is not compatible with the usual syntactic definition of transitivity nowadays, but in the late Middle Ages this usage appears to have been common. Thus, according to Siger de Courtrai, the function of prepositions is above all to establish transitivity (*Omnes praepositiones inventae sunt propter habitudines transitivas denotandas*, as he puts it, with a reference to Priscian; Siger de Courtrai 1977:62). But although Siger's claim fits examples like *vado ad plateam* and *curro ad campum*, it is nevertheless rejected by Thomas in its extreme form, on the grounds that there are both verbs and nouns which require prepositions but 'have no transitiveness' (1972:262-3). To illustrate this, Thomas uses the examples *sum in domo* (I am in the house), which has a local preposition, and *annulus ex auro*[28] (a ring of gold), where *ex auro* specifies the material, and he explicitly allows for both transitive and intransitive 'linkage' of the verb (the 'act') with the prepositional complement (the 'case form') when he says,

> This act is used for the constructible that is dependent on the case form, for the act is not always dependent on the case form by means of the preposition, although it will be frequently so. (1972:264-5)

Finally, it should be noted that Thomas does not provide a list of the prepositions in Latin, though he does indirectly say that there are 49 in all. This number is arrived at by adding up the 'thirty special types of preposition' that govern the accusative, the 'fifteen special types' that govern the ablative and the 'four types' that can govern either (1972:266-7). Among the first group, he only mentions *apud* and *ante*, under the second only the forms *a*, *ab* and *absque*, whereas all four members of the third group (*in*, *sub*, *super* and *subter*) are listed. The reader is apparently supposed to know the remaining forty prepositions.

The end of modistic grammar

We have dwelled for some time on Thomas's treatment of prepositions, chiefly because it is more detailed than most medieval accounts, but also because its incorporation into speculative grammar is characteristic of the late medieval approach to linguistic theory, which for all its shortcomings is now generally accepted as one of the important periods in the history of linguistics, short-lived though it was. As we have seen, the arguments of the Modistae are not always simple to follow, especially in view of their very sparse use of examples to underpin them, though we should understand that this is often deliberate since they operate with 'universal' language rather than with one or more particular languages, despite the fact that any examples are invariably taken from Latin.

However, once the outer framework of modistic grammar began to crumble, the whole edifice soon collapsed. It had pinned its existence on the direct correlation between the 'real' world and linguistic forms via the 'intellect' or mental representations, and when this direct link was called into question, there was nothing to prop up the theory. The *modi significandi* were the eggs that had all been put into one basket, so there was nowhere to go, once the modistic concept of universal grammar was rejected. And rejected it was, chiefly by representatives of two movements: the Nominalists and the Latin Averroists (the latter inspired by the twelfth-century Muslim philosopher Averroës), although their 'attacks' had a lot in common.[29]

The best known of the Nominalists was the English Franciscan monk William of Ockham (*c.* 1285-*c.* 1347), whose early work *Summa logicae* from around 1323 soon became known in intellectual circles on the European continent. His target was above all the heavy reliance on universals on the part of the Modistae. For him the only universals were natural signs, such as smoke from a fire, and conventional signs, such as words. What was really problematic was the overarching theory behind the modistic system, especially the interrelations between the three levels of being, understanding and signifying. Ockham makes a sharp distinction between concepts or 'mental words', which signify 'naturally' and belong to the mental sphere, and words (spoken or written) which signify by convention and agreement among the speakers of a language. A number of expressions (e.g. synonyms) can 'mean' the same, that is, have the same truth value at the mental level, but can look and sound very different. For example, Ockham finds no need for pronouns and participles at the mental level – and we are still talking about Latin – since they do not express different concepts compared with nouns and verbs. Nor do all the grammatical 'accidents' belong at the same level. While case and number are part of mental language (they change the meaning of words), grammatical gender and verbal conjugation are not; they belong to the level of signification. The standard example is *homo est alba*, which though ungrammatical has the same meaning and truth value as the correct construction *homo est albus*, where *homo* is masculine and the adjective *albus* agrees in form with the noun it modifies (cf. William of Ockham 1951:13). The conclusion must therefore be that there is no one-to-one relationship between the two levels, though this is precisely what the Modistae postulate.

The best known representative of the Latin Averroists was John of Jandun (*c.* 1285-1328), who studied in Paris, but the chief spokesman for the 'movement' in the 1330s was Johannes Aurifaber, who chaired a public discussion in Erfurt in 1332 or 1333 (ironically Thomas's new place of teaching). (An anonymous edited report of it appears in Pinborg 1967:215-32.) In it Aurifaber denies, with a range of arguments not dissimilar to those put forward by Ockham, that the *modi significandi* are either necessary or indeed that they exist. He, too, claims that mental language in principle differs from both the spoken and written language, and for him only mental language can have scientific status. However, unlike Ockham, he does not seem to have many (or any) objections to the syntax expounded by the Modistae, only to their overall theory.

The following centuries saw a growing interest in vernacular grammar, the study of individual languages, and this new approach to language studies really caught on in the Renaissance. That does not mean that the dream of 'universal grammar' in Western Europe was dead, as we shall see in Chapter IV, but the type of all-embracing theoretical framework that the speculative grammarians had so carefully erected had definitely disappeared.

III. The Renaissance

The immense influence on all areas of life which from around the middle of the fifteenth century came to be exerted by the cultural movement generally known as the Renaissance, also left its distinct mark on the language studies that were undertaken during and after this period. In the present study it is not possible to go into details about the whole background and the conditions that brought about these wide-ranging changes, so I shall confine myself to a brief look at a few of the studies of grammar that made a significant contribution to the re-orientation within this field and which had an impact on grammar writing in the following period.

We have already witnessed the shift of emphasis in the late Middle Ages away from literature and towards philosophy as the basis of grammatical studies, and although this move was not unchallenged, as may be seen from the thirteenth century poem entitled the 'Battle of the Seven Arts',[1] it was certainly widespread and reached its culmination in Speculative Grammar.

During the Renaissance period, this general trend was revoked, once again, in favour of literary studies. There were many reasons for this and some of them were interconnected, for example: (a) the discrediting of scholastic philosophy as the sustaining cultural force in society, (b) the rediscovery of classical Greek and Roman literature, facilitated by the invention of the printing press and the arrival in Western Europe of numerous 'forgotten' manuscripts following the fall of Constantinople to the Turks in 1453, (c) the Reformation with the Protestant preference for the use of the vernacular languages at the expense of Latin (cf. the Bible translations into English, German, Danish, Icelandic and Swedish by the middle of the sixteenth century), and (d) the influence that 'global' events had on people's outlook, e.g. the discovery of the new world and the gradual replacement of the geocentric with the heliocentric cosmic system. These occurrences, which took place within a relatively short span of time, also led to new views and perspectives being applied to the study of grammar as well as to other areas of scholarship. Perhaps the clearest evidence of the changes in language description is the sudden interest in the writing of grammars on, and often in, the vernaculars. Let us briefly consider some of these works as background for English grammar writing.

Most grammars written during the Renaissance or shortly afterwards adopt Priscian's eight parts of speech (though sometimes with minor modifications), even when describing other languages than Latin, but dissenting voices could be heard. Thus Peter (or Petrus) Ramus, also known as Pierre de la Ramée (1515-1572), a staunch anti-Aristotelian in Paris of all places, shows his independence of the Latin tradition by insisting on purely formal criteria, particularly the criterion of number, in establishing word classes rather than relying on the more traditional philosophical and logical, and hence semantic, classifications. This procedure enables him to distinguish nouns (incl. adjectives and participles), verbs and pronouns from the categories that are not inflected for number, which in his scheme are adverbs and conjunctions (Ramus 1971:91). Whereas for centuries case and case inflections had been seen as an important distinguishing nominal feature, which was quite natural when operating with languages like Greek and Latin, Ramus concentrates on categories, such as number, that were relevant for the individual languages in question, including the vernaculars of the time. This is seen, for example, in his French grammar (*Gramere*, 1562; see Ramus 1969), where he also uses a reformed orthography, being a member of the spelling-reform movement in France. His take on prepositions is that they (and interjections) belong to adverbs; see for example his statement: 'Those Adverbs which are called Prepositions' (Ramus 1971:55).[2] Michael (1970:66) quotes a similar assertion from *Grammaticae libri quattuor* to the effect that 'adverbs include prepositions and interjections, according to the definition' (*[a]dverbii porro definitione comprehenduntur praepositiones et interiectiones*). Vorlat (1975:46-7) goes further when she claims that Ramus only has four parts of speech, viz. nouns and verbs (which have number) as opposed to adverbs and conjunctions (which are without number), and this is echoed in Padley (1985:30ff.). Therefore when Robins (1997:120) contends that '[i]n Latin grammar [Ramus] preserved the Priscian eight word classes', this does not stand up to scrutiny. Ramus does discuss prepositions, but for him they are clearly a subcategory of adverbs.

Sanctius – the name given to the Spanish grammarian Francisco Sánchez de las Brozas (1523-1600)[3] – was another independent-minded Renaissance grammarian. He recognises only three parts of speech: nouns (incl. participles), verbs and particles, where particles consist of adverbs, prepositions and conjunctions. As justification for this tripartite division, he points to Plato's *Sophist*, but it seems to resemble more closely Aristotle's three categories, with particles corresponding to the latter's *syndesmoi*. In fact, Sanctius has an ulterior motive in setting up this system, for he claims that it applies generally, since (or so he argues) Latin, Greek, Hebrew and Arabic all at one stage had three parts of speech. However, in his own Latin grammar (*Grammatica Latina*) he operates with six parts of speech, viz. nouns, verbs, participles, prepositions, adverbs and conjunctions. In other words, he breaks up his superordinate category of particles for practical teaching purposes. But even though Sanctius himself does not apply it in practice, the idea of a general category gradually caught on and appeared in several English grammars after 1700, as well as in modern times as shown in the Introduction.

In different ways, Ramus and Sanctius both had a strong influence on some later English grammarians, mainly due to their re-examination of the criteria for establishing the primary grammatical categories.

Grammarians in sixteenth-century Italy took a keen interest in prepositions. Here studies of 'case' in contemporary Italian led some writers to claim that because certain prepositions had different functions from the majority, they should therefore be regarded as a special group and not as prepositions proper. This resulted in a lively debate throughout the century. The main points of the dispute are succinctly summarised by Kukenheim (1932:108, 140). He recounts (1932:108) the view in the anonymous *Regole della lingua fiorentina* (before 1495) that the article has the function of determining case in nouns ('E casi de nomi si notano co suoi articoli', *Regole* c. 2 A), and different combinations of preposition + (article +) noun are taken to be different cases. In Latin, cases are marked by inflections in the various paradigms, so a problem arises when grammarians, in analysing a language that has no case inflections, nevertheless attempt to see it in terms of the Latin case system and therefore look for alternative case markers. This is, not surprisingly, where prepositions come in. Pietro Bembo (1470-1547) is the first to suggest that the Italian particles *di*, *a*, *da* should be regarded as case signs ('segni di caso') rather than prepositions and draws one of his correspondents[4] into his argument in the following way (the original spelling has been preserved):

> ... et bene è che M. Hercole intenda: Ne solamente de gli Articoli; ma anchora di quelli; che segni sono d'alcuni casi; et alle uolte senza gli Articoli si pongono, et talhora insieme con essi, *Di Pietro, A Pietro, Da Pietro: Del Fiume, Al Fiume, Dal Fiume*: de quali alcuni senza dubbio proponimenti mostra [NB. in MS 'para'][5] che siano piu tosto, che segni di caso. (Bembo 1525:XLVII verso; my emphasis)
> (And it would be well that Messer Ercole [Strozzi] should say something about not only the articles but also those [words] that are signs of some of the cases, sometimes occurring without the articles and sometimes with them, [as in] *Di Pietro, A Pietro, Da Pietro: Del Fiume, Al Fiume, Dal Fiume* [i.e. Pietro's/to Pietro/from Pietro; of the flower/to the flower/from the flower]. Some of these, it appears, are doubtless prepositions rather than case signs.)

Later Pierfrancesco Giambullari (1495-1555) maintains that the noun in Italian has no case at all and cannot be distinguished by terminations, i.e. inflections, but exclusively by certain prepositions, or signs as he prefers to call them: 'Il Nome nella nostra Lingua non ha Caso alcuno, ne si distingue per alterazione di voci: Ma solamente per alcuni proponimenti o segni che noi celi vogliamo chiamare' (Giambullari 1551:61).[6] He divides prepositions into two groups: (a) 'segni de'casi' (only *de*, *di*, *a*, *da*), denoting case, and (b) 'vere preposizioni'. As he says:

> Dividonsi le nostre preposizioni in segni de'casi, ed in vere o schiette preposizioni. I segni de'casi, cioè, quelli che ci mostrano il senso di qual si voglia caso, sono quattro solamente *De, Di, A, Da*. (Giambullari 1551:106)
> (Our prepositions are divided into case signs and true or genuine prepositions. Case signs, that is, those that show us the meaning of each case are just four in number: *de, di, a, da*.)

Similarly, Lodovico Dolce (1508-1568) distinguishes between 'segni di casi' and prepositions. Under the articles of feminine gender nouns he has this comment:

> Ma a particulari Nomi si del Maschio, come della Femina, si aggiungono propriamente quelle particelle, che segni di casi di sopra ditto habbiamo. *Di, A, Da*. (Dolce 1556:34). (But to individual nouns, both masculine and feminine alike, can be added as appropriate those particles which we have above called case signs.)

But later he has a whole section on prepositions ('Della Prepositione', Dolce 1556:91-4).

However, not everybody shares this view. Thus Lodovico Castelvetro (*c.* 1505-1571) denies that such a division is valid, although he does distinguish between 'preposizioni atone' (unstressed prepositions) such as *a, di, da, per, con, in*, etc., and 'preposizioni toniche' (stressed prepositions) such as *su, verso, senza*, etc. (Castelvetro 2004:5, and footnote 10 there).

Girolamo Ruscelli (*c.* 1504-1566) strikes a finer balance by claiming that the same word forms can be 'segni de' Casi' in some contexts and prepositions in others. For instance, under his treatment of common nouns, he says:

> Et essendo troppo diverso il significamento di ciascuna prepositione, come prepositione, da quello di quei segni, che si danno solo per distintione de' Casi, non si conviene entrar'à dire, che per esser nello Articolo, Del, una D, & una L, per questo sia fatto della prepositione DI, & dall' Articolo IL, ò LO, ma che ciascuno veramente sia Articolo, ò segno per se stesso. (Ruscelli 1581:100)
> (And since the meaning of each preposition, *qua* preposition, is so different from the meaning of those signs that are placed there solely to distinguish cases, it is not correct to claim that because there is a D and an L in the article Del, it should for that reason be formed from the preposition DI and the article IL, or LO, but it is true to say that they are both articles, or signs in their own right.)

He then moves on to proper nouns ('nomi propri') and provides some examples of the difference between the two types. Thus in the examples 'Egli è padrone *di* casa' (he is the owner of the house), 'Io gli ho affitato un pezzo *di* casa' (I have rented part of the house to him) and 'Habbiate l'occhio *à* casa' (Keep an eye on the house), *di* and *à* are 'segni de' Casi'. But in 'Io non mi son' oggi partito *di* casa' (I haven't left the house today) and 'Andiamo *à* casa' (Let's go home), they can only be said to be 'prepositioni pure' (*ibid.*). In the two latter examples, of course, the prepositions have spatial meaning.

A few years later, in 1584, Lionardo Salviati (1540-1589) strongly supports Castelvetro's rejection of any difference between 'segni di casi' and (other) prepositions. First he argues that several prepositions – not only *di*, *a*, *da* – merge with the definite article to form a unit ('un corpo solo') (Salviati 1810:113, 164-73), and when it comes to 'prepositions' the uses are so varied that it makes no sense to categorise them as belonging to one group or the other. Take *a*, for example; however different functions it serves in the following two sentences: 'Io diedi a Cesare' (I gave to Caesar) and 'Questo vale a difender voi' (This serves to defend you), according to Salviati it is a preposition in both. But what about this example: 'avesse molto a così fatto accidente resistere' (might help a great deal in resisting this disease)?[7] Here, if we uphold the distinction, *a* is said to have two separate functions, namely 'per segno di caso al nome *accidente*, e al verbo *resistere* per sua vera preposizione' (as a case sign to the noun *accidente* and as the true preposition to the verb *resistere*). And Salviati concludes, 'Or fare il potrebbe, se preposizione, e segno di caso fossero diversa cosa?' (Could this be so if preposition and case sign were (two) different things?) (Salviati 1810:114).

Strangely, most of the issues in this debate are essentially confined to Italy, although the same arguments could certainly be applied to the other Romance languages derived from Latin, and it focuses, as we have seen, on the relationship between Latin and the Italian language of the Renaissance period and questions about to what extent, if at all, the usage in Latin (e.g. in the area of nominal cases and their case inflections) is relevant when analysing 'modern' Italian use of prepositions. As if to show their independence of the classical times, some of the contributors to the dispute use Boccaccio's *Decameron* (and, less commonly, Dante and Petrarch) as a linguistic reference point and offer detailed analyses of the text. The nearest it comes to a parallel debate in France is over the status of the words formed by a contraction of certain prepositions and the articles, e.g. *au*, *aux*, *du*, *des*. Robert Estienne (1558:82), in particular, includes these contractions among prepositions but does not use a French version of case signs about them or about certain types of separate prepositions (cf. Kukenheim 1932:122-3).

Despite this incipient shift towards not only writing grammars *of* but also *in* the vernacular languages, Latin continued to exert a powerful influence on grammar writing, in many cases well into the eighteenth century. For example, it is noteworthy that the first grammar of many European languages, composed between the middle of the sixteenth and the middle of the eighteenth century, was written in Latin.[8] In England, where the first grammar of and in English appeared in 1586, the Latin tradition was extremely tenacious, and this is in large measure due to one book: Lily's Latin grammar.

William Lily (c. 1468-1522), a friend of Erasmus and Thomas More, was appointed by John Colet, the Dean of St Paul's, as the first High Master of the latter's newly-founded school in 1512. His *Syntax* was revised by Erasmus and first appeared in 1513, but no edition has survived from before 1533, long after Lily's death. It seems certain that what came to be the standard reference work for many subsequent English grammarians, *A Short Introduction of Grammar* from 1548/49 (see Lily (and Colet) 1970, for convenience henceforth Lily 1970), was the result of a collaborative effort, presumably involving Lily and Colet.[9] However, in the following centuries it was almost universally known as 'Lily's Grammar', even if the spelling of the author's name varies. It was also known as the 'Royal Grammar'. The reason for this is that in 1548 King Edward VI issued a proclamation which made the use of Lily's grammar compulsory in all grammar schools in the country, thus ensuring it virtually canonical status. This helps to explain the reverence in which it was held for a very long time and consequently its huge impact on later generations of grammar writers. The royal command also resulted in a revision of the text which was to last for 'over four hundred years and through some three hundred and fifty editions' (cf. Lily 1970:Note). As far as his importance for grammar teaching and writing is concerned, Lily could thus without exaggeration be seen as a modern-day Donatus. It is therefore worth taking a look at this significant book before turning to a more detailed examination of some of the English grammars from the sixteenth, seventeenth and eighteenth centuries.

The editions from 1548/49 (in Lily 1970) both have the following wording on the title-page: 'A Shorte Introduction of Grammar, generally to be used in the Kynges Maiesties dominions, for the bryngynge up of all those that entende to atteyne the knowledge of the Latine tongue'. It was thus, despite its short title, intended as a Latin grammar rather than as a more general introduction to grammar, especially since this was taken to be two sides of the same coin at the time. Grammar in England before 1586 simply *was* Latin grammar.

Lily begins his grammar with 'An Introduction of the Eight Partes of Speache', in which he says of the parts of speech (reproduced verbatim from Lily, with his spelling, because of its enormous impact; 1970:Appendix I:7, being the second page of Appendix I):

'In Speache be these eight partes folowing.

$$\left.\begin{array}{l}\text{Noune,}\\ \text{Pronoune,}\\ \text{Verbe,}\\ \text{Participle}\end{array}\right\} \text{declined.} \left.\begin{array}{l}\text{Adverbe,}\\ \text{Coniunction,}\\ \text{Preposition,}\\ \text{Interiection,}\end{array}\right\} \text{undeclined.'}$$

This is really no different from what had been inherited from the late Roman writers and been replicated throughout the Middle Ages. There is thus a direct link back to Donatus and Priscian since the foundation it builds on is the time-honoured description of Latin. As we saw above, there was already a beginning opposition to this approach, but most of it came from people on the European continent rather than in England.

One consequence of this established scheme is that adjectives remain a subclass of nouns, which are divided into 'nouns substantive' and 'nouns adjective', while participles that feature prominently in Latin grammar, though arguably not in English, keep their status as a separate class. Articles are denied this status since Latin has no articles, but the demonstrative pronoun (*hic, haec, hoc*) is often used to help illustrate the different cases of the noun, or as Lily puts it, 'Articles are borowed of the Pronoune' (Lily 1970:8).[10]

The section 'Of a Preposition' is just over a page long. The definition found here is one that was to be repeated either verbatim or with slight modifications by many English grammarians in the following two centuries or so: 'A preposition is a parte of speeche most commonly sette before other partes, eyther in apposition: as, *Ad patrem* [to the father]: orels in composition: as, *Indoctus* [untaught]' (Lily 1970:C iii verso). This is in turn copied from Priscian's definition; admittedly, Lily does not mention here that prepositions are indeclinable, but he has already categorised them as one of the four 'undeclined' classes. He then goes on to list the Latin prepositions that govern the accusative case, with their English translations/equivalents, followed by those that govern the ablative case. He notes that two of them – one from each group – stand out because of their position *after* its 'casuall woorde' (i.e. its case-governed complement), viz. *versus* (+ acc.), as in 'Londinum versus' (towards London), and *tenus* which is also placed after its complement and governs the genitive case 'yf the casuall worde … be the plural numbre', as in 'Aurium tenus' (Up to the ears).

Lily further notes that when 'the voices [i.e. forms] of prepositions' occur alone ('without theyr casuall woordes'), they 'bee not prepositions, but are tourned into adverbes' (Lily 1970:C iiii). This claim would also often be repeated.

Lastly, the Latin prepositions that can govern both the accusative and the ablative case, i.e. *in*, *sub* ('under' or, as here, 'before'), *super* ('upon') and *subter* ('under(neath)'), are illustrated by means of *in*. We are told that these prepositions 'serve to bothe cases' and '*In*, with this signe *to* [i.e. modern-day *into*], to the accusative case: as, *In urbem*, In to the cite. *In*, without this signe *to*, to the ablative case' (*ibid.*). It is interesting that Lily mentions the presence or absence of *to* (as part of *into* in the English translation, of course) as the sole factor determining case assignment. There is no suggestion that the choice of case has anything to do with the notion of 'motion' versus 'rest/non-motion' (or a more refined distinction) in the individual examples or that this might be a pedagogically useful way of differentiating case use for this small group of prepositions.

The division into different parts of speech is not very clear in the 1549 copy. After 'An Introduction of the Eight Partes of Speache' there follows a short section on 'Godly Lessons for Chyldren', and then one with the heading 'The Concordes of latine speche'. However, the page header is still 'An Introduction of the Eight Partes of Speche' (note the different spelling of 'speech') for another ten pages and only then does it change to 'The Construction of the Eight Partes of Speche'. This is in effect Lily's section on syntax where the different parts of speech are revisited. Under 'The Preposition' (unnumbered page) he mentions two types of usage. The first one really involves 'non-usage' since it concerns examples where the preposition 'is not expressed but understood, and the casuall woorde never the lesse put in the ablative case', so that we have 'Habeo te loco parentis' (I have you in place of your parents) instead of '… *in* loco parentis'. The second point is expressed like this: 'A verbe compoun[d]ed sometime requyreth the case of the preposition, that he [i.e. the verb] is compoun[d]ed withall', meaning that when a preposition (here probably in a wide sense to include bound prefixes, though this is not clear from the examples) is part of a compound verb, the following object of the verb is in the same case as the one that the preposition would have governed. Among his examples are: 'Exeo domo' (I leave/go out of the house), where *domo* is in the ablative since this is the case that *ex* governs, and 'Adeo Templum' (I go to the temple), where *ad*, which always governs the accusative case, as a verbal prefix seems to determine the accusative form of the object *Templum*.

Some of these uses and constructions could perhaps have been explained in a more pedagogically helpful way and above all in much greater detail, but on the whole they are valid for Latin. The problem that faced grammarians writing about English in the following centuries was how much they could, or ought to, transfer from the Latin tradition and, conversely, to what extent English (as well as other vernaculars) was different in structure and needed to be analysed on its own terms. This question haunted English grammar writers at least up to the nineteenth century, but it had to be faced and the results differed widely. Consequently, English grammars, once they started to appear, displayed a zigzag course between these two poles for the first two hundred years. In the next chapter we will trace this development in English grammars up to 1801.

IV. English Grammars 1586-1801

Introduction

This chapter forms the centre of the present study, and my primary aim in it is to examine the treatment of prepositions as a part of speech within the English grammatical tradition from the late sixteenth century until the end of the eighteenth or, to be specific, from William Bullokar's *Bref Grammar for English* (1586) until John Dalton's *Elements of English Grammar* (1801).[1] It is not intended to be an exhaustive account of prepositions as a word class (or, in some cases, not) during this period, but the works included will constitute a representative sample of grammars, though sometimes I use 'grammar' in a loose sense by also including texts that cannot strictly speaking be called grammars, if they are deemed to contribute something valuable to the discussion. Thus I will look in detail at the writings of a number of English grammarians whose views on this particular topic may or may not previously have received much or any attention, and at the same time I will provide a survey of the main trends in the linguistic description of prepositions and of the parts of speech in general.

Many of the texts used are found in the extremely useful Scolar Press facsimile printings of the original texts, issued from the 1960s onwards. This is a series which constitutes a longed-for treasure trove for scholars interested in early English grammars and which is edited with bibliographical notes by A.C. Alston. Overall background information is provided, for example, in Robins (1997) and Law (2003), and I have also drawn on some specialist studies of these first few centuries of English grammar writing. Among them are the following: Poldauf (1948) is based on a selection of some 170 English grammars before 1800; Vorlat (1975) confines herself to the period 1586-1737 and has a brief summary of the Greek and Latin tradition as background to her general chapter on the parts of speech; Padley (1976 and 1985) offers a very detailed outline of the Latin tradition and the vernacular trends, respectively; and Percival's, Brekle's and Aarsleff's survey articles in Sebeok (1975) all contain important and useful information. In addition, some recent publications by Tieken-Boon van Ostade (1996, 2008 and 2011) have thrown new light on a number of relevant issues. However, the single most valuable secondary source has been Michael (1970), which offers by far the most comprehensive treatment of this topic, partly by providing background material from classical, medieval and Renaissance grammarians, but mostly by including in his account all 272 extant English 'grammars' up until 1800 (including John Dalton's grammar from 1801, thus bringing the total up to 273). Furthermore, his appendices supply the reader with complete bibliographies (alphabetical and chronological) of all the Greek, Latin and English grammatical works consulted as well as with invaluable statistical material about the numerous systems that he establishes for the parts of speech in the early English grammars.

Michael divides his systems into four main groups:

(i) Latin systems
(ii) modified systems before 1700
(iii) vernacular systems
(iv) modified systems after 1700

Intuitively, the choice of the year 1700 as a dividing line may seem arbitrary (as divisions of this kind usually are), but there is some motivation for it since, according to Michael, none of the truly vernacular grammars were published before 1700, except for the early edition of Lane (1695). This does not apply the other way round, though; some of the Latin-based grammars appeared well after 1700.

It is interesting to see how the 273 grammars[2] that Michael lists are grouped under the four headings. No fewer than 203 of them belong to group (i); only 11 to group (ii); 39 to the vernacular systems in group (iii), and 22 to group (iv).[3] So according to this division, nearly 75% of all English grammars up to 1800/1 follow (though some with certain modifications) the Latin model in their treatment of word classes in English. This figure alone clearly demonstrates the amazing tenacity of the classical tradition, but one should probably also take into account the tendency of unoriginal minds simply to copy time-honoured systems. Furthermore, although groups (ii)-(iv) account for 36 of the 56 systems listed by Michael (1970:Appendix I, 521-9)[4], they only account for 72 of the grammars, which means that the vast majority of the 36 (to be precise, all but 3) are represented by one, two or three writers only. In fact, precisely half of the systems (28) are proposed by only one writer.

Since virtually all the so-called vernacular grammars (as well as most of those using modified systems) were written after 1700, this shows how the grammarians of the eighteenth century began to question the traditional division of the parts of speech and to suggest alternative systems relevant for the English language rather than for Latin. But, as the following analysis will demonstrate, it was a very gradual process; many eighteenth-century writers continued to use some version of the Latin system, and even those who did not, often used Latin as a basis for comparison.

Michael's chronological list of English grammars (1970:Appendix VII, 588-94) bears witness to the considerable increase in the number of grammars published during the eighteenth century. A few figures will suffice to demonstrate this. Only 34 of the 273 works mentioned appeared before 1700, and another 34 in the first half of the eighteenth century, which means that the remaining 205 were published during the second half of the century (1750-1801). The 1790s alone saw the appearance of no fewer than 68 grammatical works, which is exactly the number of grammars written during the whole period 1586-1750. This is an extraordinary development, even if they were not all major studies.

As far as prepositions are concerned, a cursory glance would seem to indicate that they constitute a fairly stable part of speech.[5] Of the 271 grammars that categorise them at all, 206 take them to be a primary part of speech. In 64 other cases, prepositions are seen as a secondary part of speech, whereas – to take but one example – Cooper (1685) includes them as part of his rather eccentric noun category, together with articles, pronouns, adjectives and participles (see Cooper below).

However, this presentation is somewhat misleading, as becomes clear if we compare the number of grammars using the Latin system (203) with the 206 grammars that have prepositions as a primary part of speech. The comparison shows that hardly any of the vernacular and few of the modified systems give prepositions such a prominent status. In 57 of the 64 systems where they are relegated to a secondary part of speech, they are included under the category of 'particles'; in addition, two grammars list them under verbs, two others under adverbs and three under 'conjunctives' or 'connexives'. In modern terminology, we may talk about 'grammatical form words' as opposed to 'lexical content words'.

As a result, we can discern an emerging pattern in seventeenth and eighteenth century interpretations of prepositions as a grammatical category. As the traditional Latin system begins to lose ground to systems that are more in accordance with the linguistic data found in English, it becomes increasingly the norm to have a 'superordinate' category of particles, which besides prepositions usually includes adverbs, conjunctions and interjections, or some combination of these. This change in the categorial status of prepositions is in tune with some modern treatments, although present-day linguists, as we saw in the Introduction, do not always trace the tradition further back than to Jespersen.

The most obvious effect on the word class systems of operating with a category of particles is that, compared with the traditional system, the number of primary parts of speech is reduced. The actual number of primary categories in the 'new' systems may vary, but the vernacular systems tend to show a fourfold division – in most cases, substantives, adjectives, verbs and particles – with the secondary categories included in different combinations under these. The most extreme reduction is found in Dalgarno (1661), who accepts one part of speech only, viz. nouns, while Horne Tooke (1786) operates with two primary categories: substantives and verbs.

It should be made clear from the beginning that by English grammars I mean grammars written by native speakers of English (though this point will need to be qualified slightly) for the purpose of describing the English language, whether the grammars are actually written in English or in Latin. Hence I exclude grammars written in England by native speakers if they are not primarily concerned with English. For example, Bede, Alcuin and Aelfric were early English writers of grammar, but dealing with Latin, not (Old) English, and Roger Bacon, who wrote in and about Latin (as a universal language), belongs with the group of medieval speculative grammarians (see Ch. II). It is in this sense that Bullokar's *Bref Grammar for English* (1586) may be said to be the first English grammar. Why attempts to write grammars of English were not made until much later than in other major European countries is not clear, but Law (2003:237) refers to the 'mongrel pedigree' of the English language, due to the fact that – unlike French, Italian and Spanish – it could not pretend to have its basis in Latin (or in the two other 'sacred' languages, Greek and Hebrew) and refers to its European nickname *spuma linguarum* (the scum of languages), but it is doubtful that this represents the full story.

The first two grammars of English (by Bullokar and Greaves, respectively, both written before 1600) demonstrate in essence the wide range in the treatment of the grammatical categories over the following two centuries. Thus Bullokar's *Bref Grammar* is written in English, in line with the emerging confidence of grammarians to make use of the vernaculars during and after the Renaissance, but in many areas he follows the traditional Latin system. By contrast, Greaves's *Grammatica Anglicana* (1594), though written in Latin, is strongly influenced by Peter Ramus and is the first English grammar to reduce the number of parts of speech. Instead of the traditional eight, he seems to argue for five classes and leaves no doubt about the secondary status of prepositions.

The following survey will examine a selection of fifty English grammars, or grammatical texts in some sense, up to 1801, noting in each case what they have to say about the parts of speech in general and about prepositions and prepositional constructions in particular. They are divided into centuries: two before 1600, nineteen from the seventeenth century, twenty-eight from the eighteenth century, plus Dalton (1801). Of course, more or different texts could have been incorporated, but one has to draw the line somewhere and many of the grammars that have been excluded here are simply too repetitive or unimportant. I have chosen to examine most of the early grammars and some later ones in which the treatment of prepositions is particularly interesting and/or has in some ways influenced later grammarians, and I have attempted to strike a balance by choosing texts that express a range of different views and practices.

With this purpose in mind, I have chosen to present the texts in strict chronological order, according to their year of publication. This procedure will help demonstrate the fact that the grammatical texts used here do not constitute a step-by-step linear advance in grammatical description or in the way that linguistic analysis is handled; it is rather a kind of zigzag course that nevertheless gradually produces new and interesting results. A chronological approach of this nature means, for example, that practical and pedagogical grammars may both precede and follow philosophical or universal ones, and that important, influential works can appear next to writings that may not contain much new material about prepositions or the parts of speech in general but are nevertheless part of the whole narrative. The obvious danger of such a procedure is that it runs the risk of overwhelming the reader with a somewhat confusing and impenetrable mass of data and no clear overview, not least since a certain amount of repetition is unavoidable, but it is designed to show what actually happened in this field and in what sequence during the period in question. It is my hope, though, that the concluding comments and the cross-references in each section will help bind the text together in a way that shows both what is conventional and what is new and original in the works of the individual writers, and hence indicate the place of the various contributions within the grammatical tradition in England. By way of conclusion, the main trends in this historical account will be outlined in the Summary in Chapter V. (On a practical note, in order to avoid endless and tedious repetition of names in references, the key work(s) in each section will, after the first mention, be referred to by year and page number(s) only, rather than including the author's name in each case, in the hope that this will not compromise the clarity of the references.)

Individual grammatical works 1586-1801

(i) *The Sixteenth Century*

William Bullokar (*c*. 1531-1609)
William Bullokar was a retired soldier. His *Bref Grammar for English* (1586; see Bullokar 1977) is the earliest of the printed grammars of English to have survived (cf. Bornstein's Introduction, 1977:x).[6] Whether it was preceded by others, now lost, is unknown, but there is a reference on the last page to Bullokar's own 'Grammar at Large', from which the *Bref Grammar* is said to be 'extracted'. One therefore has to assume that this must be an 'Abbreviation' of the larger grammar (1977:67). We do not know either whether the latter has been lost or was simply never printed.

The *Bref Grammar* is strongly indebted to Lily's (and Colet's) *A Short Introduction of Grammar* and firmly based on the traditional Latin system of eight parts of speech, one of them being prepositions (cf. 1977:1). This is emphasised by Bullokar's statement that 'there is no-one word to be uttered in our speech, but it is one of the eight parts before mentioned' (*ibid.*). Although he immediately refers to articles and adjectives as well, they both come under nouns.

However, Bullokar displays some independence of mind, for example (unlike Lily) by adding the participle to the uninflected classes, in accordance with its morphological status in English rather than in Latin, and also in recognising only five cases of the noun, viz. 'the Nominative, the Accusative, the Gainative, the Vocative, and the Genitive-proprietary' (1977:3). The mysterious 'Gainative' is not explained very clearly; we are merely told that 'the sain [same?] speech being used gainatively is called the Gainative Case' (1977:4); it sounds rather like a version of the dative. We also hear that '[t]he case called ablative in Latin or other languages is in English the accusative, though governed of a preposition signifying ablative' (1977:6). This must have been done in recognition of the fact that there is no formal justification for postulating an ablative case in English.

This has consequences for prepositions since Bullokar sees them as 'always governing an accusative case' (1977:48), but whether he has both nouns and pronouns in mind here is not clear as he provides no examples. Even so, this is far removed from those of his successors – even some of those writing in the eighteenth century – who claim that prepositions in English govern the same case(s) as in Latin. We are also told that when they do not govern an accusative case, i.e. have no complement, they are no longer regarded as prepositions but as adverbs (*ibid.*). This assertion was to be repeated by many others.

For Bullokar, grammar is first and foremost an exercise in parsing and thus in aiding students to identify the different parts of speech. A preposition is defined both in positional and in relational terms as 'a part of speech properly used prepositively, that is, governing an accusative case set next after it' (1977:47).[7] (Bullokar mentions that there are exceptions to the usual positions in verse.) He adds that it can also sometimes occur 'post-positively' when it governs the relative 'that' or 'which' and the latter precedes the verb, in constructions such as 'this is the man whom we spoke of' compared with '... of whom we spoke' (*ibid.*). This type of construction with a stranded preposition became one of the test cases of grammatical tolerance in the following two centuries. It is therefore worth noting that Bullokar does not condemn it but merely records it.

A preposition can even be divided. This, we are told, sometimes happens to *toward*, in which case the now separate *to* is written <too>. As examples he mentions 'we came *too* London *ward*, or *toward* London the Monday, and rode *too* Oxford *ward* or *toward* Oxford the same day' (1977:49-50).

Bullokar then goes on to deal with compounding. A preposition may be 'compounded before a substantive ... but after an adverb', e.g. *in-sett* but *thær-on* and *her after* (1977:50). With verbs there is a distinction: when prepositions are 'compounded after a verb [they] do commonly keep their proper signification, but compounded before a verb, do often yield to the verb some other signification, not proper to such preposition' (*ibid.*). Here he gives no examples, though he mentions that 'significations of single prepositions, and their compositions before verbs ... are to be handled ... in a Dictionary' [by him?]. While it is fairly obvious that by 'compounded before a verb' he means as a prefix, as in '*under*stand', it is more uncertain what is implied by 'compounded after a verb', unless it simply means a preposition following a verb, as in 'walk *on* the ground'. In such cases the preposition would (normally but by no means always) keep its signification, i.e. meaning.

In a subsequent section, Bullokar – no doubt for pedagogical reasons – resorts to verse to drive home some of the basic rules, or as he calls it 'bref note in vers for parcing English in many points agreing with latin' (1977:56). Here we find the following lines concerning prepositions (with modernised spelling):

> The relative sometimes is ruled
> > by preposition
> In figure set after a verb,
> > other in composition,
> Or severed has this not [addition: to show(?)]
> > it set in post-position. (1977:59)

This is not crystal-clear, but may simply mean that after a relative pronoun a preposition may follow the verb, i.e. being postposed or 'stranded', as we saw above, or it may precede the relative (and thus the rest of the clause), i.e. being preposed or 'in composition', as in 'the sofa *on* which they sat'. The usefulness of verse like this as a mnemonic device is perhaps questionable.

The final section of the book, called 'A short conference of English prepositions not us[e]d in latin in on[e] meaning', shows both the importance he attaches to this part of speech and how, on the one hand, he uses Latin as means of comparison (the rule rather than the exception in the early English grammars) while, on the other hand, he is able to recognise specific English characteristics (1977:65-6).

Being a first attempt at an English grammar, it is only natural that Bullokar's work should be influenced by Lily and the Latin tradition. What is more remarkable is that he makes a conscious effort to stamp his independence on his presentation by deviating from his model in some important ways, in fact more than is the case in many later grammars of English. In this way, he blazes a trail, however modestly, for his successors in the decades, and indeed centuries, to come and shows that English as a vernacular *can* be described on its own terms and thus differently from Latin, even if it was left to others to do it much more radically.

Paul Greaves (*c.* 1570-?)

The second printed English grammar is Paul Greaves's *Grammatica Anglicana* (1594; see Greaves 1969), written in Latin. On the title page, Greaves states that what interests him are particularly the areas where English differs from Latin ('præcipuè quatenus à Latina differt'), though arguably he does not quite live up to that. He also acknowledges his debt to Peter Ramus, whose principles he broadly follows. The grammar has sections on letters, syllables, parts of speech and syntax. There is also a list of dictionary words (English into Latin), a short poem followed by word class assignments of all the words in it, and finally a list of words found in Chaucer, with translations.

Although the grammar is Latin-based, Greaves seems to operate with only five or six primary parts of speech, which is more than the four accepted by Ramus (see Chapter III above). The uncertainty arises because it is not quite clear whether he regards adjectives as an independent class (cf. Michael 1970:236). On the one hand, he mentions in the chapter 'De Substantivo' that 'Nomen est Substantivum, aut Adjectivum' (a noun is a substantive or an adjective; 1969:6), but on the other hand, adjectives are given a chapter of their own ('CAP. 4. De Adiectivo'; 1969:9-13), as are subsequently pronouns, verbs, adverbs and conjunctions. No other English grammar advocates such a system.

The short Chapter VII (1969:26-7) of the first Part is about the adverb ('De Adverbio'), but after listing a number of adverbs Greaves states that prepositions and interjections also belong to this category, though no reason is given; or as he puts it regarding the former class, 'Huc referuntur etiam quae volgo praepositiones appellantur' (To this also belong what is popularly called prepositions), followed by a selection of these, among which only *aloft* may strike a modern reader as surprising.

Chapter 4[8] (1969:34) of the syntax section ostensibly deals with adverbs in conjunction with a noun ('De syntaxi adverbii, cum nomine'). This does not sound very promising for our purpose until one realises that all the 'adverbs' mentioned are in fact prepositions, which for Greaves are after all a sub-group of adverbs. Here the Latin influence is obvious; thus we are told that *of* governs the genitive, *to* the dative, and *unto* and *fro(m)* the ablative. Some examples are provided, but there is no discussion of the fact that the forms 'a king' and 'kings' are identical in all these three cases, e.g. '*of* a king / *of* kings'; '*to* a king / *to* kings'; '*fro(m)* a king / *fro(m)* kings'. At the end of the very short chapter it is mentioned that *to* also precedes infinitives ('*to* feare; *to* be feared'), and this is repeated with reference to *to* in '*to* grow' in the later poem (no page numbers). In the latter example, *to* is glossed as 'adverbium præpositivum infinitis' (an adverb preceding an infinitive). There is thus no class distinction between *to* as preposition and as infinitive marker; both are apparently prepositions, and hence adverbs. This is an example of emphasis on form rather than function.

Like Bullokar, Greaves displays a mixture of adherence to and independence of the Latin model. However, it is Ramus rather than Lily who acts as his main inspiration, and that alone sets him apart from his contemporaries and immediate successors, and shows that he has embraced some of the new principles for analysing languages that emerged in the Renaissance. This in itself was a challenge to the grammatical *status quo* of the time.

(ii) *The Seventeenth Century*

Alexander Gill (1565-1635)[9]

Alexander Gill graduated from Corpus Christi College, Oxford, and lived for some time in Norwich before succeeding the famous educator Richard Mulcaster as High Master of St. Paul's School in London, where he had John Milton among his pupils. His work on English grammar, *Logonomia Anglica* (1619; see Gill 1968)[10] is, like Greaves's grammar, in Latin and the first proper grammar of English to appear in the seventeenth century (and to be reprinted), though it is probably better known for its section on pronunciation than for its grammatical content. Nevertheless, he shows a certain independence of mind in his grammatical analysis and cannot be ignored in the history of English grammar.

Gill only accepts three primary parts of speech: nouns, verbs and particles. He refers to the third class as 'consignificativa', cf. words that 'consignify' in the sense that they have secondary meaning. In this third class he initially includes as subclasses articles, adverbs and prepositions (1968:36), but in a later chapter (XIII) he adds to these also conjunctions and interjections (1968:67). Of the other traditional parts, adjectives as usual come under nouns ('nouns adjective') and so do pronouns (as 'personalia'), while participles belong to verbs. It is notable that in breach of the Latin tradition articles are inserted. This classification is probably based on Sanctius's tripartite system, but the secondary parts are devised in a different way. According to Michael (1970:237), it is the sole system among English grammars that consists of these three primary classes and their subdivisions, except for a grammatical manuscript by James Douglas (*c.* 1720).

Cases are dealt with under nouns and we are told that there are six (as in Latin). *Of* is mentioned as a sign of the genitive ('Genitiui signum'), *tu* (i.e. *to*) and *for* are signs of the dative, and *in*, *with*, *from* of the ablative. In other words, the Latin cases are transferred directly to English, and prepositions as case signs are introduced (cf. the Italian Renaissance grammars in Chapter III above).

Chapter XIII 'De Consignificatiuis', i.e. the 'third class' mentioned above, is extremely short and adds very little. In fact, Gill only makes a few comments on articles and adverbs and says nothing at all about the others (1968:79). However, in the case of prepositions this is rectified in Chapter XVI 'Syntaxis rectionis' (government in syntax). Gill mentions here that as far as termination (i.e. inflectional ending) is concerned English possesses only one case, but has (case) signs ('casuum signa'), namely prepositions. Nevertheless he provides a long list of those prepositions that govern the accusative and a shorter one of those that take the ablative. For each preposition he supplies the English item followed by its Latin counterpart(s). Again, this is a transfer of function from Latin and it is clear that Latin is the driving force. Gill makes this explicit when he justifies the postulation of cases by saying of the second group that others are thought to govern the ablative because they correspond to those which demand this case in Latin ('quia illis respondent quæ casum Latinum postulant') (1968:79).

A few of the examples of English prepositions under ablative are odd; thus, he lists *opnlj* (i.e. openly; cf. Latin *palam*) and *privili* (i.e. privately/secretly; cf. Latin *clam*) (*ibid.*).[11] For most people these would be typical adverbs, so how can they masquerade as prepositions here? The answer can only be that Gill works from Latin, and not from English. Both *palam* (before the eyes of) and *clam* (without) can indeed function as prepositions governing the ablative in Latin, but they can also be adverbs corresponding in meaning to the English words listed here.

There are a few further exemplifications of the use of the English case signs (1968:80), and in Chapter XVII Gill looks at prepositions with locative meaning, e.g. '*in/at/to(wards)/for/from* London', as well as those indicating other semantic categories, such as 'instrument', 'material', 'time', etc. These are translated into English, but explanations of their use are kept to a minimum.

Aspects of Gill's grammar thus demonstrate some independent thought, e.g. his view on the parts of speech, while others (as we have seen) show him to be locked into the Latin tradition and using Latin rather than English as his starting point. This is fairly typical of early seventeenth-century grammars that were trying to come to terms with descriptions of English, but Gill's influence on some later grammarians, including John Wallis, is not insignificant.

John Hewes (dates unknown)

John Hewes, who calls himself a 'Master of Arts' on the title-page, published *A Perfect Survey of the English Tongue* (with the addition, 'taken according to the Use and Analogy of the Latine') in 1624 (see Hewes 1972). He intended it to be above all a textbook for learning Latin grammar and he acknowledges his great debt to 'Lillie', i.e. Lily's Latin grammar. However, he tries for the first time to incorporate English grammar in the description of Latin, or as Alston puts it, 'The grammar reproduced here represents the earliest attempt to reconcile the rules of Latin Grammar with those of English' (1972:Note). More precisely, he finds a greater awareness of English grammar useful for learning Latin, but not for its own sake and not on an equal footing with Latin. Even so, he does not slavishly follow Latin everywhere but here and there assesses English usage separated from Latin, as also Michael (1970:155-6) points out.

From the start there is no doubt about Hewes's pedagogical intentions. The Preface is addressed 'To all Teachers of the Art of Grammar in the Latine tongue' and to others who want to learn Latin in 'a more easie and speedie way' (1972:Preface, p. 1). In it he mentions some of the obstacles that 'the younger sort' encounter when they start learning Latin, the most serious one of which is 'their defect … in the right knowledge or censure of their owne Mother tongue, in regard it holdeth a great difference in it selfe from the dialect of the Latines' (1972:Preface, p. 2).

Most of the book is structured as an explication of the examples given in three tables 'of the more general rules of the Syntax of the Cases: as they may bee conceiued in the English tongue' (1972:C2 verso), but before this there are three 'briefe notes', the first of which is 'of the parts of Speech according to the English', with the addition, 'as they lye in order' (1972:B3 verso). Presumably the last is a reference to the way the classes are normally set up in a Latin grammar such as Lily's. Here some 'rules' are presented and exemplified on the opposite page. Hewes does not give a clear list of the parts of speech, but states in the margin what class the words in his examples belong to. The problem is that some of these are sub-categories, such as 'A Verbe Actiue/Passiue', 'Gerund', 'First Supine' and 'Coniunctions Copulatiue'. He seems to recognise noun substantives, verbs, participles, conjunctions, adverbs and prepositions; adjectives are mentioned, but are they a sub-group of nouns? The examples in the 'first table' (1, no page numbering) suggest that they are, but it is not clear. Of interjections we only hear that they 'are well collected by Lilly', as are prepositions, and the reader is instructed to 'Learne first by heart your Prepositions' (1972:B3 verso). However, the term 'pronouns' does not appear, only 'Persons' and 'Relatiues', so the assumption must be that they belong under nouns.

Prepositions are dealt with in a number of places throughout the presentation. In the first syntax table on the subject of case, many of the 29 examples feature prepositions, which fall into two groups: those that constitute 'signes' of different cases (i.e. case markers) and those that are true prepositions (1972:C2 verso). For instance, *of* is a sign of the genitive in 'the labour hence *of* sundry wights', and of the genitive or ablative when 'spoken in praise or dispraise' in 'those *of* rare and noble Spirits', but 'next after a Participle' in 'as he is to be loued *of* me' and in 'to bee admir'd *of* any' it is either a 'signe of Datiue, or a Preposition', and after a verb it is a 'Preposition to the Ablative', as in 'As I have heard *of* many' (*ibid.*; I have made the emphasis more consistent here and below).

Other prepositions are treated in a similar way. Thus *at* and *in* when they denote location ('a place') are signs of the genitive, while *to* is a sign of the dative in 'inferiour not *to* any', but of the accusative when it denotes movement, as in '*to* Yorke', '*to* Carthage sent', and so on. He changes tack in example 16 where the information is substituted by an instruction: 'See what Prepositions, as *Ad, apud, ante*, etc. require an Accusatiue' (*ibid.*). Clearly, the reader is invited to find which English prepositions are the equivalents of these Latin ones, and the one example provided is '*Vnto* the walles of Rome hee hasts' (1972:C3). Furthermore, we are told that *in, with, by, through* are 'signes of the Ablatiue', but when they come 'before personall thinges', as in 'and *with* us good abide', they are prepositions (1972:C2 verso-C3).

There are more examples, but although it is not overtly specified, it seems clear from this that the distinction is one of case marker versus prepositions proper and the same 'word' can function as both. Those in the first group are closely linked to the Latin cases, while the others are more independent, probably both in use and meaning. This distinction between the roles of 'case sign' and 'preposition' is a common one in the seventeenth and part of the eighteenth centuries, but where it appears, it inevitably reveals something about the underlying view of English grammar. The notion of case signs only makes sense if grammar is considered to be invariable and uniform across languages, i.e. to be 'universal'. As long as Latin preserved its high status in comparison with the vernacular languages, English would often continue to be analysed in the light of the Latin grammatical categories, such as case and the various verb forms and conjugations. This view was soon to be seriously challenged, but it took a long time before it was completely discarded. In Hewes we see a rather timid attempt at presenting some data from the viewpoint of English only, but for many other grammarians both past and future Latin remained the yardstick, and knowledge of English grammar was first and foremost an aid to learning Latin.

Charles Butler (*c.* 1560-1647)
Charles Butler, an Oxford graduate, was at first master of the free school in Basingstoke, but from 1594 he became vicar of Laurence-Wotton only three miles away for the next 48 years of his life.

His main grammatical work was *The English Grammar* (1633; see Butler 1910).[12] In his discussion of word classes in it ('Of Words', 1910:32-54), Butler uses a system that is unique in English grammars (cf. Michael 1970:239-40). He accepts only four principal parts of speech and divides them into those with number and case (viz. nouns and verbs) and those without either (viz. prepositions and adverbs) (1910:32). This means that pronouns, adjectives and articles are dealt with under nouns, while conjunctions (mentioned very briefly) and interjections (not even mentioned by name) come under adverbs, all appearing in a very short section (1910:51-2). Basically, Butler makes the traditional separation between 'Prepositions in Apposition' (i.e. independent items) and 'Prepositions in composition' (usually prefixes attached to other words) and gives a list of prepositions in each category. Of the first group, Butler says that all these are set before 'the Rect cases of Nouns, and the obliq[ue] of Pronouns: as *by a man, without mee*' (1910:52).

This would – the word class system apart – be a fairly unremarkable treatment, were it not for two points. One is that the 'Prepositions in composition' are not confined to those items that can function as prefixes, such as 'bound' elements like *de, dis, en*, etc., most of which we would not now normally accept as prepositions, but also include (in other contexts) independent prepositions like *against, among, at*, etc. Of course, it is generally recognised that there is an overlap between the two groups in so far as elements such as *for, in, on*, etc., belong to both groups, just as *de, in, sub*, etc., do in Latin. The difference is that Butler widens the group 'in composition' by including constructions such as 'above-named' and 'beyond-sea-ac[c]ount', which allows him to supplement the 'usual' list with items like *above, beyond* and *through* that would otherwise only appear among the 'Prepositions in Apposition'.

The second point of interest is a marginal note saying that 'for *to* is sometimes used *a*, especially before verbals: as I go a fishing, a hunting, a field' (1910:52; spelling modernised). This ties in with the well-known development of the progressive verb form ('I'm hunting') from *be on/in* + *-ing* (I'm on hunting) via *a* + *-ing* (I'm ahunting') to the modern form, though the *a* + *-ing* construction was common up to the eighteenth century (cf. Schibsbye 1974:124-6; Nielsen 2005:257-

8; Hansen & Nielsen 2007:201). It is noteworthy that Butler is aware of this use of *a* and of its derivation, but also that he claims that *a* is a substitute for *to* rather than *on*, though he does not comment on the word class status of this *a*.

Lastly, a word about Butler's terminology. In dealing with prepositions in the section we have just examined, he uses no other term. As we saw, there were two types of preposition: 'in Apposition' and 'in composition'. In a section of the following Chapter, where he analyses word stress ('Of the Accent', 1910:54-8) and, for our purpose more interestingly, compounds beginning with certain monosyllables, such as *a, ad, be, de, en*, etc., he adds 'or other undeclined particles' (1910:56). Suddenly these are no longer prepositions but particles. That this is not a momentary lapse of concentration becomes clear thirteen lines further down when he informs the reader that *'en* and *enter* ar[e] French particles, answering to the Latin *in* and *inter*…'. The conclusion must be that, for Butler, 'Prepositions in composition' may equally well be called 'particles'. This term is not further defined, and in view of its rather imprecise meaning, that might be Butler's motivation for using it here.

Ben Jonson (1572-1637)
Ben Jonson, the Jacobean playwright and Shakespeare's contemporary who wrote the famous tribute to the Bard in the First Folio (1623) under the heading 'To the memory of my beloved, The AUTHOR Master William Shakespeare, and what he hath left us',[13] is not primarily associated with grammar. Nevertheless, *The English Grammar* forms part of his *Workes* (1640; see Jonson 1972), but was written before (perhaps quite some time before) 1623 when his original manuscript was lost in a fire. A second version may have been composed c. 1632. It has been said to constitute 'the first attempt in English to produce a vernacular grammar according to the principles of Pierre de la Ramée' (see Alston's pre-Preface Note in 1972), but we saw earlier that Greaves, too, was influenced by Ramus. It is more dubious when Alston (*ibid.*) claims that Jonson follows Ramus in seeking to 'make English grammatical structure conform to Latin usage', since Ramus in many respects was critical of the Latin tradition, e.g. in his attitude

to the parts of speech (cf. Chapter III above), so there is a limit to Ramus's influence on Jonson.

Jonson begins by stating that 'grammar is the art of true, and well speaking a Language' and that 'writing is but an Accident', and sets out the 'parts of Grammar' where the main distinction is between 'Etymologie, the true notation of words' and 'Syntaxe, the right ordering of them'. Then follows 'a Word' defined semantically as 'a part of speech, or note, whereby a thing is knowne, or called: and consisteth of one, or more Syllabes'. A 'Syllabe', in turn, is 'a perfect sound in a word, and consisteth of one, or more Letters' in the 'Orthography, or right writing by the form', whereas its 'Prosody [i.e. its spoken realisation], or right sounding is perceiv'd by the power [i.e. the mind]'. However, 'Prosodie' (Jonson's spelling varies) and 'Orthography' are specifically said not to be 'part of Grammar' (1972:35).

In Chapter IX onwards – and in contrast to Ramus – Jonson accepts the eight parts of speech found in Latin (nouns, pronouns, verbs, participles, adverbs, conjunctions, prepositions and interjections), to which he adds the article that is divided into 'Finite' (definite) and 'Infinite' (indefinite). He thereby continues the Latin tradition of identifying participles but not adjectives as an independent class. Instead, adjectives appear briefly under nouns while their syntax is examined later in a separate chapter. However, not all the classes mentioned are dealt with separately in the following sections; thus there are chapters on nouns, pronouns, verbs ('words that have number', 1972:67), adverbs and conjunctions (the latter two said to be 'without number'), but none on participles, prepositions or interjections. Participles come under verbs, whereas both prepositions and interjections are considered to be subgroups of adverbs and therefore appear under this heading. Of interjections it is stated that they 'are in right Adverbs' and a little later we learn that prepositions 'are also a peculiar kind of Adverbs' (1972:68). No reason is given for treating prepositions as a sub-class of adverbs; they are merely divided into separable items (a list of fourteen is provided) 'for the most part of Time, and Place' and inseparable items, which 'signifie nothing, if they be not compounded with some other word', e.g. *re* in 'release' and *un* in 'unlearned'; in other words, bound prefixes. In view of the joint influence from Ramus, it is hardly surprising that there is more than a passing resemblance to Greaves in this presentation.

The second part (called the 'Second Booke') deals with the syntax of the different classes, and although here too prepositions are placed under adverbs, their syntax covers a whole (large) page (1972:80-81). On the subject of prepositions and case, we hear that prepositions combine with the accusative case of pronouns ('for the love that you have borne *to* me'), but Jonson quickly shows that his analysis is modelled on Latin by stating not only that *of* may have 'the force of the Genitive' ('the praise of God'), but also that *to* can have 'the force of the Dative' ('be thankfull *to* God') and among others *from, of, in* and *by* that 'of the Ablative' ('take the cock *of* the hoope // I was saved *from* you / *by* you / *in* your house'). This is another example of Jonson's basic view that English should be analysed on analogy with Latin.

Position is mentioned briefly. 'Prepositions follow sometimes the Nounes they are coupled with', we are told; this concerns prepositional stranding in relative clauses, cf. the second occurrence of *in* in the following example: 'to direct them *in* the way, which they have to walke *in*'. Jonson adds that '*ward*, or *wards*; and, *toward*, or *towards*, have the same Syntaxe that *versus*, and *adversus*, have with the *Latines*: that is, the latter coming after the Noune, which it governeth, and the other contrarily'. His examples are: 'For, his heart being uncleane to God-*ward*, and spitefull *towards* men...' and 'And south-*ward* runneth to Caucasus...' (*ibid.*). It is interesting that Jonson should consider *ward(s)* prepositions when his examples in both cases show -*ward* to be part of a noun – and no other position was possible even in the early seventeenth century – but it is not very different from regarding prefixes such as *re* and *un* as prepositions, as others do. That is merely part of a long tradition, though the parallel with the Latin 'equivalents' is not exact.

Jonson's last points are noteworthy. For one thing, he observes that when prepositions combine with 'Participles present', the latter become ('supply the place of') a gerund, e.g. '*in*/*of*/*by* (etc.) loving', and also that prepositions can govern adverbs, as in 'sent *from* above'. Furthermore, it seems almost modern that he treats words like *touching*, *concerning* (etc.) as prepositions. These, he says, can even be omitted; e.g. in '[Touching, etc.] riches, and inheritance, they be given by Gods providence...'. Another example of deletion of a preposition, because it is 'understood' in the context, is found in the case of *of* missing after 'Universitie' in 'The whole Universitie, and City of Oxford' (1972:81).

Lastly, a curious point: Jonson finds that *if* is 'somewhat strangely lacking' in examples such as 'Unwise are they, that end their matters with, Had I wist', where a 'less strange' version would presumably be '…with, if I had wist [i.e. known]'. What seems peculiar here is (a) that Jonson finds this construction (i.e. the deletion of *if* and consequent inversion of subject and finite verb) odd as it has a long history and appears very often in contemporary language,[14] and (b) that he should count *if* among prepositions, especially since it is mentioned in Chapter XXII ('Of Conjunctions') of Part I (1972:68), together with *unlesse* and *except*, under 'conditioning' conjunctions.

Jonson, then, recognises and operates with prepositions, and deals with aspects of their syntax, but at no stage does he explain why he considers them a sub-group of adverbs.

Joshua Poole (*c.* 1615-*c.* 1656)

Joshua Poole attended Wakefield grammar school and Clare College, Cambridge. A few years after graduating he became a teacher at Dronfield grammar school near Sheffield before taking charge of a private school near Barnet, Middlesex. It was due to his dissatisfaction with the prevailing teaching conventions that Poole wrote *The English Accidence* in 1646 (see Poole 1967). As the title suggests, it is overwhelmingly concerned with establishing and analysing the different grammatical forms of English, with the overall purpose of facilitating the learning of Latin through awareness and a sound knowledge of the English language. The contemporary trend was to teach English by means of Latin, not the other way round (cf. 1967:Note), but Poole argues passionately for his approach since he has noticed

> how Children have been puzled and counfounded, by being set to the construing, parsing, and making of Latine, before they had the least knowledge of their Mother Tongue, or were able at all therein to distinguish the parts of Speech: so that I have had some, that would in construing give me the right English of a Latine Noune, or Verb, yet could not then distinguish by the signification which was the Noune, and which was the Verb. (1967:To the Reader, A2)

Poole adopts the standard Latin system of eight parts of speech and begins his book with a 'First Praxis', a short text of 16 words which are parsed into separate parts of speech, with expanded comments on each of the words (1967:B). It contains two instances of *of* and both are described, not as prepositions but as 'the signe of the Genitive case'; in the expanded version with the somewhat circular explanation 'because the Genitive case is commonly known by this sign *of*' (in the second instance written '… by this signe, *of*).

In the short section on prepositions (1967:19) there is a concise definition as 'a part of Speech undeclined, most commonly set before the words which they govern', and a number of prepositions are listed, including *as*. They are divided into three sub-groups: (i) those that 'govern/serve an Accusative case only' (e.g. *against, about, towards, between*, etc.); (ii) those that 'govern/serve an Ablative case only' (i.e. *in, with, from, of, concerning*); and (iii) those that 'govern/serve both an Accusative and an Ablative' (i.e. *for, under, upon, before, without, out of*); much as we have seen it done earlier with Latin prepositions.

However, it is in the later section 'Certaine Rules for the easier turning of English into Latine' (1967:24-37) that Poole's distinction between 'proper' prepositions and 'signs' becomes evident. On these pages he deals with a number of words that apparently present some problems for learners when compared with equivalent Latin words or constructions. The fact that a third (11 out of 33) of them are prepositions shows how seriously Poole takes the correct use of this class in a Latin context. The order seems rather haphazard, but placed in alphabetical order the following prepositions occur: *about, at, by, for, in, of, on/upon, over, to, under, with*.

It would be tedious to look at all of them in detail, so we will concentrate on Poole's approach to, and analysis of, prepositions by examining his entry for *of* (1967:24-5), which even in the English of the seventeenth century was the most semantically 'bleached' member of the class. The description of it bears all the hallmarks of being a teacher's presentation and, as so often, the explanation used can sound rather primitive to a modern reader. For example, we are told that 'when *of* comes between two Substantives, the Substantive following must be the Genitive case' (for 'Substantive' read noun phrase), as in 'the learning of the Master'.

Even more vague is the 'rule' that 'when *of* comes before the English of the Present tense, the word following must be a Gerund in *-di*' (i.e. in Latin), as in 'The way *of* Writing well, is joined with the Art *of* speaking well' (here and below I highlight the relevant preposition(s) in the examples). This is rather difficult for us to interpret (not to mention for schoolchildren at the time), especially since the example contains two instances of *of*, each followed by a verb form (in *-ing*). It is not clear what Poole means by saying that '*of* comes before ... the Present tense'. Presumably, he thinks of 'Writing' and 'speaking' as present tense forms which have been turned into the *-ing* form (cf. his definition under 'A Participle': 'A Participle of the present tense, signifies the time present, and endeth in [ing:]'; 1967:17), but this relationship is not obvious and the mention of 'present tense' does not seem to apply to 'is (joined)'.

If we conflate a few paragraphs, the reader is informed that the preposition *e(x)* + an ablative case must be used in Latin 'when *of* comes before a word signifying the matter of which a thing is made', e.g. 'a cup (made) *of* gold', and 'after Verbs of making, consisting [etc.]', e.g. 'it consists *of* two parts'. Similarly, when *of* means 'from or concerning, it is a Preposition serving to the Ablative' and must be expressed accordingly in Latin. The last instruction is interesting (a) because no Latin example is given (and thus no information about which, if any, preposition is required in Latin), and (b) since, despite its vagueness, the wording 'a Preposition serving to the Ablative' must refer to English. However, this should not surprise us; it is merely a practical example of Poole's insistence on ascribing the Latin case system (six cases in both the singular and the plural) to English nouns (cf. 'Cases of Nounes', 1967:4).

In other constructions, e.g. 'after the signification of a passive', *of* can be rendered in Latin either 'by the Dative case, or an Ablative with the Preposition *a* or *ab*', as in 'He is loved *of* all' (again without any Latin examples); in others, 'after words of eating, unloading, spoiling [etc.]', *of* is defined as 'the signe of the Ablative case'. On the other hand, when '*of* belongs to the word going before', which may be verbs ('to smell *of*), nouns ('to aske counsel *of*), adjectives ('to be glad *of*), or other classes ('out *of*, 'because *of*), we learn that 'it is not the signe always of the Genitive case'. This is a somewhat unexpected statement since the previous definition of *of* as 'the signe of the Genitive case' occurred when it appeared between two nouns (NPs).

Poole's (pedagogical) summing up distinguishes three functions of *of*: (i) as 'the signification of the word going before' (as in 'to smell *of*'); (ii) as 'a Preposition'; and (iii) if it is neither of these, 'it is most commonly a signe the word following must be put in the Genitive case' (1967:25). In other words, in (iii) it must be 'the signe of the Genitive case', and thus not a preposition. One could adduce similar examples from the sections on the other prepositions dealt with by Poole, but it would be merely repetitive.

Since Poole's ostensible aim is to facilitate the learning of Latin via English for young learners, it is natural that he should emphasise how English words and constructions compare with, and can be turned into, Latin, but this inevitably has consequences for his understanding and analysis of English, and a case in point is his treatment of prepositions. Thus by imposing the Latin grammatical system, including the case system, on English and thereby not distinguishing between English and Latin grammar, Poole – unquestionably from the best of motives – brings some confusion to his treatment of prepositional use in English. The problem is not that he operates with concepts such as 'signs' of cases, for example – this has been shown to be common practice at the time and, in essence, it is not too far removed from some modern treatments[15] – but that his descriptions and distinctions of English prepositions are completely dependent on Latin usage. However much this approach was in vogue with some grammarians in the early centuries of English grammatical description, it was not conducive to a proper analysis of the English language.

Francis Lodowyck (1619-1694)

Francis Lodowyck (spelt Lodwick by some writers, cf. e.g. Cram & Maat 2001:5; Law 2003:263; Robins 1997:137) belonged to the group of grammarians who attempted to construct a new universal language. In two short works within the space of five years, *A Common Writing* (1647 (or perhaps 1646); see Lodowyck 1969 and the Note there) and *The Ground-work of a New Perfect Language* (1652; see Lodowyck 1968), he laid the foundations for this task. His aim was to create a language (or 'writing') which, as he says, 'hath no reference to letters, or their Conjunctions in words, according to the severall Languages, but, being rather a kind of hieroglyphical representation of words, by so many severall Characters, for each word a Character, and that not at Random...' (1969:Introduction A2).

This is in fact the earliest published seventeenth-century attempt to establish a universal writing system, or a 'universal character'. The idea of creating a universal language that could solve the problem of communicating across the increasingly expanding international community was a preoccupation of the seventeenth century. It was in part motivated by continuous reports from explorers of the discovery of new and 'strange' languages, but also by the gradual replacement of Latin as the international language of scholarly communication with a range of vernaculars. There is no doubt that Lodowyck's works influenced those of his contemporaries who in later works showed a similar interest in universal language, such as Cave Beck (cf. his book *The Universal Character*, 1657), George Dalgarno and John Wilkins (for the last two, see below) and several others.[16]

Lodowyck thus tapped into the spirit of the time, even if his own schemes in these works remained somewhat fragmentary. It is an obvious drawback that he was not particularly careful or precise in his definitions; even his statement above hardly stands up to scrutiny, unless by 'letters' he means 'English letters', for the first five prepositions he lists (seemingly, in no particular order), viz. *above, under, about, before, behind* (1969:24), are represented by the first five letters in the Greek alphabet, which can hardly be a coincidence. On the other hand, it may help to explain some of the rather idiosyncratic features in his treatment of the parts of speech, which is not easy to follow in all details.

Thus, in *A Common Writing* he begins by dividing the different classes into 'Radixes' and 'Derivatives', and 'Radixes' can signify 'Action' or 'No Action'. Apparently only verbs ('Verball Radixes') belong to the former, while 'Nouns Substantives', 'Nounes Adjectives', pronouns plus the 'foure undeclined parts of Grammar' (i.e. adverbs, prepositions, interjections and conjunctions) belong to the latter group (1969:1). Another word for 'Radix', it seems, is 'Radicall', or words are 'radically characterized', and it later transpires that 'the Radical

Characters' (1969:31) are really the symbols invented for each word that is a 'root', with additional signs (e.g. dots at different heights, lines in different directions, etc.) for inflections and derivations. That the distinction is a purely morphological one becomes clear in Section 11 on adverbs where we learn that 'Adverbs Radicall' are 'simple' adverbs, such as *now* and *there*, whereas 'Adverbs derivative' have their 'distinctional addition' (no doubt the inflectional ending *-ly*), though no examples are given (1969:15).

It therefore comes as no surprise that prepositions are described in Section 13 as 'undeclined radixes' which, somewhat tautologically, 'are to be radically characterized' (1969:16). A (deliberately incomplete) list of prepositions follows, the most surprising of which are *out*, *some*, *none* and *same (or) self-same*. As if anticipating objections, Lodowyck issues what looks like an extraordinary disclaimer under adverbs by admitting lack of knowledge: '… and if among the number of them [i.e. "the Adverbs Radicall"], be found any which are Prepositions, Conjunctions, &c. or among those … be found which are Adverbs, and so misplaced, this may be *ascribed to our want of skill in Grammar*, and will be no materiall defect' (1969:15; my emphasis). Faced with such endearing frankness, it would be churlish not to forgive Lodowyck the odd lapse.

However, all this is merely a precursor to Lodowyck's primary aim in this study, viz. the allocation of signs or 'distinctional marks' to each word and word form in order to create a universal language. The minutiae of this – for it is a very intricate system – need not concern us here, except the fact, as hinted at above, that each preposition is assigned a symbol, some of them letters from the Greek alphabet.

In *The Ground-work of a New Perfect Language*, Lodowyck's approach is somewhat different. He now divides all words into three categories: (i) words of action; (ii) words of quality; and (iii) words of help (1968:4). In contrast to his previous work, he includes nouns under words that signify action. Very little is said about the third category, later named 'The Auxiliary Words' (1968:12). All we hear is that this 'third sort of Radicall words' comprise pronouns, adverbs, prepositions, interjections and conjunctions. Compared with *A Common Writing*, it might look as if pronouns have been assigned to a new category, but that is hardly the case. The difference is that the emphasis here is on function, while in the former work the division was one of form (declined versus undeclined). The remainder of this short volume (19 pages in all!) is dedicated to the further work on universal symbols and is of no direct relevance to us.

John Wallis (1616-1703)
There are good reasons for claiming that John Wallis possessed the most original grammatical mind in seventeenth-century England. His education at school and later at the University of Cambridge included an impressive variety of subjects, such as classical languages (Greek, Latin and Hebrew), logic, ethics, theology and mathematics as well as several natural sciences (physics, medicine, astronomy and geography), and his later publications reflect this extraordinary range. They include works on theology, mathematics, physics and medicine plus his English grammar. In addition, he acquired the skill of deciphering letters and in later life devoted much time to the teaching of the deaf. He was one of the founding members of the Royal Society in 1660, but he was chiefly a mathematician and was appointed Savilian Professor of Geometry at Oxford in 1649.

Wallis's English grammar *Grammatica Linguae Anglicanae* (1653; see Wallis 1972)[17] was written relatively early in his long career, at the age of 37, and five editions of it appeared during his lifetime. Wallis himself maintains that he wrote his grammar of English 'because there is clearly a great demand for it from foreigners, who want to be able to understand the various important works which are written in our tongue', and for this reason he wrote it in Latin rather than in English (1972:105). Wallis points in particular to 'foreign theologians, whose great ambition is to study *Practical Theology*, as it is normally taught in our tradition' (1972:105; his emphasis), but he also has native speakers in mind, as is clear from his later summing-up in which he links his stated approach to his envisaged readership: 'I aim to describe the language, which is very simple in essence, in brief rules, so that it will be easier for foreigners to learn, and English people will get a better insight into the true structure of their native tongue' (1972:109).

The fact that the grammar is aimed at foreigners poses some problems for Wallis. On the one hand, he considers it a mistake that previous writers have 'forced English too rigidly into the mould of Latin' (*ibid.*), thereby 'giving many useless rules' about a number of grammatical phenomena 'which have no bearing on our language, and which confuse and obscure matters instead of elucidating them' (1972:111). Or, as he puts it a little later, 'So in our language, where the situation is quite different from that in Latin, there is no reason at all for introducing a collection of cases, genders, moods and tenses which are artificial and wholly inappropriate, and for which there is no need and no basis in the language itself' (1972:113). In the context of what we have observed so far, this reads like a strikingly modern statement.

On the other hand, he informs the reader that he will not, after all, adhere strictly to these principles: 'I thought I had better keep the Latin terminology normally used in this Art, even though it is not entirely suited to our language' (*ibid.*). One reason for making this compromise is that 'the meaning of it [i.e. the Latin terminology] is well known', and another is 'an unwillingness to make any unnecessary innovations' (*ibid.*).

This attempt to strike a balance between theoretical considerations and practical guidance seems to have influenced his treatment of the parts of speech. In general, he accepts the traditional classes although he also has a short chapter on the articles, but in practice his presentation differs on some points from previous works on the word classes, presumably for pedagogical reasons. One such deviation is seen in his treatment of the verb, where he devotes more space to dealing with auxiliary verbs (two separate chapters) and irregular conjugations (one long chapter) than to an analysis of more general aspects of verbal usage.

Another variation concerns the presentation of prepositions and the ambiguity of Wallis's purpose is perhaps seen most clearly in his discussion of this class. In his last chapter (Chapter XIII) he very briefly summarises adverbs, conjunctions, prepositions and interjections. As we have witnessed earlier, it was quite common to see these four classes as one group, either for semantic reasons (they were often said to have no independent referential meaning) or from a morphological point of view (they shared the property of being indeclinable in Latin, in contrast to the 'major' parts of speech). The inclusion of prepositions under this group must be seen as a bow to tradition, for it is clear that for Wallis they differ from the three other classes. Indeed, he had already devoted a separate chapter to prepositions (Chapter IV), which is why he merely refers to this analysis in Chapter XIII. Moreover, under conjunctions he observes that there is an overlap between adverbs and conjunctions so that 'the same word is often to be interpreted as an adverb in one place and a conjunction in another' (1972:375). This leads Wallis to conclude that 'there would be no great harm in putting adverbs, conjunctions and interjections all in the same class' (*ibid*.). The wording here is characteristic of his undogmatic approach, but the really interesting thing, from our point of view, is that prepositions do not really seem to belong to this group, even though they are mentioned in the heading of Chapter XIII.

This apparent contradiction is explained in the separate chapter on prepositions where they are said to be closely linked with substantives, in fact almost part of them: 'Prepositions are used only before substantives, or words acting as substantives, and are as it were a common property of them' (1972:291). He also makes the strong claim that once 'you have learnt the meanings of these few small words [i.e. prepositions] you can immediately understand practically the whole syntax of nouns' (*ibid*.), or as he states elsewhere, 'The whole syntax of the noun depends almost entirely on the use of prepositions' (1972:111). It is for this reason that Wallis 'contrary to normal custom' (1972:289) decided to have a special chapter on prepositions immediately after the chapters on substantives and the articles, respectively. For him, they belong with nouns.

This alleged close link between prepositions and nouns is a consequence of case. Thus, according to Wallis, prepositions in English are used to 'convey all the meanings which in Greek and Latin are expressed partly by different cases and partly by prepositions' (*ibid*.). They have, we are told, 'the same characteristics as in other languages', only 'they are commoner in English than in Latin because we have no differences of case' (1972:377).

For Wallis, the main function of a preposition is 'to indicate logical connections' (1972:291), which, surprisingly, seems to be synonymous with 'local relationships' ('the current term', we are informed). This may perhaps help explain an otherwise rather puzzling passage:

> When a preposition is prefixed to a substantive governed by another word, it shows what relationship exists between the substantive and the word by which it is governed, whether it is a verb, a noun or another part of speech. (*ibid.*)

First of all, the expression 'prefixed to' can, in the context, only mean 'precede', not 'be part of one and the same word' (i.e. a prefix), but if so, some confusion arises as to the precise meaning of 'governed by another word'. It would, of course, be natural to assume that the relationship between preposition and noun in a prepositional construction is one of 'government', so that the preposition governs its complement. This was the traditional view and it may be what Wallis wants to imply, but it is interesting that he does not once use the word 'govern'[18] to describe this relationship, although he uses it in other contexts (cf. 1972:38).

The most likely interpretation of Wallis's statement is somewhat reminiscent of the one we considered in connection with a similar problem in Thomas of Erfurt's analysis (see Chapter II above). In both cases, a syntactic relationship is said to obtain between the prepositional complement (which in Thomas's terminology is a 'terminus' or 'terminant') and a word other than the preposition, but they differ considerably in their use of the term 'government'. For Thomas, a preposition 'governs' its complement, but a verb does not 'govern' its direct object (or vice versa). Wallis, on the other hand, lets a prepositional complement (the 'substantive') be 'governed by another word', but not, it seems, by the preposition.

However, in spite of the difference in terminology, the two analyses are similar in that they are both chiefly concerned with logical relations. So although both writers would strongly deny that prepositions are devoid of meaning, they are nevertheless committed to the view that the main function of prepositions is that of logical connectors between the prepositional complement and another element of the sentence, i.e. they are what Thomas calls 'linking' elements and Wallis sees them as the English equivalent of Latin case endings (or as case signs).

In the rest of the chapter Wallis lists the English prepositions in arbitrary order, in each case stating the most common meaning(s) and, wherever possible, comparing them with the semantically equivalent prepositions or cases in Latin. The use of the prepositions is illustrated by examples, though often rather inadequately considering that this is intended to be a practical grammar aimed at foreigners. It is worth noting, however, that Wallis distinguishes between prepositions proper and words that 'are often used as prepositions' (1972:301). Examples of the latter kind are 'touching, concerning, according to, belonging to', which are 'really participles', though here one should remember that participles are not a separate part of speech for Wallis, unlike for so many others, but verbal forms (1972:331).

Finally, two syntactic points made by Wallis deserve to be mentioned. The first one merely emphasises the close relationship between prepositions and adverbs that in antiquity Diomedes commented on (see Chapter I above) – and in the English tradition, Lily (see Chapter III above) – namely that 'prepositions ... become adverbs ... when they occur without being followed by the appropriate case' (1972:301). This was a common view in the seventeenth century – which is still held by some linguists – and Wallis apparently feels no need to provide any examples.

The second point is more original. Wallis shows that there is a correlation between two types of 'adjective construction' and constructions with prepositions. Indeed, he goes so far as to say that the 'two kinds of adjectives ... can take the place of almost any preposition' (1972:305). The first of these correlations was quite familiar, viz. between a genitive construction, as in 'man's nature' (Wallis calls the genitive a 'possessive adjective') and the equivalent *of*-construction 'the nature of man', but the second one was a less common observation at the time. It concerns the relationship between what Wallis calls 'respective adjectives' (i.e. the first part of a compound noun) and the alternative construction with a prepositional phrase, the latter construction type expressing 'these relationships ... much more clearly' (1972:311). This correlation is found, for example, between 'a wine-vessel' and 'a vessel for wine', between 'a sea-voyage' and 'a voyage by sea' and between 'a gold-ring' and 'a ring of gold'. Wallis does not, however, point out that the preposition in examples such as these is often idiomatic, cf. *'a voyage for/in/of/on/over (etc.) sea' (not even 'at sea'), though sometimes a substitution is possible – with a resulting change of meaning – as in the difference between 'a vessel for wine' and 'a vessel of wine'; only the former is a true paraphrase of 'a wine-vessel' since, in contrast to the latter, it does not imply that there is wine in it.

In view of Wallis's wide knowledge and experience in many academic fields and his general attitude to language description as expressed at various places in his grammar, one can only deplore the fact that he did not undertake to write a truly theoretical grammar as well as this more practically oriented one. His influence on later grammarians would no doubt have been even greater than it was, for although he inspired some grammarians such as Cooper, Gildon & Brightland, and Greenwood (the last two incorporating whole chunks of Wallis's grammar in translation), it was chiefly for his work on sounds that he came to be remembered by posterity. In fact, it was not really until the twentieth century that Wallis, with his general view of grammatical description and his analysis of specific areas of English grammar, became recognised as an innovator and a forerunner of a formalist or structural approach.[19] Even if his treatment of case is not wholly original (e.g. Greaves pointed out in 1594 that English has no cases in nouns, see above), he undoubtedly helped to make this view more accepted and widespread in the time that followed.[20]

Jeremiah Wharton (dates unknown)
Hardly anything is known about Jeremiah Wharton, but it is believed that he is the Jeremiah Wharton who obtained a BA from Trinity College, Cambridge, in 1625, followed by an MA in 1633. He is known from one work only, *The English Grammar* (1654; see Wharton 1970), which is an example of a 'school book grammar' and on its title page refers to the author as 'M^r of Arts'. In the introduction ('To the Courteous Reader', 1970:unpaginated), Wharton makes it clear that the *Grammar* is partly meant as a guide to young people's understanding of their own language, and partly (like Poole's *English Accidence*) as preparation for learning Latin ('or any other Grammatized language'). Consequently, he is mainly concerned with outlining the basics of letters, syllables and not least the parts of speech of which we are told that '(like as in the Latine) there bee eight parts', viz. the eight conventional Latin classes.

Of prepositions, though they are given a separate mini-section, he has fairly little to say, and what he says has a by now familiar ring to it: 'A preposition is a part of speech set before other parts; either in apposition, or composition' (1970:58) and he then provides a number of examples of each type. For example, like Ben Jonson, he lists *concerning* and *touching* under 'Prepositions in Apposition' (influenced by Jonson?). He certainly seems to echo Butler (1633/1910), when he has 'beyond-sea-' under 'Prepositions in Composition'. Whether it is for reasons of space (the list is set out in narrow columns) or lack of understanding is difficult to say, but it is the only example that is not complete (cf. Butler's 'beyond-sea-ac[c]ount'). One also notices that *fro* (in 'fro-ward') is included along with *for* (for-swear) and *fore* (fore-tell). Chapter 9 (1970:71-84) is entitled 'Composition of words' and features a long (but, compared with the earlier number of 'Prepositions in Composition', not complete) list of such initial elements with examples of the words they form part of. Here it is interesting to note that his entry

> '*En* and *Enter*.
> Are French particles, answering the Latine *in* and *inter*...'

deviates only in spelling, capitalisation and the omission of *to* from Butler's formulation, down to the term 'particles', which was discussed above under Butler. This is an early example of the rather extensive 'borrowing' that took place in these centuries, as we shall see later.

William Walker (1623-1684)

William Walker was headmaster of two grammar schools, first Louth and then Grantham. He was a quite prolific author of textbooks, of which *A Treatise of English Particles* (1655; see Walker 1970) is now the best known. He also wrote, among other things, the first treatise on English and Latin idioms, a revised version of Lily's Latin grammar and a treatise on education (cf. 1970:Note).

A Treatise of English Particles stands out among the contemporary works mentioned in the present study. It is not a grammar, nor strictly speaking a monograph, but rather a 'Dictionary of Particles', which is how Walker himself refers to it (1970:Preface, p. 4). It has been called 'the first systematic treatment of English particles for students of Latin' (1970:Note) and by 1720 fifteen editions of it had been printed. It contains a 'Preface to the Reader', which lists six possible uses of the book from learning the rules in it by heart to rendering the Latin examples into English. Walker informs the reader that he has entered the particles in alphabetical order (as would be expected in a dictionary) except for some late insertions. It is, however, a major deficiency that Walker at no point defines what a 'particle' is. The nearest that he comes to doing this is when he mentions apologetically that 'some words and observables are here inserted, which perhaps may be thought by some not to come so properly under the name of Particles; but being few and very useful I would not omit them' (1970:Preface, p. 5). It is for this reason that the book is of more limited value to us than its title would suggest. I shall therefore confine myself to a few comments on the choice of the words included and on some of the entries.

The entries in their entirety (all in the name of 'particles') are a rather mixed bag and each entry is a separate chapter. At first glance, one is tempted to deduce that the term 'particle' tacitly stands for everything that is not a noun (substantive or adjective) or a verb, since the list includes traditional pronouns, adverbs, prepositions, conjunctions and interjections. However, even this is uncertain. For example, we come across an entry that reads 'Of the Verb *Becometh*' (Ch. IX, 1970:16) and wonder why it is there if it is not a particle. Chapter XXI has 'Of the Particle *Long*', which can be justified in examples such as 'All my life long' but hardly in 'He longs to see you' (1970:56). The following entry 'Of the Particle *Man*' (Ch. XXII, 1970:57) is even more bewildering since all the examples show it to be a noun. Chapter XXXIV (1970:95-102) is named 'Of the English of the Participle of the *Present* Tense' and distinguishes ten uses (or meanings) of the present participle, but it does not seem to be a particle; rather, there are examples of the use of participles *in construction with* particles (e.g. 1970:98). Similarly, an entry (listed under the letter 'a') has 'Of Adjectives and Adverbs compounded with *Dis*, *In*, or *Un*' and offers four examples of compound adjectives, but none of adverbs or of other constructions with adjectives/adverbs and particles (1970:4). Chapter

XL (1970:118) is entitled 'Of *Substantives* becoming *Adjectives*' and demonstrates the phenomenon we may call functional shift, i.e. that a word which usually belongs to one class (here, a noun) in a certain environment 'becomes', or takes on the function of, another class (here, an adjective) in examples such as 'a Louth-Scholar' or 'a crystal-glass', where 'Louth' and 'crystal' modify the following noun in the way that an adjective normally does. This may have been an interesting observation at the time, but why include it in this book, and how does it fit in alphabetically between the entries for 'such' and 'that'?

One could go on, but there would be little point in doing so. This does not mean that Walker's book is a bad one. On the contrary, as a dictionary it provides a wealth of information on each of the entries and it is particularly helpful in enumerating a number of different meanings and, often subtle, uses of the words listed. But it is not a 'treatise' in the usual sense and its lack of definitions remains its most serious shortcoming. For each example, Walker supplies the Latin equivalent, often adding relevant quotations from the ancient Roman writers. It may be argued that this dual aim of exemplifying English words from 'minor' parts of speech and rendering these in Latin is somewhat confusing, but again one has to acknowledge the important role that Latin played at the time. Walker has thus created something new, but with a little more care and consistency it could have been a good deal better, not just for our purposes but also for those of his contemporary readers.

George Dalgarno (*c.* 1616-1687)

George Dalgarno follows in the footsteps of Lodowyck in his interest in, and attempt to devise, a symbolic system of signs or a 'universal character' that could be used for all languages, but he goes a lot further. Not satisfied with creating an international set of symbols, he and some of his contemporaries strove to produce nothing less than a universal language; that is, a new artificial language based on logic to replace the 'imperfect' existing languages, which included even the classical languages Greek and Latin, in order to facilitate communication and debate across linguistic borders. His most important work is the treatise *Ars Signorum* (or *The Art of Signs*, 1661, see Dalgarno

2001), which in many ways is an impressive achievement, but was all but ignored and soon overshadowed by John Wilkins's monumental work, *An Essay towards a Real Character, and a Philosophical Language* (1668). It is only in recent years that Dalgarno's originality has been recognised, along with the degree to which he collaborated with Wilkins before serious disagreements between them on some substantive issues put a stop to further cooperation (cf. 2001:Introduction).[21]

On the question of word classes, Dalgarno's stance is extremely idiosyncratic, and it does not help that he changes his mind and recasts his thoughts part of the way through *The Art of Signs*. Furthermore, his wording seems to add to the confusion. First, it should be mentioned that Dalgarno in his established lexicon distinguishes between 'radical words' and 'compound words'. Radical words make up a small set of 1,068 words, and each one includes at least a partial description of the 'thing' in the real world that the word denotes; hence the term 'real character'. Equally, compound words can contain information of this kind by combining the meaning of two or more radical words (cf. 2001:35, 177-89).

Normally these words would be divided into different classes, in the time-honoured fashion, and that is indeed what Dalgarno does, to a certain extent, in the early stages of his studies. Thus in Chapter X he tells us that he 'divided all the primitive notions into classes – namely, material and formal' (2001:241). As material elements he counts 'the nouns and verbs and their cases', while the formal elements are the 'particles'. In notational terms, the particles are 'arranged around the capital character of the noun and verb' (2001:243).

However, in *The Art of Signs* Dalgarno radically breaks with tradition in terms resembling a 'road to Damascus' moment, or as he puts it: 'But finally clearer light dawned on me' (*ibid.*). His alleged discovery is 'that there is no particle that does not derive from some … noun, and that all particles are really cases or modes of nominal notions'. Therefore, in a sense, they are all nouns. This 'discovery' underpins his earlier claim and his rejection of the traditional view set out in Chapter VIII:

> Grammarians teach that there are *eight* parts of speech; Logicians say rather that there are only *two*. I myself, following the freedom to philosophize I have

claimed for myself here, acknowledge only *one* primary part of speech properly so called – namely, the Noun. For the others that are traditionally so termed should be counted as inflections and cases of the noun. The reason for this assertion is as follows: every *Being* of whatever kind must of necessity have a place in the predicamental series; but every predicamental notion is a noun. From this it follows that the Verb, no less than the other parts of speech enumerated by Grammarians, is only a case or inflection of the noun. (2001:225)

Ultimately, then, by applying substantive rather than formal criteria, Dalgarno recognises only one (primary) part of speech: nouns. However, there is some confusion in his presentation. Going back to his treatment of 'the particles' in Chapter X, he is at pains to emphasise the importance of these elements. Here he talks in glowing terms about how he discovered 'the key to this invention', by which he means 'the notions usually known as *particles*', and not only that but his description of the particles could hardly be more graphic in its use of body and house metaphors:

> ... particles, which are to speech what the soul is to man, what the nerves and ligaments are to the body, or what cement is to the building. For, if particles are taken away from speech, what remains? What else but a dead body without the form of a man? Or unconnected limbs without the form of a body? Or a pile of stones without the form of a house? And, just as the particles constitute *the formal and most primary part of speech*, and indeed likewise the most difficult one (the whole practice of logic and grammar residing in their correct use), so they also constitute *the most important part of speech*. It is for that reason that I call the analysis of the particles, and their reduction to rules of art, the key to the invention. (2001:241; my emphasis)

Admittedly, this passage is followed a page later by the previously quoted information about the clearer light dawning on Dalgarno, but it does seem to muddy the waters somewhat. He appears to stress several things simultaneously about the particles. On the one hand, they are 'formal'; they are like binding materials ('cement'), presumably to nouns; and they can be reduced to 'rules of art'. On the other hand, they 'constitute the formal and most primary part of speech'; indeed, 'the most important part of speech'. It is hard to combine these rather contradictory statements, even if we uphold the distinction between 'material' and 'formal' elements. In practice, Dalgarno really operates with two classes – a primary class, nouns, and a secondary class, particles – in much of his subsequent presentation. His pride in his alleged discovery of the importance of particles is simply too strong for him to ignore it.

So where do prepositions come in? Well, later in Chapter X Dalgarno remarks: 'It should be noted that included under the heading of particles are the notions commonly called conjunctions, prepositions, and interjections by grammarians' (2001:249).[22] It is clear that he distances himself from the traditional terminology of 'grammarians' and speaks of 'notions' rather than of classes or (syntactic) functions, and as part of his argument for a universal language he states that 'the main feature that makes the vernacular languages difficult is the great ambiguity of the particles', since these 'are so varied and uncertain in their meaning that no fixed rules can be given by which their meaning can be determined' (2001:245). It seems that the main difficulty that Dalgarno creates for himself is precisely that his definitions of word classes are based on semantic rather than functional criteria, which causes a lot of ambiguity.

In one of the rare instances where Dalgarno discusses the use of a preposition, though under the name of 'particle' of course, he claims that the 'particle *in* is extremely ambiguous in its signification'. In addition to the logicians' 'eight modes of in-ness [modi inessendi]' (which are not exemplified), he adds a ninth: 'a thing *in time* [res in tempore]'. However, as he says 'there is only one of these modes that can properly be called the mode of *in-ness*, that is a thing *in a place* [res in loco], e.g., Peter is *in the house*; the wine is *in the goblet*' (2001:249). This amounts to saying that the core use (or even meaning) of *in* is spatial/locative and the other uses/meanings (including temporal) are derived. This is contrasted, among other things, with 'a wall with respect to whiteness', which cannot be said to be a 'subject of *inhesion*', unlike mud 'when someone is immersed *in* it', i.e. something can 'be inside' mud, and inside a house, but this is not the relationship between a wall and a colour. Dalgarno does not say that it is basically the difference between a three-dimensional and a two-dimensional structure, but that seems to be implied.

Although Dalgarno's main preoccupation of creating a universal language is not directly relevant for our purposes, it has some interesting ramifications for his view of word classes. His contemporary John Wilkins has much more to say about prepositions, but both in Wilkins's writings and in those of some subsequent grammarians such as John Horne Tooke over a century later much of Dalgarno's argumentation is prevalent.

John Wilkins (1614-1672)
John Wilkins was a friend of Wallis and, until they fell out, of Dalgarno, and like the former he was one of the founders, and indeed the first secretary, of the Royal Society. He later became Bishop of Chester and is often known as Bishop Wilkins. His principal work on grammar, *An Essay towards a Real Character, and a Philosophical Language* (1668; see Wilkins 1668), is very close to Dalgarno's work both in conception and in its declared aim. Like Dalgarno, it was Wilkins's ambition to construct a universal, international language ('Real Character') and to describe language in universal terms.[23]

The *Essay* is divided into four parts: I. Prolegomena, II. Universal Philosophy, III. Natural Grammar,[24] and IV. A Real Character and a Philosophical Language. For our purposes, Part III of the *Essay* ('Concerning Natural Grammar', 1668:297-383) is the most relevant section. Here Wilkins distinguishes two kinds of 'grammar' (1668:297):

(i) Natural Grammar, i.e. general or universal grammar;
(ii) Instituted and Particular Grammar, concerning particular languages.

Whereas the work of Wallis and most other grammarians falls under (ii), Wilkins claims to deal with (i) only. In this approach, he finds few predecessors – by this time he refuses to acknowledge any influence from Dalgarno and before him Lodowyck – but he mentions Verulam,[25] Scotus,[26] Caramuel[27] and Campanella[28] and in part also Scaliger[29] and Vossius[30] (1668:297). Wilkins divides grammar, in sense (i), into three parts (1668:298):

1. 'Concerning the kind of words', i.e. the parts of speech, including morphology and etymology;

2. 'Concerning the proper union or right construction of these into Propositions or sentences', i.e. syntax;
3. Orthography and 'Orthoepy', i.e. writing and speech.

In practice, Wilkins keeps most of the traditional word classes ('the Doctrine of Words'), but he divides them up in a new way in accordance with his commitment to universality. Here all words are either 'Integrals' or 'Particles'. 'Integrals' comprise nouns (substantives and adjectives including participles) and derived adverbs.[31] The verb is explicitly excluded from the 'Integrals' on the rather unusual grounds that 'it is really no other then [i.e. than] an adjective and the Copula Sum affixed to it or contained in it' (1668:303).[32]

The class of particles is more complex. First, Wilkins distinguishes between (a) particles that are 'essential in every complete sentence', i.e. the copula (cf. the above characterisation of the verb), and (b) particles that are grammatical and 'not essential, but occasional'. The latter group is subdivided into the following three subgroups (1668:298):

(i) 'substitutive in the room of some': pronoun and interjection;
(ii) 'connexive', expressing
    (a) 'the construction of word with word': preposition;
    (b) 'the contexture of sentence with sentence': adverb and conjunction;
(iii) 'declarative of some Accident belonging to'
    (a) Integral: article;
    (b) Copula: mode;
    (c) Integral or Copula: tense.

(Wilkins's last group 'transcendentals' can be ignored for our purposes.)

Wilkins's treatment of prepositions is found in Part III, Chapter III (1668:309-12). Being 'connexive particles', they are defined in the following terms:

> Prepositions are such Particles whose proper office it is to joyn Integral with Integral on the same side of the Copula; signifying some respect of Cause, Place, Time, or other circumstance either Positively or Privately. (1668:309)

Wilkins observes a close link between prepositions and nouns and provides an interesting comparison by stating that prepositions have 'such a subserviency to Nouns ... as Adverbs have to verbs' (*ibid.*).

According to Wilkins, there are 36 prepositions in English, which form 18 pairs. These 18 pairs are further divided into six 'combinations', each consisting of three pairs, i.e. six prepositions, and the six 'combinations' fall into two main sections: the first two containing 'Causal Prepositions' and the last four 'Local Prepositions'.

Such an overall pattern is obviously much too neat and does not stand up to scrutiny. For example, it is characteristic of Wilkins's general approach, and also quite common at that time (cf. e.g. Wallis above), that against each preposition he lists its Latin counterpart(s) in the margin, even when it happens to be a case rather than a preposition, as with *of* (the genitive case) and *with*, *by* (the ablative/instrumental case).

This makes one wonder whether the Latin prepositions, rather than the English ones, have determined Wilkins's classification, and a closer look at some of his choices seems to confirm this suspicion. For example, seven prepositions (*by, for, on this side, out of, upon, with, without*) are entered twice, which alone makes Wilkins's claim that 'there are thirty six Prepositions' more than dubious. Another difficulty is that in seven cases two parallel entries seem to count as one (*with, by; concerning, upon; without, void of; for, on this side; against, opposite unto; betwixt, between; against, over against*).

The criteria for grouping and pairing the prepositions in this way remain obscure, and it would not be difficult to show the inadequacy of such a presentation. It is therefore reasonable to surmise that an attempt to provide something approximating to a one-to-one relationship with Latin prepositions (or cases) has been the overriding principle in Wilkins's description, but his attempt to aim at universality in his description may also have played a part in devising a system that was as symmetrical as possible.

As a result, there are many inconsistencies. For instance, it is hard to justify the inclusion of *on this side* (but not *on that side* or *on the other side*, cp. *beyond*), except as the English equivalent of Latin *citra* (as opposed to *ultra*), for it is clearly (for us, at least) a prepositional phrase, not a preposition, though admittedly such distinctions were less clear-cut then. Furthermore, it does not seem obvious to match *over* with *about* or *under* with *upon*. Nor were *upwards* and *downwards* commonly seen as prepositions in the seventeenth century, though they were 'used Adverbially' (1668:312). So one suspects that they are included here in order to provide a match for *sursum* and *deorsum*, respectively, and so on.

Moreover, a number of prepositions seem to have been omitted for no other reason than the fact that they would spoil the neat pattern. That must be why *until* is listed under adverbs where it is paired, rather strangely, with *yet, still, hitherto* (1668:313), but not under either prepositions or conjunctions. *Beneath*[33] appears in the diagram (see Fig. 1) but not in the list, and *towards* is placed under adverbs, as a synonym of *always* (!), though there is no syntactic justification for this, to mention but a few examples.

There are, then, a number of shortcomings in Wilkins's presentation. His obscure criteria and vague notional distinctions, the undue importance attached to the Latin counterparts and the complete lack of examples all detract from the value of his ambitious undertaking. Nevertheless, there are enough interesting points to make a study of it worthwhile.

In general, it may be said that the very attempt to give a structured analysis of this part of speech was in itself something of a novelty in those days and therefore deserves some attention, but more specifically, its chief merit lies in the overall distinction between 'causal' and 'local' prepositions and, in particular, in his treatment of the 'local' prepositions, however much one may disagree with the details. In addition, Wilkins schematises all the 24 'local' prepositions that he mentions in a fairly complex diagram (reproduced in Fig. 1), and hence anticipates the now fashionable interest in localist analyses of prepositions.

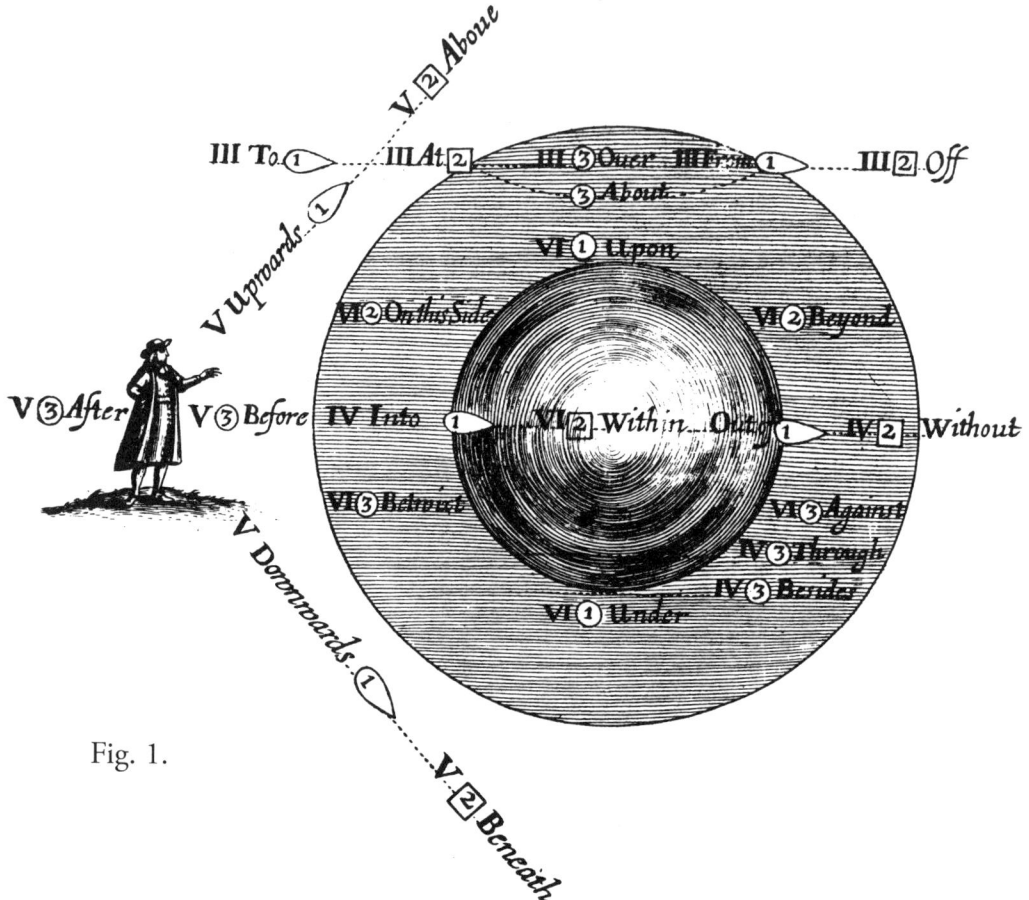

Fig. 1.

The main division into causal and local prepositions allows Wilkins to subdivide the local prepositions into three groups as follows (recall that they all appear in pairs):

1. Prepositions 'absolutely determined to motion': *to, from; into, out of; upwards, downwards.*[34]
2. Prepositions 'absolutely determined to rest (or end of motion)': *at, off; within, without; above, below.*
3. Prepositions 'relative to both motion and rest': *over, about; through, beside; before, after; upon, under; on this side, beyond; betwixt (between), against (over against).*

Group 3 forms a kind of link between groups 1 and 2, so that Wilkins's threefold division resembles some modern distinctions between 'locative' (including 'end of motion') and 'directional' prepositions, or between the semantic notions of 'source', 'path' and 'goal'.[35] Wilkins says of the non-causal prepositions that they 'primarily refer to Place and Situation; Secondarily to time; And some of them, by way of Analogy, to Comparison', and he finds an interesting asymmetry between prepositions of motion and of rest in the sense that those of motion cannot signify rest, but those of rest 'may likewise signifie motion in the Terminus' (1668:310). Again, this foreshadows modern analyses like Bennett (1975), where 'locative' (L) is embedded under 'goal' (G) (Wilkins's 'end of motion'), but clearly not the other way round. This aspect of Wilkins's treatment of prepositions is arguably the most relevant one from a modern point of view.

Thomas Lye (1621-1684)
Thomas Lye was a nonconformist minister and at one time Headmaster of Bury St Edmunds School. He wrote two school-books on the English language: *The Child's Delight* (1671; see Lye 1968) and *Reading and Spelling English made easie* (1673), but only the former is of relevance to us.

The second of the two main sections of *The Child's Delight* has the subtitle 'Containing an Essay towards an English Grammar' (1968:69ff.), and in Chapters XI-XIX he deals briefly with the parts of speech. Lye adopts the traditional eight-part division, including participles as a separate class and nouns divided into 'substantives' and 'adjectives'. Prepositions (Chapter XVIII) cover two and a half (small) pages and are defined as 'words set before other words, either in composition, being joined with other words, or in apposition, i.e. only set before them: And Terminations, or endings of words' (1968:134). The rest of the treatment consists in examples of these three uses, i.e. in composition, in apposition and terminations. In view of the fact that this is a book for schoolchildren this definition cannot have been very helpful and when it comes to the examples, anyone reading this presentation must have been confused. It is certainly a very flexible use of the term 'preposition'.

The first section does indeed, as so often in the past, include a few prepositions used as the first part of compound verbs, nouns and adjectives, e.g. 'infect' and 'undergo', but the vast majority do not contain (English) prepositions at all, only different kinds of prefixes, such as 'mistake', 'unwise', etc., or elements that can function as prepositions in Latin, such as 'circumcision', 'excell', 'substance', 'translate', etc.

The section called 'In Apposition' is a list of prepositions that are presumably supposed to precede and 'govern' a noun, though this is not made clear. It is alphabetical in so far as each sub-section contains a key example followed by other prepositions that either include that word or begin with the same letter (or one that is alphabetically close to it), the key words being: *above, because-of, concerning, farr-from, in, near, of, through, under* and *ward* (!). It is thus a mixture of 'genuine' simple prepositions and complex ones, e.g. of these three types (a)-(c) – using modern terminology:

(a) prep. + and/or + prep.: *over and above, except-or-saving-that*, etc.
(b) conj./adj./adv. + prep.: *because-of, but-for, hard-by, next-after, privy-to, well-near*, etc.
(c) prep. + NP + prep. (*of*): *at-the-point-of, by-reason-of, for-the-sake-of,* and even *in-the-possession-and-power-of*, etc.

A few examples have no end preposition, which may be an oversight, e.g. *in-comparison, in-a-manner, on-this-part-or-side*, and the more outlandish *behither-on-this-side*. Nevertheless, this is by far the most usable sub-section, even if it is nowhere stated that these prepositions precede a noun (phrase). In fact, it is not clear what 'in apposition' means; since nouns are not mentioned, one might assume that it refers to the status of each element of complex prepositions, but that would not account for all the simple prepositions.

One's pedagogical misgivings are tested even further when confronted with the third and final sub-section, 'Terminations, or distinct endings of words'. Here the implied definition of a preposition is stretched so far that it reaches breaking point. There is no explanation, only a list of seven such 'terminations', which can be rendered in full, as set out by Lye (cf. 1968:136):

y Air, air-y. Earth, earth-y
ish, child-ish, wolv.ish (*sic*)
full, care-full, fruit-full
less, care-less, use-less
ness, great-ness, white-ness
some, burthen-some, trouble-some

These are all perfectly good examples of adjective (and, in the case of *-ness*, noun) suffixes, but one can only sympathise with the pupils who found it hard to see what they have to do with prepositions and therefore why they should be mentioned in this section at all. School grammars rarely deviate much from at least one of the traditional systems, but Lye's presentation certainly carries its own personal stamp.

Mark Lewis (1621/2-1681)
Mark Lewis was a schoolmaster, according to Michael (1970:570) 'probably in Mr Bret's "reformed school" at Tottenham'. His publication *An Essay to Facilitate the Education of Youth*, which is, as stated on the title-page, 'Fitted to Childrens Capacities, for the learning, especially of the *English*, *Latin* and *Greek* Tongues: but may be as a general Grammar, and a Foundation to any Tongue', appeared in 1674 (see Lewis 1674).[36] The *Essay* carries a one-page dedication to 'the Right Honourable Anthony Earl of Shaftesbury, Baron Cooper of Paulet',

asking for his patronage since 'Your very Approbation will be a sufficient Protection against all the slander and envy of prejudiced Persons'. This is a reference to Lewis's 'two grand didactick Principles, the sense of seeing (in regard of the thing signified) and Syncrisis',[37] which are 'accounted by many ... very ridiculous' (cf. the dedication, but also mentioned on the title-page). Lewis expounds his views of grammar further in the introductory 'Synopsis' to the reader which, as mentioned in endnote 36, may be a summary of the first edition. At the end of it Lewis claims that he 'did never intend this Grammar for Public View', but explains why he decided to publish it and predicts that even if his grammar does not succeed, 'sooner or later a Grammar founded upon these Principles ... will prevail in the Nation' (1674:23). This pride and confidence in his 'new principles' must be the reason for an intriguing short passage (below 'Errata') on the reverse side of the dedication, which may at the same time throw a little more light on Lewis's workplace, informing the readers that 'Mr. *Lewis* the Author, or some Person on his behalf, may be spoken with at the *Academy* in *Chancery Lane*, at the *Grammar-School*, on *Thursdays* in the Afternoon, from Three till Six of the Clock, to give an account of this Method to any that desire it' (his emphasis). This is public service beyond the call of duty for a grammarian, but it demonstrates how keen Lewis was to disseminate the content of his grammar.

In the 'Synopsis' Lewis sets out his stall. Most of it is a fierce criticism of Lily's[38] Latin grammar for being far too complicated for young (or any other) learners with its profusion of forms and, not least, rules based on unhelpful semantic criteria. Despite this, it is not exclusively a demolition job; Lewis offers his own alternative approach, but it would take us too far to go into details. In general, his attitude to grammar teaching at an early stage can be summed up as a step-by-step or first-things-first method which, according to his presentation, Lily's grammar is decidedly not. This should not, of course, blind us to the fact that this *Essay* is not merely a grammar of English; the title itself refers to both Latin and Greek as well, with Latin the predominant factor in it. The intention is clearly to *replace* Lily as an introductory textbook. It is also worth mentioning that the wording of the 'Synopsis' is surprisingly Saussurean when Lewis blames Lily's grammar for not being 'plain ... either in the word signifying; or in the thing signified' (1674:23). This is an important distinction which, among others, Richard Johnson and Anne Fisher fail to observe (see R. Johnson and Fisher below).

He expands on this on the first page of 'The English Grammar' ('The First Part or Accidence'), though less clearly, by stating that 'Words are the marks of our Thoughts. As is the thing, so is its representation: therefore the subject of all Discourse is a Substantive, thing, or matter, called the Nominative Case …' (1674:1). A little later we are told that '[t]he Substantives are tackt on to words influencing them by Signs of Cases, or Prepositions' (*ibid.*). This vacillation between being 'Signs of Cases' and 'Prepositions' runs through the whole grammar and appears in connection with establishing the parts of speech. Here Lewis proves to be a traditionalist, presenting us with the usual eight parts, set out precisely as in Lily's grammar: four declined (noun, pronoun, verb, participle) and four undeclined (adverb, conjunction, preposition, interjection) (1674:6). It is also mentioned, though, that some are 'integral words, as *Book, love*; some are Particles, bits of words, appendents to these, as the signs of Cases; the signs of Comparisons, the signs of Moods and Tenses', and he adds that '[t]hese are not to be accounted as distinct parts of speech: but to be added to the next integral word', giving as examples 'of a Book' and 'does Love' (*ibid.*). However, it is not obvious what all this means. For instance, are only nouns and verbs ('Book, love') integrals, and all the other classes not? And what is a 'Particle'? It does not seem to be a superordinate category for (some of) the undeclined parts.

Towards the end of 'The Accidence' Lewis mentions prepositions. He offers a long list of English prepositions, followed by the Latin ones divided into those that govern the accusative, those that govern the ablative and a few that can govern either, but before that there is a brief characterisation of prepositions, according to which 'they express the circumstances of things: their use is to tack on Substantives to Verbs, or other words governing them: they have the same common nature as signs of Cases have' (1674:16).

At the beginning of 'The Second Part, or Grammar' Lewis revisits the parts of speech. After stating that 'Grammarians may reduce all words in our English Tongue to eight Parts or Heads', he enters into a curious argument by claiming that '[s]ix are sufficient in any Language distinctly to express our thoughts', of which the 'Substantive' and the 'Verb' are 'the most material, and principal' (1674:18). By maintaining that 'Adverbs are the manners of Verbs, as Adjectives are of Substantives' he seems to have reduced the number by two to six, but adjectives are not a separate class in his earlier list. Prepositions and conjunctions are also brought into focus here. He repeats the function of prepositions, but not before clearly equating 'signs of Cases' with prepositions: 'Prepositions and signs of Cases (which we may reckon as Prepositions) tack on Substantives to the word influencing, or governing them', and prepositions and conjunctions are contrasted in the following way: 'Conjunctions tack on Sentences to Sentences in a Period, as Prepositions do words to words in a Sentence'. Both are apparently vital to language structure, for if they are removed from 'Periods and Sentences', respectively, these 'will be but a parcel of stones, tumbled on a heap, that make no structure' (*ibid.*). The cohesive nature of these two classes could hardly have been described more graphically, so they are presumably *not* the two redundant classes. In fact, shortly afterwards we are back to eight parts of speech again: 'I shall speak to these eight Parts of Speech in the method I have done in the Accidence' (*ibid.*). This page is not a model of clarity.

Prepositions, in this part of the book, occur in two places. First as 'signs of Cases' under 'Substantives', where they are treated in exactly the same way as the equivalent Latin prepositions, e.g. *of* is 'a sign of the Genitive Case', *to, for* are 'signs of the Dative Case', while *with, by, from* and *than* are of 'the Ablative Case' (1674:24-6). The second place does not contribute anything new and deals exclusively with prepositions in Latin. The definition is the standard one of being 'put before other words, either in apposition before a Substantive … or else they are put before other words in composition' and much of the previous information about them governing different cases in Latin is repeated. There is no attempt to distinguish between English and Latin.

Despite his expressed opposition to Lily and the wording in certain parts of his *Essay*, Lewis seems in essence very conventional in his presentation of the parts of speech in general and of prepositions in particular. His comparison of prepositions and conjunctions shows glimpses of what he might have been capable of, had he freed himself more from the straightjacket of the Latin tradition. Whether the missing section on 'Critical or Idiomatic Grammar', promised on the title-page, would have been different, we shall probably never know. As it stands, it is difficult to see how this account can justify Lewis's claim to have discovered 'new principles' for a grammar.

Christopher Cooper (1655?-1698)[39]

Christopher Cooper was Master of the Grammar School at Bishop's Stortford and a vicar. His *Grammatica Linguae Anglicanae* (1685; see Cooper 1968)[40] is exceptional in several ways. First of all, it is the last English grammar written in Latin. It is also well known for its sections on phonetics, and Alston cites E.J. Dobson for claiming that Cooper's work in this area was, if anything, superior to Wallis's (1968:Note). In the long Preface ('Præfatio'), Wallis is mentioned as an inspiration for the work, together with Gill and Wilkins. A new version of the chapters on pronunciation and spelling was published under the title *The English Teacher* in 1687, but this does not include the grammatical sections. Grammar ('Etymologia') is tackled in the third part of the book ('Pars Tertia'), including syntax ('De Syntaxi').

But the grammar is remarkable, too, for its treatment of the word classes, not least of prepositions. In fact, it is difficult to make out exactly what Cooper regards as genuine parts of speech. In Chapter I of 'Etymologia' he seems to set up a division into principal words or *integrals* ('integrales') and circumstantial words or *particles* ('particulæ'); a distinction that no doubt owes much to Wilkins. He further adds that integrals are either nouns or verbs, but nothing else is said at this point and he does not mention this classification again (1968:96). On the following pages it is clear, though, that adjectives, as so often, come under nouns. In Chapter II (1968:116-32) he focuses on the properties or 'accidents' of (noun) substantives. These comprise articles, pronouns, gender, number and – unusually – prepositions. It is not often that we find prepositions classified as an accident of nouns, unless we apply this term to the 'case signs' found in many grammars at the time. However, there is no distinction between different types of preposition in terms of their functions; they are all accidents of nouns.

Chapters V-VII (1968:162-71) contain separate analyses of adverbs, conjunctions and interjections, respectively, and it looks as if they are granted status as parts of speech, in contrast to what we were told in Chapter I. If so, Cooper ends up with a five-part word class system that consists of nouns, verbs, adverbs, conjunctions and interjections. Such a system is not only unusual but unique among English grammars (cf. Michael 1970:251-3).

The prepositions in Chapter II (1968:127-32) are divided into different categories according to function and/or meaning. First, we have some uses of *of*, e.g. authorship ('the works *of* Cicero'), possession ('the Palace *of* the King'), subject ('a cup *of* water') or relation ('the son *of* an earl'), but also material ('a building *of* marble') and the object of something (= concerning) ('a treatise *of* philosophy') (my emphasis). *With* and *by*, we hear, take the ablative case in Latin, but it is not specified if they also do that in English, as there are no examples featuring them or the other prepositions mentioned here, such as *without, for, according to, instead of* and *against*; only their semantic role is stated ('agent', 'concomitant', 'opposition to', etc.).

Another group denote motion in space or time, e.g. *to, from, into, out of, up*(*wards*), *down*(*wards*), but again with no exemplification, as is also the case with the two last groups, namely those that express position or non-motion (*at, off, within, without, above, below/beneath*), and those that can denote either motion or position, e.g. *over, about, before, after, upon, under, between, against*, etc. At the end of the chapter we are told that prepositions often do not appear with case, i.e. case-marked complements, if they function as adverbs.

There is thus a clear attempt to establish various groupings of prepositions in terms of their use, function or meaning, but the lack of examples makes the presentation rather abstract, and the semantics of the prepositions in some of the groups is not easy to reconcile with their alleged status as properties of nouns.

Finally, it is worth mentioning a few points under syntax in Chapter VIII. The very first sentence maintains that 'English syntax nearly always depends on prepositions' (1968:171), but this is not substantiated. There are some other scattered remarks about certain prepositions, the most interesting one relating to their position in the clause. Although they are generally placed before their complement, they can also be found after it, in a type of construction that we have heard of before and which came to be mentioned with increasing frequency, namely in certain relative (and, in other grammars, interrogative) clauses like 'The man, whom I spake *of*' or the 'ellipted' form 'The man I spake *of* is dead' (1968:177). There is no indication here – unlike in some later grammars – whether such usage is acceptable or indeed recommended, but the very absence of a judgemental attitude is notable.

Guy Miege (1644-1718 or earlier)
Guy Miege was born in Lausanne, Switzerland, and came to England at the age of seventeen. He soon became under-secretary to Charles Howard when the latter was ambassador extraordinary to Russia, Sweden and Denmark. Apart from journalistic and historical works, Miege is known for a French-English dictionary and in addition he wrote three grammars, of which *The English Grammar* (1688; see Miege 1969) is relevant in this context, though its popularity at the time was limited despite being reprinted in 1691. What makes Miege's treatment especially interesting is the fact that his is apparently the only English grammar written by a non-native speaker before 1800 (cf. Miege 1969:Note).

In his initial address to the Reader, which is in part a sales advertisement, Miege makes the point that it is 'very proper, before a Young Man be turned over to the Latine Tongue, to know the Nature and Principles of his own' (1969:A3). In a way this sets the tone for the whole book. Miege recognises the usual eight parts of speech, but it is noteworthy that he talks of 'eight Sorts of Words, whereof a Language does consist' (1969:1). This strongly implies the then common notion that the parts of speech are universal and not established according to what is appropriate for each language.

Another early statement is worth quoting. Having distinguished between monosyllabic, dissyllabic and polysyllabic words, Miege continues, 'And a short word, whether it be a Pronoun, Adverb, Conjunction, Preposition, or Interjection, is commonly called a Particle' (1969:2). There is nothing strange about using 'particle' as an umbrella term for at least some of these classes, but there seems to be an odd implication that the other classes (nouns, verbs, participles) do not have 'short words'. There is a clear hierarchy among these classes, for we are told that 'Nouns and Verbs are the most considerable', that 'Pronouns and Participles are in their nature half Nouns', and 'what are [the last four], but Accessories to Nouns and Verbs, and as it were their Attendants?' (1969:7). In essence, this almost boils down to three major classes: nouns, verbs and particles.

Prepositions are dealt with in three different places in Part I of the *Grammar*. First, the class appears as part of a brief introduction of the eight parts of speech, where it is simply given this definition: 'A Preposition is a Word that expresses some Circumstance or other of the Noun' (1969:7), which is followed by 31 (simple) prepositions, with alternatives in two cases. On the positive side, prepositions are explicitly related to nouns, but by any standards this is a very vague definition.

The second place where prepositions are discussed is under the section 'Of the Composition of Words' (1969:20ff), where prepositions are given a prominent role. In his initial statement Miege says that 'the Way of making Compounds in English is Twofold, either with a preposition, or with some other previous Part of Speech' (*ibid.*). He makes the additional point that 'the Prepositions used in this Case are either Separable, or Inseparable. That is, they are either such Prepositions as may be used by themselves, or such as are only used in Compound Words' (*ibid.*). He then gives examples of the two groups, and it becomes clear that by 'separable' he means items that can function as independent prepositions, such as *after* (in 'afternoon'), *in* (in 'to inhabit'), *under* (in 'undervalue'), etc., but also some that are more debatable, such as *cross* (in 'cross-grained'), *forth* (in 'forth-coming'), *out* (in 'outlandish'), and a few more (1969:20-21).

The 'inseparable prepositions' are divided into those that are 'properly English' and those 'of Greek and Latine Origine'. However, it turns out that the English ones are bound prefixes, such as *a*, *be*, *fore*, *mis*, *un*, with the exception of *over* that is said to 'signify both Eminency and Excess', as in 'overrule' and 'over-cautious', respectively (1969:21). The Greek and Latin examples are a mixture of prefixes and words that can act as independent prepositions. Though one can quibble with the terminology and definitions (prefixes or prepositions), it has to be said that Miege's analysis of these compounds that include 'prepositions' is extremely thorough and runs to eight pages (1969:20-8), while the remaining compound words cover just another page and a half.

Finally, the 'Use of Prepositions' is dealt with in the later section 'Of Adverbs, Conjunctions and Prepositions', which is introduced with the somewhat dismissive remark: 'I shall speak of these three Parts of Speech under one Head, because I han't much to say of any of them; and leave out Interjections, as the most barren of 'em all' (1969:77). Nevertheless, the three classes are looked at separately on the following pages, ending with a two-page treatment of prepositions. Here Miege makes some brief but salient points, for example by distinguishing between 'local Motion' and 'no local Motion', as seen in *to*, *into* (e.g. 'he goes to School, he is gone into his Chamber') versus *at*, *in* (e.g. in 'he is at School, he is in his Chamber'). This distinction is still central to any modern study of prepositions, and so is the extended locative use where the movement is figurative. Miege does not use any such terms, but this is clearly implied in his observation 'concerning the emphatic Use of these two Prepositions, *Out* and *Into*, wherein the English does far outdo the French', giving as his examples 'to work a Child out of his roguish Tricks' and 'to whip him into better manners' (1969:80), whatever they might suggest about the attitude to, and upbringing of, children.

Another relevant observation concerns stranded prepositions with the prepositional complement fronted in interrogative and relative clauses, as mentioned above under Cooper. Miege states that 'although the Prepositions took that name from their being commonly placed before Nouns, yet in English they are often placed at the end of a Sentence; especially after these two Pronouns, *Who* and *What*', as in 'who did you dine with? What place do you come from?' (1969:80-81). He even notes, half apologetically, that here 'the Preposition becomes, if I may say so, a Postposition', though he feels that he needs a comparable Latin example ('Ore *tenus*', by mouth) for support. Given that this 'definition', i.e. 'commonly placed before Nouns', is a little more informative than his first one, i.e. 'a Word that expresses some Circumstance or other of the Noun', it sounds odd when he immediately afterwards seems to suggest that being part of a compound is somehow more natural for a preposition than being used independently, for that is how one must read his comment in relation to verbs: 'Whereas in Verbs Compound [i.e. compound verbs] the Preposition goes first, and makes but one Word with the Verb, the English has another Way besides of using Prepositions, viz. after the Verb, and distinct from it', as in 'to look upon', 'to look for', 'to put out' and 'to go after' (1969:81). At no stage does Miege consider that an important function of a preposition might be to link a verb and the (nominal) prepositional complement.

The rest of his account makes two points. One is to draw attention to some examples where 'the Preposition is left out', which include (a) genitives (e.g. 'God's Glory', cp. 'the Glory of God'); (b) 'after some Verbs', in fact, with indirect objects (e.g. 'send it me', cp. 'send it to me'); and (c) in expressions such as 'to go home' (cp. 'house'), 'a House forty foot high' (cp. 'a House to the height of forty foot'); 'to go ten miles' (cp. 'to go to the end of ten miles'), etc. (*ibid.*), which vary in explanatory quality. The other point is more poignant, namely 'that there are Prepositions sometimes used Adverbially, that is, without a Substantive', as in 'he went before, and I came after' or 'He was above, and I below'. Like others before him, Miege says that they are 'used Adverbially', but not that they *are* adverbs in such examples. It was often a bone of contention then whether there was identity of word class or merely similarity of function in these cases.

In summary, Miege provides a more comprehensive account of English prepositions than one finds in some of the treatments we have looked at so far, and the fact that he writes about English from an outsider's perspective gives it a different slant. His strength does not lie in his definitions, but a few interesting and relevant points are considered in some detail.

John Locke (1632-1704)
John Locke was a philosopher, not a grammarian, and his main philosophical work *An Essay on Human Understanding* (1689; see Locke 1975) is obviously not a grammar. Nevertheless, the *Essay* contains a presentation of some fundamental aspects of language from a philosophical point of view, which bears comparison with some of the philosophical grammars of the time.

In the section entitled 'Of Particles' (1975: Book III, Ch. VII 1-6, pp. 471-3), Locke distinguishes between 'words, which are names of Ideas in the Mind' (discussed in the previous Chapter: Book III, Ch.

VI) and 'a great many others that are made use of, to signify the connexion that the Mind gives to Ideas, or Propositions, one with another' (1975:471).

These other words, we are told, by which the mind 'signifies what connexion it gives to the several Affirmations and Negations, that it unites in one continued Reasoning or Narration, are generally call'd Particles' (*ibid.*). This is, as we have seen, in tune with other treatments of the time and especially with an increasing tendency in philosophical grammars to conflate some, if not all, of the 'minor' parts of speech to form a general category of 'particles'.

Locke attaches great importance to the stylistic role played by the 'particles', e.g. when he says that in 'the right use of these ... consists the clearness and beauty of a good Stile' (1975:471-2), and he is careful to point out that they are not merely ornamental, since they are if 'not truly, by themselves, the names of any Ideas', at least of 'constant and indispensible use in Language'. In fact, according to Locke, this part of grammar 'has been, perhaps, as much neglected, as some others over-diligently cultivated' (1975:472).

Locke acknowledges that prepositions, conjunctions, etc., are 'names well known in Grammar' as categories, and he accepts the view that 'the Particles contained under them [are] carefully ranked into their distinct subdivisions' (*ibid.*). Human beings, he contends, think 'in train', and by doing so they must 'observe the dependence of ... Thoughts and Reasoning, one upon another'. It is in this context that he emphasises the important role of particles, for in order 'to express well such methodical and rational Thoughts' it is necessary to 'have words to shew what Connexion, Restriction, Distinction, Opposition, Emphasis, etc. he [i.e. the speaker] gives to each respective part of his Discourse' (*ibid.*).

So far, Locke seems to echo the often expressed view that particles (in particular, prepositions and conjunctions) essentially have a connecting function, i.e. they 'bind together' the discourse. However, in the rest of the chapter he invests them with semantic properties that go well beyond the notion of a merely supporting role.

First, he claims that 'they are all marks of some Action, or Intimation of the Mind', so that 'to understand them rightly' we must study 'the several views, postures, stands, turns, limitations, and exceptions, and several other Thoughts of the Mind, for which we have either none, or very deficient Names' (*ibid.*). Unfortunately, all of these greatly exceed 'the number of Particles, that most Languages have, to express them by', which, according to Locke, explains why 'most of these Particles have divers, and sometimes almost opposite significations' (*ibid.*); that is, they are polysemous. This is exemplified by *but* (1975:473). Locke does not consider the opposite situation when the same relation is expressed by different prepositions.

Secondly, he goes even further when he says of the particles that 'some ... constantly, and others in certain constructions, have the sense of a whole Sentence contain'd in them' (*ibid.*). This potentially makes the particles more semantically relevant to the discourse than 'referring words' such as nouns ('words, which are names of Ideas in the Mind', see above), but such a claim is not really substantiated, since Locke confines himself to the example of *but*. (A parallel here might be the so-called 'pro-forms', e.g. *it*, *do*, *so*, etc.)

It must be admitted that the paucity of convincing examples detracts from the weight of Locke's general argument, and some of his claims are certainly open to question. The importance of his contribution to language studies, in terms of prepositions, is, however, partly that he lends his authority to an analysis that operates with particles as a general category, and partly that he sees this category as semantically more important than is usual in most previous accounts.

William Clare (dates unknown)
Hardly anything is known of William Clare, but his work *A Complete System of Grammar English and Latin* (1690, note that there is no comma in the title; see Clare 1971) is introduced by an 'Epistle Dedicatory' to William, Duke of Gloucester, followed by an 'Advertisement to the Reader'. However, the latter is not very informative so, as the Editor's Note rightly points out, 'when "the Advertisement" and the main text are considered together the underlying scheme of the work is not at all clear' (1971:Note). The aim seems to be to facilitate the learning of Latin via English, but Latin is the dominant language in that explanations relevant for Latin are generally transferred to English whether they suit English grammar or not.

The book is organised as parallel English and Latin texts, each page being divided into two columns, but what is included under each language varies. Throughout the book, the text is presented as a dialogue between a pupil M(artin) and a teacher J., where M. asks the questions and J. answers them. This can be a pedagogically useful approach and does make many definitions and grammatical issues clear. It was to be copied in many later grammars, but the device goes right back to Donatus and the *Schulgrammatik* tradition in the Middle Ages.

The framework is a traditional one, treating grammar as one of the seven medieval Liberal Arts, consisting of the four parts – orthography, etymology, syntax and prosody – that emerged in the late Middle Ages (see Chapter II above), though like earlier 'etymology' is not to be understood in its modern sense. 'Of Etymology' makes up by far the longest section and is, as was customary then, mainly concerned with the parts of speech. Here, too, the overall system operates with the customary eight parts of speech.

The sub-section 'Of a Preposition' is just over one page long. Prepositions are defined as 'an undeclined part of Speech, which is out before other parts of Speech either in composition, or else in apposition' (1971:97), which was the mantra since the Roman grammarians. Clare, to his credit, provides examples for most of his statements; in this case, composition is exemplified by 'he has admonished' and apposition by 'he sitteth at the right hand'. The Latin influence is seen in the former example: *ad* is not a preposition in English, but it *is* in Latin, so as a preposition it may more accurately be said to be part of the 'composition' in the Latin word form *admonuit* (*ibid.*).

This procedure of transferring examples and explanations from Latin to English becomes even more questionable when Clare states that 'sometimes Præpositions[41] are used both ways' (he must mean in the same example or sentence) and illustrates this with the clause 'I am going to my Father'. The reader can only make sense of this by looking at the equivalent Latin clause 'adeo ad patrem' where *ad* appears with both functions. Similarly, when he informs us that 'these five Præpositions are usually set after the Cases they govern', we have to look across to the other column to see that he means the Latin prepositions *cum, penes, tenus, versus, asque*, as in 'quibus cum', 'Anglicam versus' and 'ad occidentem asque', for the prepositions are not listed in English and their alleged behaviour certainly does not apply to the English translations 'with which', 'towards England' and 'even to the setting of the Sun' (*ibid.*).

From these examples alone it is clear that English is treated as if it were identical to Latin in structure and grammatical categories and this fundamental view clearly informs Clare's handling of cases, too. We are told that 'to a Præposition belongs Case, Government or Construction', and as far as case is concerned, prepositions are divided into those that govern 'an Accusative Case', those that require 'an Ablative Case' and those that take one or the other, depending on whether they signify 'motion' or 'rest'. Of course, this is only relevant for Latin, not for English, so it is perplexing when we read M's question: 'Why do you say, *up to the legs*, by a Genitive, or an Ablative case indifferently?' and find that the answer is: '*Tenus* governs a genitive case plural, also an ablative in both Numbers' (1971:98). Once again, we must look at the Latin text to understand that it is the difference between 'crurum tenus' and 'cruribus tenus' (to the legs) and the fact that the preposition *tenus* can govern both the genitive and the ablative that explains the otherwise mystifying information. And so on.

The relationship between prepositions and case is also dealt with under case. For example, we hear that 'the Ablative case hath a Preposition either expressed or understood which in English are *at, by, for, from, in, on, thro, with, than* after an Adjective of the Comparative degree, and *of* after a verb passive' (1971:29; my emphasis). Despite the syntax and the missing punctuation, the meaning is clear enough, i.e. *than* is used after a comparative form and *of* after a passive verb form. However, what is interesting is partly that a preposition can be 'expressed or understood', i.e. the claim that it is found in the relevant sentence's deep or underlying structure (for those who operate with this notion), and partly that, once more, it is postulated that English prepositions can govern the ablative, here without any matching Latin prepositions being found in the opposite Latin column.

Finally, prepositions 'become' adverbs when they have no prepositional complement or, as Clare puts it, 'And Præpositions also when they govern no Case are changed into Adverbs, as, &c. *I came at length*' (1971:96). So, firstly, they 'are changed into' adverbs (cf. Miege above, for instance, for whom they are used adverbially in such cases) and secondly, the example – like so many others – only really works in Latin, 'longo post tempore veni'.

There is no doubt that Clare sets out to explain the intricacies of Latin grammar for those who want (or have) to learn it, and it may to some extent be unfair to blame him for not distinguishing more clearly (or at all) between the two languages if his main aim is to illustrate Latin, but there really are many points of confusion in his use of parallel texts, with English being totally subservient to Latin, and his handling of prepositions is a good illustration of this.

Joseph Aickin (dates unknown)
Joseph Aickin was a schoolmaster in London and wrote *The English Grammar* in 1693 (see Aickin 1967). In a way it is an ambitious undertaking and has at the front a fulsome verse eulogy by a friend of Aickin's, known only by his initials S.H. In it, S.H. praises the *Grammar* for its emphasis on English ('No more on Latine now our Tongue depends') and sees Aickin as the pinnacle of a long tradition that started with 'Great Chaucer' and in his view continued with John Wallis, Jeremiah Wharton and Christopher Cooper, though in later years Aickin has been suspected of plagiarising Cooper and, through him, Wallis. Following that, there is an 11-page Preface addressed to 'the Schoolmasters of the English Tongue and other Candid Readers'. Here Aickin is at pains to establish the importance of learning grammar in order to master not just foreign languages but also one's own, 'For no Tongue can be acquired without Grammatical rules'; and, as he adds, 'since ... all other Tongues, and Languages are taught by Grammar, why ought not the English Tongue to be taught so too' (1967:Preface, p. 1). He bemoans the poor standard of native English, even in boys who have been to school for 10-11 years ('Nay, some scarce learn to read and write in that time'), and attributes this partly to a failure to teach them grammar, and partly to 'the want of an English Grammar', although, as we have seen above, this is something of an overstatement. Even so, filling this 'gap' is Aickin's overt reason for writing his grammar.

The *Grammar* is divided into the familiar four sections, and the First Part (on Orthography) is much longer than the three others combined. The Second Part of the Grammar contains the three other sections: Etymology (Chs 1-6, pp. 2-16), Syntax (Chs 7-8) and Prosody (or Poetry, Ch. IX), with the parts of speech appearing under Etymology.[42]

Aickin preserves the eight parts of speech that we have become accustomed to, including participles but excluding adjectives. Prepositions are dealt with in just over two pages (1967:Ch. 1, Section 5, pp. 5-7) and given the traditional definition: 'a part of Speech, which is commonly set before other parts of Speech, either in *Apposition*, as *of me, to God*: or else in *Composition* as, *toward, upward, forward*, etc.' (1967:5-6; his emphasis). But if this has a familiar ring to it, Aickin deviates markedly from, for example, Clare when he remarks that nouns in English 'cannot be said to have Cases, as in the Latin and Greek Tongues' and adds that this 'defect in our Tongue is supplied by the aid of Prepositions', giving some examples of nouns in both singular and plural, with and without prepositions. He also comments that 'this defect of Declensions and Cases, makes the English Tongue easie to be learned'; and seeing that 'Prepositions supply the same you must', he admonishes his readers, 'learn the Prepositions perfectly' (1967:6).

His wording here is worth paying attention to. His rejection of cases in English nouns – even the genitive, it would seem – was not commonplace at the time; nor was the assertion that the 'same' functions are served by prepositions. Although it was often recognised that there is a connection between cases and the use of prepositions, most contemporary grammarians postulated that the Latin nominal cases applied to English, too. Secondly, he does indeed see the lack of declensions and cases as a 'defect', but not only is this linguistically remedied by means of prepositions, he also spots the advantage that it allegedly has for learning English more easily. This was not a usual way of looking at the phenomenon.

In the rest of the section Aickin divides prepositions into two groups: 'Causals' and 'Locals'. Among causal prepositions we find possessive *of*, as in 'The works of Cicero' and 'the Palace of the Emperour'. These examples with *of* are 'sometimes ... changed into an adjective possessive', cf. 'Cicero's works' and 'the Emperour's Palace' (*ibid.*). *Of* may also denote a 'material cause', cf. 'a Building of stone' versus 'a stone building', or 'the object', as in 'He is writing a Treatise of Logick', where presumably 'Logick' is seen as the object – or part of it? *With* and *by*, we hear, 'expresse the instrument, cause, or way of an action', cf. 'He killed him with a sword' and 'He did it with care', where the notion of 'cause' may not be obvious, unless one claims that the sword caused the man's death. Finally, *for* 'denotes the Final cause or end of an action', as in 'He taught for profit'; *according to* the rather vague 'likeness or idea of a thing', as in 'According to his patterns'; and *against* opposition, as in 'Against God' (1967:6-7).

The remaining prepositions are then, by definition, 'Locals', denoting 'the place, the time, or motion and rest'. They fall into the usual three groups: (i) those that 'signifie motion' (e.g. *to, from, into, out of*, etc.); (ii) those that 'signifie rest' (e.g. *at, off, within, without,* etc.); and (iii) those that can do either (e.g. *over, about, beside, before,* etc.) (1967:7). Those in group (i) include *downwards* and those in (iii) a number of words in *-ward*, such as *forward, upward, thitherward* and even *heaven ward* (written in two words). Aickin's last point is to separate *between/betwixt*, used of two entities, from *among*(st), used of more than two. This latter distinction has long ceased to be observed, but it shows the precision which Aickin tries to bring to his writing.

Aickin's *Grammar* is certainly not a bad one for his avowed purpose. The first part, Orthography, is extraordinarily detailed, while the remaining ones – despite many good observations – are less so. But all in all, Aickin managed to produce a grammar of English without direct reference to Latin, and that in itself was an achievement for the time. One can only deplore the fact that it apparently did not reach as wide an audience as the author clearly hoped for, since it was never reprinted.

A. Lane (?-between 1700-1705)
Little is known about A. Lane (including his first name) other than the fact that he was master of the Free-School of Leominster in Herefordshire and later a teacher in a private school near Stepney (cf. Lane 1969:Note).

Lane wrote two grammars; first, *A Rational and Speedy Method of attaining to the Latin Tongue* (1695; see Lane 1972) and five years later *A Key to the Art of Letters* (1700; see Lane 1969). *A Rational and Speedy Method* is in two parts: the first (short) one (1972:1-24) concerns general grammar, while the much longer second part (1972: 25-124) deals exclusively with the grammar of Latin. We shall therefore concentrate on the first part.

The *Method* opens with a consideration of the parts of speech. From the start Lane rejects the traditional view and shows his independence of mind by stating that 'there are four kinds of Words, a Substantive, an Adjective, a Verb, and a Particle', having already defined 'Words' as 'commonly called Parts of Speech' (1972:1). Compared, for example, with Miege, who among others also operates with a class of 'particles', Lane's particles do not include pronouns and interjections, but only 'three Sorts; Adverbs, Prepositions, and Conjunctions' (1972:22). Lane seems very sure that this four-part division is correct 'because there are but four kinds of Things to be signified by Words: For whatever is in the whole Universe, is either a *Thing*, or the *Manner* of a Thing; the *Action* of a Thing, or the *Manner* of an Action' (1972:1). In other words, Lane's definition of the parts of speech is made on notional grounds with reference to the external world, which has echoes of the medieval Modistae (cf. Chapter II above). According to Michael (1970:254), Lane is the first grammarian to use what Michael calls a 'vernacular' fourfold system, but by no means the first to operate with a class of 'particles'.

Under the heading 'Of a Particle', a preposition is described as 'a Particle that denotes some Circumstance of an Action, and cannot make compleat Sense with one Verb without some oblique Case after it', and as prepositions he lists *of, to, with, from, against* (1972:22). He expands on this by saying, 'I know the Particle *of* is a Preposition, because I cannot say in compleat Sense, I spoke *of*, but I spoke *of him*' (1972:22-3). The point here is not just that the sense is 'completed' in the second sentence by a pronoun (though Lane does not use this term), but that it is in an oblique case, not 'of he' because that is a 'Nominative, with which no Preposition can make Sense' (1972:23). Maybe it could have been said more clearly and more elegantly, but the 'rule' is not in doubt: a preposition combines two elements, so as well as a verb (or another element, see below) there must be a nominal element governed by the preposition and therefore in an oblique case. Only then do we have a 'compleat Sense'.

Lane's Latin grammar is' of no concern to us, but his second book, *A Key to the Art of Letters*, certainly *is*, if more for its general purpose than for its treatment of prepositions, some of which is a repetition of what was said in the previous book. Like Clare's *Complete System* (see above), it carries a dedication to 'the Most Illustrious Prince William, Duke of Glocester',[43] and the title page explains the purpose of the book very concisely. It is 'a key to the art of letters' but also to 'English a Learned Language, Full of Art, Elegancy and Variety'. This is normally the kind of praise that is heaped on the classical languages, not on a modern vernacular. In fact, the book will, the reader is told, 'enable both Foreiners, and the English Youth of either Sex, to speak and write the English Tongue well and learnedly, according to the exactest Rules of Grammar'. Only then may they 'attain to Latin, French, or any other Forein Language in a short time, with very little trouble to themselves or their Teachers'. Obtaining a proper command of 'the rules of grammar' is thus a prerequisite for speaking good and 'learned' English, and once that is achieved it will be easy to learn other languages. So despite having written a Latin grammar, Lane strongly advocates an intimate knowledge of English before tackling any foreign language. Although he is not the first to advocate this, it is still very different from those of his predecessors or contemporaries who recommended learning Latin early and the grammar of their own language via Latin, or not at all. One may also notice that for once a grammar is aimed at girls as well as boys, which was not usually mentioned either, but became gradually more and more common in the eighteenth century, as we shall see. Finally, Lane refers to his Preface as 'shewing the Necessity of a Vernacular Grammar' (1969:Title page).

Already in his Dedication, Lane talks of the 'excellency and usefulness of the English Tongue', which 'is as capable of all the Art and Elegancies of Grammar and Rhetorick, as Greek and Latin, or any other Language in the World, whether Antient or Modern' (1969:iii-iv). Therefore, Lane concludes, 'it seems to be contrary to Sense and Reason, as well as to Antiquity, to put English Youth to toil in any Forein Tongue whatever for the attainment of good Learning, while their own Excellent Language lies neglected and uncultivated' (1969:iv). He also points out to the young prince that even Aristotle wrote in his mother tongue and probably 'knew no other', so why should the

English not embrace theirs? The 14-page long Preface continues in this vein. Thus, the purpose of learning grammar is not to have 'an Instrument to acquire some unknown Tongue'; on the contrary, 'the true End and Use of Grammar is to teach us how to speak and write well and learnedly in a Language already known', i.e. in the vernacular, and he adds that 'the unalterable Rules of right Reason … are the same in all Languages how different soever they be' (1969:x). Lane, then, views grammar as universal and therefore finds it natural, indeed preferable, first to obtain a thorough grounding in it in one's own language, which after all was what the Greeks and the Romans did. He puts it in even stronger terms when he asks rhetorically, 'Can any thing be imagined more absurd and ridiculous, than to put Children to learn Latin and Grammar at once?' (1969:xi). It is hard to imagine a stauncher defence of the vernaculars *vis-à-vis* the classical languages in the neo-classical period.

Great expectations were thus created both by Lane himself and also by the two writers whose panegyrical verses about the book appear just after the Preface, and Lane deals succinctly and competently with many aspects of grammar that were not mentioned in *A Rational and Speedy Method*. He deliberately uses the same technique of a question-and-answer dialogue that we observed in Clare's *Complete System*, and the answers are usually clear and to the point. It is not surprising that he recognises the same four parts of speech (or rather, 'kinds of Words'; 1969:20) and the same 'three sorts of Particles' (1969:56) as in his earlier book, and when he comes to prepositions, it is only the question-and-answer format that is different, not the content.

However, there is mention of prepositions and their functions in a few other places. For instance, under nouns – apart from using *of* before a 'Substantive' as one way to form the genitive – the question 'How is the Dative known in English?' is answered in this way: 'In English the Dative is usually known by the Preposition *to*, and sometimes *for* before it, and then the applied Word comes before the Preposition', with the following examples (not without moral overtones): 'Strong Drink is hurtful *to* Children or *for* Children' and 'I said my Lesson *to* the Master' (1969:27; my emphasis). First, it is notable that Lane uses the full Latin case system (cf. 'There are six Cases [of the noun]' (1969:26)), also when applied to English grammar; there are apparently limits to the independence of the vernaculars. Secondly, the 'applied Word' is not the prepositional complement but the word *before* the preposition, here 'hurtful' and 'Lesson', respectively, although we have immediately prior to this heard that 'a *Noun* is in the dative case, when it is the thing to which any other thing is applied by some *Verb* or *Adjective*' (1969:27; his emphasis). Despite this limitation, the 'applied Word' clearly means the element that is linked to the prepositional complement by the preposition, which, as we saw in the above example with 'Lesson', can also be a noun. Similarly, we are told that 'a Noun is in the Ablative Case, when it comes after any of these Prepositions, *with*, *from*, *in*, or *by*, etc., *as with my Master, from my Father, in the School*, etc.' (1969:28; his emphasis). Prepositions, then, are generally seen in terms of Latin cases and as having relational function.

Much of this is repeated in the later section on syntax ('Of a Sentence'; 1969:74ff). On the whole, the treatment in *A Key to the Art of Letters* is largely an expansion of Lane's previous book, but it is set out in far greater detail. It is clearly an attempt to 'stand up for English' and other vernaculars but English is largely described within the framework of Latin grammar. However, this was to change in many eighteenth-century presentations, some of which were influenced by Lane.

(iii) *The Eighteenth Century*

Richard Johnson (1656/7-1721)

Richard Johnson's *Grammatical Commentaries* (1706; see R. Johnson 1969) is a polemic and very ambitious work. On the one hand, it is a strong attack on Lily's Latin grammar; on the other hand, it is constructive in so far as Johnson, by criticising Lily, seeks to create nothing less than 'a New National Grammar' though, like Lily's, intended for those who 'would Attain to the True Knowledge of the Latin Tongue'. Both aspects are evident from the title-page since the full title is: *Grammatical Commentaries: being an Apparatus To a New National Grammar: by way of Animadversion upon the Falsities, Obscurities, Redundancies, and Defects of Lilly's System Now in Use*, and it goes on to mention that errors by other 'Eminent Grammarians' will also be corrected. That this strikes at the core of grammar writing in England is clear when we remember that Lily's grammar was not only the most influential grammar up to this time, but also, in Alston's words, 'the only authorised text, and prescribed by Royal edict to be used in all grammar-schools' (1969:Note). It is no wonder, therefore, that Johnson was keen to enlist the support of some of his distinguished contemporaries, whose strong recommendations appear before the actual text.

Johnson is included in the present study more for his overall definition of grammar than for his account of prepositions which is very modest indeed. His book had an impact on several of his successors, e.g. James Harris and William Ward, but it remained a controversial work and came in for a fair amount of harsh criticism (see e.g. Buchanan below and the discussion in Michael 1970:192-3). The seriousness with which Johnson approaches his topic can be seen from his initial, very densely argued four-page attempt to provide a full definition of grammar ('Of the Definition of Grammar', 1969:1-4), but this is, in a sense, where he comes unstuck. After taking issue with Lily's and other earlier definitions, including Lily's opening statement 'Grammatica est recte loquendi atq; scribendi Ars' (Grammar is the art of speaking and writing correctly), which stands as a kind of motto for this short section, Johnson works his way carefully through perceived pitfalls. Johnson's explanation of this point is very detailed, but in essence his argument is that 'recte loquendi', or even 'recte loqui', in the sense of the (correct) choice and meaning of words, is something that belongs to the dictionary and not to grammar. What is important in grammar is the *relations* between words or, as he puts it at this point of his argument, 'That we observe the Relation that Words have to one another in Sentences, and represent those Relations by such Variations, and Particles, as is usual with Authors in that Language' (1969:3). Note that Johnson specifically talks about the relation between *words* in a way that is almost verbatim what his namesake Dr Johnson postulates half a century later. But now something virtually inexplicable happens, for half a page further down Johnson arrives at the following 'True Definition of Grammar': 'Grammar is the Art of Expressing *Relations of Things in Construction*, with due Accent in

Speaking, and Orthography in Writing, according to the Custom of those, whose Language we learn' (my emphasis). True, he has just prior to this used the term 'Things' when he explains that 'Syntax … treats of the Use of those Things in Construction, according to their Relations', but elsewhere, as we saw, he seems to understand that the relations are between words, not things; indeed, he all but repeats his former statement a little later when he blames Lily for not considering that 'Grammar was the Art of expressing the Relation of Words in Sentences to one another' (1969:4). So is Johnson simply confused in his terminology? This is what Michael seems to imply by also quoting from a later text by Johnson (*Noctes Nottinghamicae*) where he similarly talks about '… Ways of expressing the *Relation* of *Things* …' (Michael 1970:193; his emphasis). The use of 'Things' rather than 'Words' recurs, for example, in Gildon and Brightland, Collyer and Fisher (see below), while Buchanan's criticism of this usage seems to be influenced by John Newbury's *An Easy Introduction to the English Language* (1745; cf. Michael 1970:193).

Johnson then moves on to the parts of speech and reproduces the established Latin scheme with eight parts, as found in Lily, but only to suggest an improvement. He wants to separate the adjective from the noun and to see it as an independent class, and at the same time to include the participle under the adjective.

The rest of the book is an extraordinarily detailed discussion of the declined classes (including the participle) covering more than 400 pages, leaving little more than a page for adverbs, conjunctions and prepositions (interjections are ignored). In fact, prepositions are merely accommodated in the last paragraph of the book. At the beginning of that short section he reproduces Lily's definition, which in all its brevity sounds like this: 'A Preposition is a Part of Speech most commonly set before other Parts, either in Apposition, as *ad Patrem* [to the father]; or else in Composition, as *indoctus* [unlearned]' (1969:407; for Lily see Chapter III above), but this is only to condemn it for being 'imperfect' by 'not naming what other Parts of Speech it is set before, nor for what end, which in this case is an indispensible Part of a Definition' (1969:408). His own suggestion is as follows: 'A Preposition is a Part of Speech us'd to shew the Relation of Nouns Substantives in Discourse', and one can in turn discuss how comprehensive that is.

However, he leaves us with the impression that he could have said so much more by claiming that if he wanted to 'shew the Reader the Defectiveness of this [Lily's] Grammar in the account it gives of the use of the Prepositions, it would make a little Volume' (*ibid.*). It is a pity that he did not discuss at least some of this 'Defectiveness', for Johnson – despite his confusion of 'Words' and 'Things' – is very scrupulous in his criticism as well as in (most of) his alternative proposals. After all, even his ardent critic James Buchanan refers to him as 'judicious' (Buchanan 1968:1).

Charles Gildon (1665-1724) **and John Brightland** (?-1717)
In 1711 one of the most influential English grammars of the eighteenth century, *A Grammar of the English Tongue* (see Gildon and Brightland, henceforth G&B, 1967), was published, with a dedication to Queen Anne. At the bottom of the title page it states that it is 'Printed for John Brightland' and sold by a number of booksellers in London as well as others around the country. However, there is some dispute about the authorship of this grammar (see 1967:Note); for example, Sir Richard Steele has been credited with the work, including in the 1782 reprint entitled *Youth's Preceptor*. Before then, eight editions of *A Grammar* had appeared, which shows its popularity throughout the century. The main inspiration for the authors seems to have been John Wallis's *Grammatica Linguae Anglicanae* from 1653 and the French Port-Royal Grammar from the same year (see Lancelot and Arnauld 1968). Both are mentioned on the last page of the Preface (unpaginated), where the authors claim to have consulted all previous grammars (and not only the 'about Thirty' English ones they mention). Another name put forward is that of 'Mr Lane' (1695; see Lane 1972), whose work(s) they 'read over more than once', but they blame him – along with Ben Jonson and most other writers of English grammars – for having 'extended and tortur'd our Tongue to confess the Latin declensions, Conjugations, and ev'n Construction, whereas there is nothing so different' (1967:Preface, last page). In the same vein, they criticise Lane for his extensive use of Latin terms, but despite these misgivings we are nevertheless told that 'his [Lane's] is the best English Grammar, except Dr. Wallis who has indeed justly cast off all, that was superflu-

ous' so as to make it 'Entirely English' (*ibid.*), though Wallis's grammar was of course written in Latin.

G&B follow Wallis in emphasising the importance of basing the rules of grammar on each individual language and in rejecting the usual deference to the classical languages: 'the Rules of our Tongue are only to be drawn from our Tongue it self, and as it is already in Use … and that we are to have no manner of Regard to the Proprieties of other Tongues, either Ancient or Modern' (1967:Preface, p. 6). They also state, somewhat unconventionally, that their *Grammar* is 'for Children, Women, or the Ignorant of both Sexes, who must be the most numerous Teachers of it in this Nation' (1967:Preface, p. 7). In other words, it is intended to improve the general level of education and awareness of the English language (a) for those who use it for everyday purposes, and (b) for those (in particular the women) whose lot it is to raise the future generation; hence the reference to 'the most numerous Teachers'.

G&B open their *Grammar* with the following definition: 'Grammar is the Knowledge or Art of Expressing our Thoughts in Words join'd together in Sentences according to the Use, Form and Propriety of every Tongue either in Speaking or Writing' (1967:i). As for so many other grammarians at the time, the close link between thoughts and words is a crucial one, but both the use and the form of languages are also prominent here, as is the distinction between the spoken and the written language. Grammar, in turn, consists of four components or – one is tempted to say – layers: letters, syllables, words and sentences. This is quite close to the modern concepts of phonology/orthography, morphology (including the notion of 'words') and syntax, and G&B clearly see this division as a hierarchy, each level acting as 'building blocks' for the next level up:

> The *Second* is produc'd by the various Conjunction of the *First*; and the various joining of the *Second* begets the *Third*; as the different putting together of the *Third* does the *Fourth*. (1967:ii; their emphasis)

This is rounded off by the conclusion that 'in the perfect Knowledge of these four Heads consists the Whole Art of Grammar' (*ibid.*) and is exemplified in some detail.

In Part III 'Of Words', G&B turn their attention to the parts of speech. Words, we are told, 'convey something to the understanding' (1967:67), which apparently is not the case with 'syllables' in Part II, so here any parallel to morphs/morphemes appears to break down. Their view of the parts of speech is rather complex and can only be understood by considering the different stages of their argument. In fact, this part – as well as whole chunks of text under some of the individual parts of speech – is largely copied from the Port-Royal Grammar (cf. Lancelot & Arnauld 1966:26ff., 1968:22ff). First of all, the view presented is notional, not to say philosophical, and based on the alleged operations of the mind. Following Lancelot & Arnauld, they claim that 'all Philosophers' are in agreement that 'there are three Operations of the Mind, *viz. Perception, Judgement,* and *Reasoning*' (1967:70; their emphasis). However, the third operation ('Reasoning') 'is but an Extension of the second', so they confine themselves to the first two. A proposition, such as 'the Earth is round', 'naturally includes two Terms, viz. the 'Subject' (here: 'the Earth') and 'the Attribute' (here: 'round'), with 'is' as 'the Connection betwixt these two Terms', but both 'Terms do properly belong to the first Operation of the Mind', i.e. perception, whereas 'the Connection belongs to the second', which they call 'the Action of the Mind, and the Manner in which we think' (*ibid.*).

From this G&B deduce that 'the greatest Distinction of that which passes in our Minds, is to signify, that we may consider the Objects of our Thoughts, and the Form and Manner of them'. Therefore, when we want 'Signs to express what passes in the Mind, the most general Distinction of Words, must be of those, which signify the Objects, and Manners of our Thoughts' (1967:70-71). It is significant that G&B distinguish between things/objects and the words that represent them; for the latter they use the term 'signs'. This forms the basis for stating that 'there are four Parts of Speech, or four Heads, to which every Word in all Languages may be reduc'd', viz. 'Names, Qualities, Words of Affirmation, The Manner of Words' (1967:69). In other words, it is a fourfold division like Lane's and, despite the different terminology, not too dissimilar to his. This division is not explicitly made in the Port-Royal Grammar.

Referring back to the two operations of the mind, the words that belong to the first class are (personal) names, participles, prepositions (or, to use their preferred term for them, 'fore-plac'd Words') and adverbs (also called 'added Words'), while the second class consists of verbs (which are 'Words of Affirmation'), conjunctions ('Joining Words') and interjections (which, they state, is an absurd term, and they condemn establishing these as a separate word class since they are 'only added Words of Passion') (1967:71). There is thus some overlap and some criss-crossing between the four parts of speech and the two types of operation of the mind. What cannot be denied is that G&B's system is quite original, and they are not afraid of rejecting a number of traditional terms and divisions. For example, they explicitly decline to use the term 'Noun Adjective' for adjectives; for them, 'adjectives' come under 'Qualities', just as 'nouns' are placed under 'Names' (1967:72, 88ff.). However, all in all it is fair to say that their presentation of word classes is not a model of clarity.

Like the previous argument, the particular treatment of prepositions (let us retain this term rather than use G&B's 'fore-plac'd Words' except in quotations) is both complex and fairly sophisticated. Aspects of it are found in different places in the book, and the first ones appear under 'Cases' as part of 'Names'. Having mentioned some 'Signs', e.g. articles, that distinguish nouns from adjectives (or 'Names' from 'Qualities'), we are told that 'there are other Signs Peculiar likewise to Names, which denote their State and Reference to each other, or to a Word of Affirmation, or to a Quality, etc.' (1967:79). After another few pages, due to G&B's use of extremely long footnotes, we are at last informed that 'these Signs are *of, to, for, o, by, with, from, in*, etc. and express several States [read: Cases] of the Name' (1967:82). We can here ignore *o*, which is only relevant for the vocative, but the rest are subsequently explained in more detail. Thus, *of* 'signifies Relation between the Name that follows it, and that which goes before it, and joins the following Name to the former, as the *Son of Adam, the House of God*'. Next, '*to* and *for*, import the Thing or Person *to*, or *for* whom any Convenience or Inconvenience is meant by the Name, the Quality, or Word, etc. as a *Friend to the Mules; Good for the Stomach* ... etc.' (*ibid.*). Finally, '*By, with, from, in* and the like, express the Instrument by *which*, or *wherewith*, the *Manner how*, etc.' (1967:83).

This is further expanded in another footnote over several pages. As we have seen, G&B are well aware of the danger of transferring Latin concepts and terms into English grammar; they suggest the term 'State' for 'Case' (which is followed by some later writers) and they argue that the Greek and Latin case systems only really, and then only in part, apply to pronouns (or 'Personal Names') in English. Nevertheless, for convenience they stick with the Latin names for cases in dealing with each case in turn. Of relevance to prepositions is, first, the genitive where it is said that the vernaculars ('the Vulgar Tongues') 'make use of a Sign to express the Relations of this Case, as *of* in English, *de* in French, etc.' (1967:86); that is, *of* as a functional link between two nouns is emphasised. Secondly, under the dative case we find that 'in English, we express this Case, or that which is equivalent to it, by the Sign *to*, or *for*', but they add that 'the same Signs are likewise us'd to what is the Accusative, and the Ablative in the Latin' (*ibid.*). This information is not followed up or repeated under the accusative case, but from a more general grammatical point of view it is interesting that G&B here contrast Latin case usage with word order in English, especially in order to explain how to identify the subject and the object in a clause without the help of case endings, e.g. by means of the examples 'the King loves the Queen' versus 'the Queen loves the King'. Finally, we hear that in Latin they 'have invented another Case, call'd the Ablative, to be join'd with several other Prepositions, from which it is inseparable in Sense', whereas it is pointed out that the accusative often appears without prepositions (1967:87).

In Chapter VIII 'Of the Manner of Words', it is initially stated that '[a] Manner of a Word, is a Part of Speech or language, that signifies the Manner, Circumstance, or Connection of Words, and are join'd to other Parts of Speech' (1967:117). A footnote informs us that 'I have already observ'd that Cases, and Prepositions ... were invented for the same Use, that is to show the Relations, that Things have to one another. In all Languages, these relations are shown by Prepositions' (*ibid.*).[44] (For the use of 'Things' in this context see comments under R. Johnson above.) This part of speech is divided into three sub-classes: (i) 'Added Words', i.e. adverbs; (ii) 'Fore-Plac'd Words', i.e. prepositions, 'denoting some Circumstances of Actions, and join Words to Words, and little members of a Sentence to each other'; and (iii) 'Joining Words, join Sentence to Sentence, as greater Members of a Period', i.e. conjunctions (1967:117-18). G&B point to a correlation between adverbs and prepositions, in that the rise of adverbs can be explained by economy of language, or as they put it, 'The Desire Men have to shorten Discourse', since the alternative expression is one of a preposition plus a noun. Here they claim that we should make a distinction between English and Latin since 'in the vulgar Languages, the greatest Part of the *Adverbs*, are generally more Elegantly explain'd by the *Noun* and the *Preposition*', e.g. 'with Wisdom' and 'with Pride' instead of 'wisely' and 'proudly', etc. (though they admit that 'it holds not always'), whereas 'in *Latin*, it is generally more Elegant to use the *Adverbs*' (1967:118; their emphasis). Whatever one's attitude to this may be, at least it demonstrates their policy of treating languages individually.

As an element of this 'part of speech', prepositions are given a separate paragraph. Here it is said that they 'take their Denomination from their Situation, both in Words compounded of them, and being plac'd before *Names* in Construction, or Sentences, denoting the Circumstances of an Action, as, *To, for, from, with, in, by*, etc., and it may be known by making compleat Sense with a *Word*, or a *Quality* deriv'd from a Word before it, and a *Name* with some of the *Signs* of its States after it' (1967:121; their emphasis). This definition, which is undoubtedly influenced by Lane, seems to state that prepositions link two elements, usually two nouns or an adjective and a noun. As in Lane, it is also shown that prepositions combine with an oblique case form (hence, 'a *Name* with some of the *Signs* of its States after it'), e.g. 'me, him', not 'I, he'.

Finally, in an Appendix to the *Grammar* G&B deal with French specifically and here they make some general comments about prepositions; they even use this term. However, it is mainly a re-statement of their previous definitions, albeit in a wider context involving not only French but also Hebrew and Latin.

G&B have thus gone further than Lane. They are not content merely to recommend the learning of English grammar by ordinary people; unlike Lane, they also try to explain the workings of English grammar on its own terms and using a terminology that is independent of Latin. This was a big step forward in the description of English and one that was to prove influential for at least some of their successors. The fact that in some of their exposition they rely heavily on other works – not least, as we have seen, Wallis, the Port-Royal Grammar and Lane – is another matter and should not detract too much from their significant achievement.

James Greenwood (1683?-1737)

James Greenwood was High Master of St. Paul's School from 1721-37. He published *An Essay towards a Practical Grammar of English* in 1711 (see Greenwood 1968), the same year that Gildon & Brightland's grammar appeared. It must have been popular since five editions of it had appeared by 1753, and an abridged version entitled *The Royal English Grammar*, published in 1737 (the year of Greenwood's death), ran to four editions, the last one in 1750. In addition, a small vocabulary of Latin, *The London Vocabulary*, from *c.* 1700 was reprinted more than thirty times right up to 1830 (cf. 1968:Note; Michael 1970:564-5).

Greenwood's aims seem modest, right down to the title of the book; since he does not believe that a 'Compleat Grammar' can 'be expected from any one Person', he chooses to call it 'an Essay' instead (1968:Preface, A4). He wants to 'explain the Principles of Grammar in such a perspicuous and familiar way, as may rather incite, than discourage the Curiosity of such who would have a clear Notion of what they speak or write' (1968:Preface, A3). In order to do this, he sets out three goals: first, 'to excite Persons to the Study of their Mother Tongue'; secondly, to give an easy and at the same time 'delightful' account of English grammar to 'our English Youth', who in his view have for far too long found such a study 'irksome, obscure and difficult', partly because of the way it was taught, but especially because of exposing them to 'Grammar in Latin, before they have learn't any thing of it in English' (in this, he is in obvious agreement with some of his more recent predecessors); and thirdly, he too wants women to have a thorough understanding of their mother tongue and therefore sets out 'to oblige the fair Sex whose Education perhaps, is too much neglected in this Particular' (1968:Preface, A3-4). His main inspiration is John Wallis, whose principles he follows, if not his method as Wallis wrote 'for Foreigners and in Latin', and whose preface to *Grammatica Linguae Anglicanae* is reproduced in English translation at the beginning of the book. He also mentions Bishop Wilkins's *Essay towards a Real Character* and 'Dr Hick's *Saxon Grammar*'[45] and admits to having 'in two or three Places ... made use of Mr Lock's Expressions, because I like them better than my own' (1968:Preface, A4). The last point must refer to John Locke's examinations of particles (see above); a term which Greenwood introduces later in his book although, unlike some of his contemporaries, he does not recognise them as a separate part of speech.

Greenwood's *Essay* is very detailed. It provides clear definitions and explanations and afterwards tests these in the familiar pedagogical manner by means of question-and-answer sections, not unlike those that formed the composition of the grammars of Clare and Lane (1700). First, Greenwood divides grammar into 'two Kinds' (with a clear nod to Wilkins): (a) 'Natural and General Grammar', which deals with the universal aspects of language, and (b) 'Instituted and Particular Grammar', which describes individual languages on their own premises. The second type is the one that Greenwood himself applies to English, and again he points to Wallis and his criticism of those grammarians who try to force 'our English Tongue too much to the Latin Method' and consequently 'have delivered many useless Precepts concerning Cases, Genders and Declensions of Nouns; the Tenses, Moods and Conjugations of Verbs, as also the Government of Nouns and Verbs, and other such like Things, which our Language hath nothing at all to do with' (1968:34-5).

Secondly, he identifies the usual 'four Parts of Grammar': Orthography, Etymology, Prosody and Syntax. He is also, like Gildon & Brightland, acutely aware of the hierarchical structure of language; for example, he calls syntax 'the End of Grammar' (cf. Sanctius's *finis grammaticae* in Chapter II above), i.e. the most important part, 'for to what purpose is it to have Words, if we do not join them together', which in turn is only 'sufficient, [if] we rightly join them, that is as the best Speakers us'd to do' (1968:35). Stylistic elegance through an imitation of the good practice found in past writers thus forms part of his description of syntax. In Chapter II, Greenwood adopts the traditional division into eight parts of speech without any modifications. In view of some of his later more individual observations, he seems rather uncritical in copying these eight classes and in accepting that they are 'the same in English as in Latin' and that 'that which is a Noun in English is a Noun in Latin, and so of the rest', but he stands by his previously stated principles by adding, 'But as for Numbers, Cases, Genders, Declensions, Conjugations, etc. These are not the same in both Languages' (1968:39-40).

This latter point is picked up in his treatment of case in nouns. Case is defined as 'changing the Ending of a Noun'. For that reason, Latin is acknowledged to have six cases, while English only has one, namely 'the Genitive Case', which is shown 'by putting s, or es … to the Singular or Plural Number' (1968:58-9). Since the 'nominative' is unmarked, by definition it is not a case; nor is the *of*-construction an example of case, as in 'of God' 'for they are two Words; *Of* is a Preposition, and *God* is a Noun' and, we are re-instructed, 'Case is the Alteration of the Noun' (1968:59).

The chapter on prepositions (Ch. VIII, pp. 69ff.) is 25 pages long and very detailed. Most of it provides information on individual prepositions, which space does not permit us to go into, but before that part Greenwood makes many interesting points about prepositions in general. He repeats the anatomical metaphors of some of his predecessors when he describes prepositions, along with conjunctions, as 'the Nerves and Ligaments of all Discourse', without a good understanding of which 'we cannot attain to a right Knowledge of any Language'; and he replicates the former comparisons of language with a building and the 'minor' parts of speech with the materials binding it together, for they function as 'the Mortar and Lime which are to cement and join those Materials together' (1968:69). Greenwood then does what so many others in the past failed to do: he makes a clear distinction between separable and inseparable prepositions; indeed, the latter (e.g. in 'overcome', 'withstand') are not really to be regarded as prepositions in English as most of them derive from other languages (e.g. in 'subscribe', 'transpose'). In fact, he devotes a whole section under 'Etymology' ('Of the Prepositions used in Composition'; 1968:195-202) to compound words of this kind, under which he also includes prefixes such as *be-* and *mis-* and the Latin *di(s)-* and *retro-*.

After trying to explain some of 'the Great Mr. Lock's' observations on particles and quoting his statement that 'this Part of Grammar has been, perhaps, as much neglected, as some others over diligently cultivated' (1968:69-70; see also Locke above), Greenwood finally arrives at a definition of prepositions: 'A Preposition is a Part of Speech, which being added to any other Parts of Speech, serves to mark or signify their State or Reference to each other' (1968:71). He specifies that he uses the expression 'added' because prepositions (in English) can appear both 'behind a Word, as well as before it' and mentions (and exemplifies) that they can be added to other parts of speech than nouns. Again, he contrasts English with Greek and Latin by stating that 'the English Tongue has no Diversity of Cases … but does all that by the help of Prepositions' and adds that when a preposition interacts with a noun, it 'shows what Respect or Relation that Substantive hath to that Word which went before it, whether it be a Verb, a Noun, or any other Part of Speech' (1968:72). This means that the function of prepositions is essentially relational, linking two other classes (i.e. elements), the second of which is most frequently a noun. At this point, he presents a long list of individual prepositions and tries diligently to include under each all their 'Significations'.

The last point that Greenwood makes is on the relationship between adverbs and prepositions. He mentions the commonly held view that prepositions 'when they do not govern a Word or come before it, do become Adverbs' (1968:93). However, he thinks 'that in almost every Example that is produced, some Word is understood', and if that is the case, there is no reason why 'the Preposition should part with its own Nature or Property', that is, why we should not see them as prepositions. This is an argument that has also been advanced in recent times (see the Introduction above).

So despite Greenwood's modest intentions and his partial dependency on other writers, he comes across as a rather 'modern' grammarian in many ways and his views on prepositions are not simply adopted from others, but represent an attempt to improve contemporary knowledge and awareness in that field. Certain parts of his treatment consequently make him stand out from his time and surroundings.

Michael Maittaire (1668-1747)
Michael Maittaire was a master at Westminster and later ran a private school at Mile End in the East End of London. He is described as

'a learned classical scholar', but published only two books of note: a work on Greek dialects in 1706 and *The English Grammar*, with the subtitle 'An Essay on the Art of Grammar Applied to and Exemplified in the English Tongue', which appeared in 1712 (see Maittaire 1967), only a year after the grammars by Gildon & Brightland and by Greenwood (cf. 1967:Note; Michael 1970:573).

Maittaire is thus one in the long line of schoolmasters who wrote a grammar in order to assist pupils in their understanding of their own language. In the preface to *The English Grammar* he joins some of the earlier writers in condemning both the standard of grammar teaching in schools ('It is now a-days the miserable Fate of Grammar to be more Whip't than Taught; and the Children, like Slaves, are bred up into the hatred of it'; 1967:Preface, pp. iii-iv) and the custom of teaching Latin to pupils who have little formal knowledge of English ('the Youths are forced to learn, what they can't understand; being hurried into Latin, before they are well able to read English'), for as he argues, 'The Ignorance of English can never be a good foundation or ingredient towards disposing of Youth for the learned Languages' (1967:Preface, p. iv). He is also in agreement with those who think that it is especially important that young women should learn 'the accomplishments of Speech and Understanding' and that the 'tender Sex' should not be treated as if it was 'weak and defective in its Head and Brains' (1967:Preface, pp. v-vi). He is a strong advocate of the usefulness of general learning rather than concentrating narrowly on what young people may need to know in their later careers. His pedagogical awareness reveals itself when he ensures that those 'things, which are above the understanding of the young beginner … are printed in a smaller Character' and when he shows how the different parts of the grammar can be taught in stages (1967:Preface, p. ix).

However, in many ways Maittaire is a traditionalist, for example in adopting the Latin six-case system for English and in his division of grammar into the familiar four parts. Nevertheless, his view of the parts of speech differs from most previous presentations. He recognises eight parts, but not entirely the long established ones and at any rate they are not of equal status. The main parts, as before, are the noun (including the adjective) and the verb (later he even invokes Aristotle for this view and summarises Quintilian's discussion of it; cf.

1967:35), while the article and the pronoun are subordinate to the noun and the participle to the verb. Finally, he uses 'particle' as the umbrella term for the adverb, the preposition and the conjunction. The class that stands out here is the article, which was not part of the Latin tradition; on the other hand, by excluding the interjection he still ends up with eight parts. Nor was it in tune with contemporary convention that he provides a separate treatment of 'Inseparable Particles' between the sections on the adverb and the preposition, but it is certainly refreshing that these elements (e.g. *be-*, *dis-*, *mis-*, *re-*, etc.) are not dealt with as prepositions (though see also Greenwood above).

The first definition of a preposition is as 'a Particle, which qualifies and explains the signification of some part of speech, by going before a word, which it governs or brings into the clause or sentence' (1967:93). This definition in itself only relates the preposition to its complement, and does not – as in several previous grammars – see it as a link between the complement and another element in front of the preposition. On the other hand, as we have just seen, he does not equate prepositions with prefixes.

The actual section on prepositions (1967:110-20) does not confine itself to English; much of it is devoted to compounds with Latin and Greek prepositions, which we shall ignore. From the start, Maittaire makes some basic but quite acute distinctions: between 'Primitive' prepositions (e.g. *on*, *out*) and derived ones such as *at* from Latin *ad*;[46] between 'Simple and Uncompounded' words like *up* and 'Compounded' ones like *upon* and *into*; and between 'Simple and Uncontracted' forms, such as *thorough*, and 'Contracted' ones like *through* (1967:110). Another contrast is between monosyllabic (*at, for, from*, etc.) and dissyllabic prepositions (*above, after, before*, etc.), and it is mentioned that 'the Casual Signs [i.e. the 'case markers' *of, to, unto, by* and *with*] are very often prepositions' (*ibid.*). This 'relegation' to signs clearly lies behind his comment under nouns that 'the Cases in each number are only varied by signs' (1967:40), so the same forms can for Maittaire have two distinct functions: either as case signs or as prepositions but apparently not both at the same time.

Although it is not part of the above definition, prepositions are here seen as part of 'the Composition of Words', i.e. of compounds, but admittedly only some of them. In this connection Maittaire shows how their meaning can change according to whether they form part of a compound verb or appear after the verb (e.g. 'stand with' versus 'withstand', 'stand out' versus 'understand', 'run out' versus 'outrun', etc.), but he also calls them 'compound words' when the preposition is 'put after, without governing a word', as in 'to go on/out', 'to run in', 'to get up', etc. Note that he does not label *on*, *out*, *in* and *up* adverbs here, though he does mention that adverbs, such as *back* and *away*, can function in the same way (1967:110-11). This is why he can claim that 'the Particle, which compounds the verb by following it, does not always go next to the verb; but the Noun, which is governed by the verb, is often placed between', which is illustrated by examples such as 'I keep in my breath' versus 'I keep my breath in' (1967:111). However, for Maittaire 'some English Prepositions, with some addition or composition, become Adverbs', viz. those ending in '-ward' (*toward(s)*, *forward*, *upward*, etc.) and *underneath*. Apart from *toward(s)*, these of course cannot govern a noun, which is presumably his rationale for assigning them to the class of adverbs.

Finally, some mention of prepositions is made under Syntax. First we hear that all prepositions 'govern words without the help of any Signs', except *out* which needs an *of* (cf. 'out of the town'), and sometimes *up*, compare: 'he is gone up the hill' with 'he is got in the water up to his neck'. The last of these examples is explained in this intriguing way: 'the Particle *up* seems to compound the Verb more than govern the Noun', and therefore in such a case 'it may admit another Sign or Particle besides', e.g. in 'he has gone up to the hill', which is compared with 'he went down the hill' or 'down from the hill', which in turn are contrasted (more metaphysically) with 'he came down from heaven', not *'he came down heaven', and 'he went up to heaven', not *'he went up heaven' (1967:162). In other words, when the particle is more closely attached to the verb than to the prepositional complement, i.e. in constructions that are now usually called 'phrasal verbs', a preposition ('Sign or Particle') is inserted before the complement. This is a very acute observation that was rarely made at the time. The rest of this section is concerned with particles (mainly prepositions) and cases in English as well as in Latin and Greek, but we have already seen that some 'prepositions' are designated as 'case signs'; such as, *of* for the genitive, *(un)to* for the dative and *by*, *with* for the ablative (cf. 1967:41).

Although Maittaire is more careful in his wording than some of the previous grammarians, there is no doubt that, unlike Gildon & Brightland and Greenwood, he operates with the same cases in English as in Latin and (where they match) Greek. This causes some problems for his explanations, but to his credit he does provide many useful details and insights that do not seem to have been borrowed from earlier presentations.

Thomas Sheridan (1687-1738)

Thomas Sheridan was a schoolmaster in Dublin. His work *An Easy Introduction of Grammar in English. For the Understanding of the Latin Tongue* from 1714 (see Sheridan 1714) is, as the title suggests, aimed at (young) people learning Latin rather than being specifically about the English language. Nevertheless it contains some general grammatical points and exerted a certain influence on later writers, e.g. J. Wilson (see below). It is in tune with attitudes in the early eighteenth century that the grammar is '[c]ompil'd not only for the Ease and Encouragement of Youth, but also for their Moral Improvement' with examples taken 'from the Choicest Pieces of the best Authors' (1714:title-page).

Grammar, according to Sheridan, 'is the Art of True Writing and Speaking' (1714:1) and falls into the usual four parts. A word is 'the Sign of some inward Conception', which neatly distinguishes real phenomena from their linguistic representation. Since this is in part a Latin grammar, it is no surprise that the parts of speech consist of the traditional classes modelled on Lily and are presented in exactly the same way.

Under 'Of a Preposition' it is not only the heading that echoes Lily; the definition is also a carbon copy of Lily's, though 'an undeclinable Word' is inserted (1714:128). The use of prepositions with cases is postponed until the following part on 'Syntaxis', and when he resumes his treatment there, he continues to copy Lily virtually verbatim. This is seen in his three classifications of prepositions that govern accusative, ablative or either, respectively, though some illustrative examples have been added. But it is characteristic that no extra explanatory information is provided; in fact, where Lily at least used the English translation with (*in*)*to* to explain the difference between the use of accusative and ablative for the four prepositions that can govern both in Latin, even this is missing in Sheridan. It is up to readers to deduce from the examples which case should be used, or indeed which case is used in the examples.

Finally, Sheridan repeats the two points that Lily makes about prepositions in his section on syntax (or 'Construction'), namely where he claims that a 'Compounded Verb', i.e. a verb prefixed by a preposition, retains 'the Signification of the Preposition [and] will have after it the Case of the Preposition' (1714:163). In other words, the meaning or 'force' of the preposition is so 'strong' that the word it would have governed, had it appeared in front of it, is nevertheless found in the case that the preposition governs. As illustration, he uses Lily's example, 'Adeo Templum' (I go to the temple), where *ad* as a verbal prefix seems to determine the accusative form of the object 'Templum'.

The reason for including a grammar like Sheridan's, which is more geared to teaching young people Latin rather than English, is partly that it was used and referred to by later grammarians, and partly to show how much some grammarians were still in thrall to Lily's grammar more than a century and a half after it was made mandatory for use in grammar schools. At the same time it demonstrates very clearly that there was no smooth step-by-step development in consecutive English grammars. Some of the 'new' grammars may contain added example material, but the essential classifications and definitions often remain largely the same as in the traditional type of grammar writing.

Hugh Jones (dates unknown)
Hugh Jones was professor of mathematics at Willliam and Mary College, Williamsburg, Virginia, and *An Accidence to the English Tongue* (1724; see Jones 1967) is, as far as we know, the first English grammar written in America (but printed in London). It is modest in size – 69 small pages – and seems to be intended as an all-purpose account. At least the author describes it as being 'for the Use of such Boys and Men, as have never learnt Latin perfectly, and for the Benefit of the Female Sex; Also for the Welch,[47] Scotch, Irish, and Foreigners', and he calls it 'a Grammatical Essay upon our Language' (1967:title-page). So to some degree it is meant to make up for any deficiency in the

instruction of Latin, which women would not normally have learnt anyway, but whether the same assumption can be extended to the Scotch, Welsh, Irish and to foreigners is another matter.

English grammar, we are told, 'teacheth the Grounds, and Use of the English Language' and 'the Grounds' consist of the following familiar hierarchy: letters, syllables, words, sentences and discourses (or speeches) (1967:1-2). Jones distinguishes three parts of speech (or 'Kinds of English Words'): nouns, verbs and particles (cf. 1967:22). Some of the other conventional classes relate either to nouns (thus adjectives, which – like participles – come under 'Nouns Epithets', and pronouns, here also called 'Nouns Adjutants') or to verbs (such as participles, despite being 'Noun Epithets'), while particles are divided into 13 sub-classes according to various criteria. 'Prepositions' are distributed over several of these; for example, *of* and *thro'* are said to be 'Signs of Nouns', *after* 'of Time', and *at, in, out, upon, under, up, down* 'of Manner and Position'. At the end there is a small schema, showing that particles relating to verbs are termed 'Adverbs'; those relating to nouns 'Prepositions', and those relating to sentences 'Conjunctions'. These 'minor' classes are thus sub-categories of particles (1967:28-38).

Under the short Part IV ('of English Sentences') there is a page on 'the Position of Words in Sentences' where most of the classes and sub-classes are mentioned, but not prepositions except that it is pointed out that 'the Noun is oft removed from its Signs' using the following examples: 'this I agree to' versus 'I agree to this' and 'that I allow of' versus 'I allow of that' – in other words, preposition stranding – but there is not a word about the positional (or any other) relationship between prepositions and complements or verbs.

Of course, one must accept that this is meant to be a concise grammar, providing a brief overview of a range of linguistic, stylistic, etc., areas, but for anyone hoping to learn something about the nature and use of prepositions Jones's *Accidence* can only have been disappointing. Not even the most basic coverage is attempted.

Daniel Duncan (dates unknown)
The one thing known about Daniel Duncan is that he was Master of Islington School, and only because it says so on the title-page of

A New English Grammar (1731; see Duncan 1967). This is a grammar in a narrow sense, excluding – for different reasons – the areas of 'Etymology, Orthography and Prosody' (1967:Preface, p. vi) which feature so prominently in many other grammars. The problem with 'Etymology' is that it 'supposes a greater Knowledge of other Languages than can be found in Boys' (*ibid*.), which suggests that Duncan uses the term in its modern sense, whereas for many others it covers 'grammar' and especially the parts of speech. Like other teachers, he intends his *Grammar* to be a short introduction to English for the pupils in his own school before they move on to Latin. He seems to speak from personal experience when he states that 'the Learning of dead Languages is a Yoke, that neither we nor our Fore-fathers could ever bear, when we were Children' and surmises that 'the Loathsomeness of that dry Study comes for want of reasoning previously with them enough about the Nature of Words, and their Dependency on one another, in their own Mother Tongue' (1967:Preface, p. v). (His stated plan of issuing a Latin grammar after this one seems to have come to nothing.) If, however, he can give the pupils 'an Idea of their Mother Tongue, *in every Part of Speech*, before they enter upon learning of Latin', that will make Latin 'much easier to learn' (1967:Preface, p. vii; my emphasis).

Duncan adopts the traditional eight parts of speech (cf. 1967:1). Prepositions are discussed in several places. First, it happens under nouns when he deals with cases. Here he takes over the six cases of Latin and, again like others before him, sees certain 'prepositions' as 'case signs'. Thus *of* as the sign for the genitive case, *for* and *to* for the dative case, *at*, *to* and *into* for the accusative case, and *from*, *by*, *in*, *with*, *through*, *for* for the ablative case. This procedure of fitting English data into the Latin schema is generally adhered to, but Duncan once reveals that he is aware of the differences between the two languages when, in the section 'Of Prepositions', he refers back to his treatment of cases but adds that there, 'tho' we gave different Names to the States of Nouns, as these were joined to this or that Preposition, yet … there is properly but two Cases in English, the right Case, including the Nominative and the Vocative; and the oblique Case, comprehending the Genitive, the Dative, the Accusative and the Ablative; for *him* and *them* are all these Cases' (1967:43). Whether it is the fact that he is laying the groundwork for the later study of Latin that prevents him from following the strength of his conviction is unclear, but it is a good example of the dilemma in which so many grammarians found themselves in the seventeenth and eighteenth centuries when the straightjacket of Latin still had a restricting effect on their description of English (and other vernaculars).

Prepositions are next mentioned as part of the 'Indeclinables' where it is claimed that their nature (and that of conjunctions) is 'to signify the Form of our Thoughts, by joining Words to Words, Sentences to Sentences', the first applying to prepositions, the second to conjunctions. In general, indeclinable particles seem to have a range of functions, including that of providing linguistic economy: 'These indeclinable Particles serve to shew the Dependence of Thoughts and Reasonings among themselves, as their Connection, Extension, Restriction, Distinction, Opposition, Emphasis, Relations, etc., or save Multiplicity of Words, by saying in one what otherwise must be express'd by many' (1967:37).

The section on prepositions in this part offers the following basic definition: 'Preposition is an Indeclinable that governs the Nouns that follow it. It serves to modify or circumstantiate the Noun' (1967:43). They are contrasted with adverbs, interjections and conjunctions by taking 'the oblique Case *him* or *them* after it' (*ibid.*). A list of 'the chiefest Prepositions' follows, but it is more interesting to note that the words *notwithstanding, concerning, according, pursuant to* and *touching* 'are used as Prepositions, [but] are nothing else but Participles governing the same Case as their Verbs' (*ibid.*). On the one hand, Duncan acknowledges that these words function as prepositions, which seems a valid observation; on the other hand, what case(s) do they govern, and in what sense is *pursuant* (*to*) a participle, the form of which was previously said to be *-ing, -ed* or whatever form the past participle may have in strong and irregular verbs?

The last important mention of prepositions is in the last part of the book called 'Syntax of Regimen'. Here the reader is given more precise information about their position: 'The natural place of Prepositions is before the Noun they govern', and they are 'always added to Substantives, either express'd or understood' (1967:66). This statement is so categorical that some explanation is needed when they quite patently interact with other word classes — he himself mentions adjectives, pronouns, verbs, participles and adverbs – and Duncan duly delivers this by stating that in such cases 'these Words must be taken in a Substantive Sense, or resolved by others governable by a Preposition'. One cannot help wondering what his pupils will have made of that justification. He only supplies two examples: 'from whence' is said to be equivalent to 'from what Place' and in 'I love to read' '*to read* is a Substantive for *reading*' (*ibid.*; his emphasis). Neither claim is unreasonable – 'to read' clearly has nominal function here – but it would have been helpful to see examples of *all* the classes listed, not least verbs. The 'joining power' of prepositions is illustrated by 'This is the Book of John' where '*of* joins *Book* and *John* under the Notion of Possession' (*ibid.*; his emphasis). The rest of the section consists of lists of 'separable' and 'inseparable' prepositions with examples of their use and meaning and at the end a list of the Latin prepositions that can act as prefixes in English, which is also the role of the 'inseparable' prepositions.

One is left with the feeling that Duncan had it in him to be more radical both in his analysis of prepositions and about the parts of speech in general than his adherence to Latin would permit, but in this he was of course not alone.

John Collyer (dates unknown)

John Collyer is another grammar writer of whom we know little, apart from the fact that he taught in a school in Nottingham and that he published *The General Principles of Grammar*, with the subtitle 'especially Adapted to the English Tongue', in 1735 (see Collyer 1968) and explicitly stated to be 'For the Use of Schools'. The address 'From my School' at the end of the Preface to the book is taken by Alston to mean that he ran the school in Nottingham (1968:Note). He, too, complains about the educational standards in schools and refers to earlier writers such as 'Mr. Walker' and 'Mr. Lane' (for both see above) who had made the same point. He is even more scathing about the teaching of Latin than those we have mentioned previously, believing that 'to mend the matter' of not providing proper teaching of English grammar the pupils 'are sent to trifle away three, four or five Years to get a smattering of Latin, which they usually forget in as little time as they learn it' (1968:Preface, p. iv). He is thus yet another advocate for teaching pupils the foundations of English before moving on to Latin or other languages for those who do so. One of his arguments for this is that 'the Essential Parts of Grammar being the same in all Languages, they would have little more to do than to learn the Peculiarities proper to each' (1968:Preface, p. vii). By this time Collyer had already published *The English Spelling Book*, to which he refers, but he claims that he 'could not find any Grammar that answered my end, as being in any tolerable measure fitted for the use of Schools', an argument we have heard before from schoolmasters, including those mentioned by Collyer, as justification for writing their own grammar, in this case ostensibly in order to retrieve 'the Credit of the *English School*, which has been debased and discredited by unskilful Teachers' (1968:Preface, p. viii; his emphasis). There was clearly no love lost between colleagues of the teaching profession! In his own presentation Collyer tries to apply pedagogical principles and for that reason admits to having 'not always expressed my self in the usual Grammatical Terms, choosing rather to do it in plainer Words, that may be readily understood by Children' (*ibid.*).

Having already dealt with orthography in his *English Spelling Book*, Collyer starts with etymology (the second 'Part of Grammar'), and first tackles the parts of speech. It is no surprise that there are eight in number, but in one respect he deviates from the usual pattern, in that adjectives are now recognised as being a class of their own at the expense of participles. However, traditions die hard and Collyer is almost apologetic for not having adopted the traditional system. He atones for it by including participles under adjectives, thus preserving the canonical number of eight parts: 'I have followed as near as possible the Common Latin Grammar, yet could not entirely fall in with it, especially as to the Adjective coming under the Class of Nouns, yet that I might not encrease the Number, I have joined the Participle with it, and made them one Part of Speech' (1968:3). He even conjures up some 'great Authorities' in his defence, but his arguments are quite rational. Each part of speech is 'explained' in a few words, e.g. nouns are 'Names of Things', verbs 'Affirmations of Being', and prepositions display 'Relations of Things' (1968:2), the last of which repeats Richard Johnson's *faux pas* in mixing up reality and representation. Nevertheless, some parts of speech are more equal than others; nouns and verbs are said to be 'the two principal parts of Speech', while the other parts are 'occasional Attendants, being used to represent, explain, and shew the Relation of Words to each other, or to connect to them', prepositions 'shewing the relation of Nouns to each other' (1968:3-4). Here Collyer at least has amended his terminology to 'Relation of Words'.

When it comes to case, Collyer adopts a surprisingly traditional view. He acknowledges that various 'relations are frequently expressed in Latin and Greek by particular variations in the ending of the Noun called Cases; but English having no such variation, hath occasioned our Grammarians to deny them the use of all Cases except the Genitive' (1968:12-13). He cannot endorse this view, mainly because 'its [viz. the genitive's] relations are the same in English with other Languages'. He therefore wonders why 'so many great Men' have reduced cases in English to two and argues, with reference to Latin (though this is not entirely clear from the context) that 'if the use of [cases] was only to express such variations, how comes it about that there are more cases than there are variations to express? and that some of the cases are alike', pointing out that the forms of the (Latin) nominative and vocative cases are often identical, as are those of the dative and the ablative. The consequence of this stance is that Collyer joins the band of grammarians who operate with some 'prepositions' as case signs along the familiar lines: *of* for the genitive, *for* and *to* for the dative, and no fewer than nine for the ablative. This is set out in a table showing all six cases of the noun 'Man' in both the singular and the plural (1968:16).

Prepositions or (as he calls them, following Gildon & Brightland) 'Fore-placed Words' are given a chapter of their own, in which they are described as 'either little Words joined with other words in Composition [i.e. as prefixes]; or such as being put betwixt other Words, (chiefly Names) shew their relation to each other, in affinity, distance, or some other casual circumstance' (1968:40). In the latter use as independent words, when they are 'put between Words, they shew the relation they stand in to each other, usually called Case' (*ibid.*). The rest of the section consists of a list of individual prepositions with examples of their use and their various meanings. At the end of the chapter on conjunctions, Collyer quotes Greenwood's metaphors about the adhesive function of conjunctions and prepositions and furthermore the latter's citations from 'the great Mr. Lock' (i.e. John Locke) which were mentioned under Greenwood above.

The section on syntax adds nothing new about prepositions, while the one on 'the Derivation of Words' concentrates on those prepositions used as prefixes ('in Composition'), some of which cannot function independently, e.g. *dis, en, un* and some Latin prepositions. In general, there are glimpses of independent insights in Collyer's book, but the shackles of the tradition are often too strong, and the quotes from, and deferential references to, some of his predecessors demonstrate his inherent insecurity.

Thomas Dilworth (?-1780)

One of the few things we know about Thomas Dilworth is that he was a schoolmaster in Wapping and that he first published *A New Guide to the English Tongue* in 1740. However, the earliest surviving copy is from the fifth edition in 1744 and that sole copy is in a very poor condition. In fact, the earliest perfect copy is from the thirteenth edition in 1751, which is the one used here (see Dilworth 1967). However, as it is no doubt ultimately based on the first edition, it seems reasonable to enter it at this place in the chronology. The bulk of the book is quite simply a spelling-book and this is almost certainly what accounts for its immense popularity (cf. 1967:Note), but it also contains a short section called 'Of Analogy' which deals with the parts of speech ('Analogy teaches us how to know distinctly all the several Parts of Speech in the English Tongue', 1967:97). This part is composed along the lines of the question-and-answer exchanges that we have come across before.

The parts of speech are the traditional eight, and the case system is borrowed from Latin. The chapter on prepositions (Chapter IX) defines a preposition as 'a part of Speech regularly set before a Word of another Part of Speech, either separated from it or joined to it, to signify its Rest, Alteration, and Manner of Motion' (1967:114). This is almost a classic definition although the terminology at the end deviates a little. As so often before, a separate preposition is said to be in 'Apposition' and, when it is 'joined to the Noun', in 'Composition'. A fairly comprehensive list of separate prepositions is provided, followed by lists of those 'in Composition' (i.e. functioning as prefixes in compounds) with examples, both in English and in Latin.

Little else is said of relevance for us, and the reason for incorporating this work at all is, apart from its obvious popularity and consequently enormous circulation, that it is typical of many similar, very short treatments of grammar at that time, for which this may stand as a representative.

John Kirkby (1705-1754)

Traditional and conformist are not words that one can use about John Kirkby's *A New English Grammar* (1746; see Kirkby 1971). It has the subtitle 'Guide to the English Tongue, with Notes' and is dedicated to 'Edward Gibbon of Putney, Esq; Representative in Parliament For the Town of Southampton … in Acknowledgement of the many Favours Received'. Gibbon was the father of the Edward Gibbon famous for *Decline and Fall of the Roman Empire*, and prior to the appearance of his *Grammar* Kirkby had been tutor, in 1744-5, to young Edward who later admitted writing with Kirkby's works in front of him (cf. Michael 1970:569).[48]

There is no preface explaining the purpose of the book, but more than the first quarter of it (Chapters I-VI) is concerned with spelling and pronunciation and the last quarter is a Latin grammar. In between, Kirkby deals with the parts of speech and with syntactic and stylistic issues. Regarding the parts of speech he says from the start that 'All words may be reduced into three Kinds or Classes' (1971:55). This has, of course, been done before; indeed, it is Aristotelian in origin, but Kirkby's terms are different. He calls his three classes 'Substantives, Adjunctives, and Particles' and these may be subdivided in the following way: (a) Substantives include 'Names', such as 'Appellative[s] or Common' and 'Proper', and 'Alternatives', i.e. pronouns; (b) 'Adjunctives' are verbs and adjectives; and (c) 'Particles' comprise adverbs, prepositions and conjunctions (and later, we hear, interjections), whereas participles are merely mentioned under the chapter on verbs (1971:55-7). There are further, terminologically interesting, divisions that we cannot go into here. It is the second group that is the surprise package; not only because of its name but it was highly unusual to place verbs and adjectives under the same label. In fact, according to the definition an 'Adjunctive' is 'a Word, which being joined with a Substantive expresses it under some Quality, Action, or Condition' (1971:57). Kirkby thus conflates the relationship between a noun and an adjective, which were traditionally two items of the same class, with that existing between a noun and a verb, or in functional terms between subject and verb. He even sees, as a special case, verbs (under the name of 'Alternative Adjunctives') 'joined to an Alternative' (i.e. again pronoun) in, for example, 'I live' and 'he hath' (*ibid.*). Compared with this, the grouping of the 'minor' classes into particles has a much longer history.

When classifying particles, Kirkby defines a preposition briefly as a word 'by which we express some Relation to a Substantive' (*ibid.*). In Chapter XIII ('Of Prepositions') it seems that there is also a hierarchy among the particles for now we are told that 'A Preposition *is an Adverb*, which may also come before a Name, expressing it to have some particular Relation or Situation with respect to another Thing' (1971:104-5; my emphasis). This sounds strange. Are prepositions, then, a sub-group under adverbs that can *also* appear in front of nouns? And is 'Thing' used advisedly? (Cf. the discussion in the section on Richard Johnson above.) In this chapter, Kirkby's penchant for long footnotes becomes a real problem for the reader, as there are only 2-10 lines of actual text per page, which results in a several pages long footnote with an extensive list of prepositions.

Another striking feature of Kirkby's approach is his cocksureness of numbers; it is difficult to find another term for it. For example, he confidently states that 'there are principally forty and four prepositions', and under the individual prepositions he is equally sure that *about* 'has seven Significations', *at* has six, *by* twenty, *of* twelve, and so on (1971:104-6). It takes a very brave man to be so categorical! In between, Kirkby makes some valid observations. For instance, he notes that '[m]any verbs include a Preposition along with them', i.e. that there is often a fixed collocation (not his term) between the verb and the following preposition, e.g. 'to play at', 'to send for', 'to meet with', etc. He also has a few examples of prepositional alternation, such as 'angry with/at them', 'to rejoice in/at', as well as some of preference for one preposition over another, as when he claims that 'we rather say *wroth with them* than *wroth at them*' (1971:107).

We are informed that '[w]hen a Name is not expressed after a Preposition, it is often understood', exemplified by 'I wrote before', i.e. 'before that Time', and 'We live below', i.e. 'below the Stories above us' (1971:108). However, in view of his earlier definition, there is no mention that the preposition here functions as an adverb, let alone that it might have 'become' one. It gets more cryptic when he writes that 'A preposition before an Adjective is often used before an Adverb', as in 'at all', 'for certain', 'in earnest', etc., and then rather abruptly says that 'So often before an Appellative', as in 'at Hand', 'in Jest', 'on Purpose', etc. What can the reader make of that?

There is a more traditional short section on 'Prepositions used in Composition', with examples not only of English elements but also from French, Latin and Greek. Finally, there are brief references to prepositions in the chapter on syntax (Chapter XV, 'Of Construction'). First, it is said that 'A Preposition has the Implicit State after it'. There has been no prior treatment of case; hence this statement here. It should be mentioned that in Kirkby's terminology an 'Explicit' means the subject or other element in the base (or nominative) form, while an 'Implicit' refers to a word in an oblique case, e.g. the direct or indirect object or the prepositional complement. However, we are told that a preposition can also precede an 'Explicit' in cases such as 'They came before we' if the verb is 'understood'; cp. 'They came before we came', but if it is not, then an 'Implicit' must be used, as in 'They came before us'. Furthermore, it is said that 'Some Names are seldom or never used, but after a Preposition', e.g. 'For your sake', 'In my Stead', 'In a Trice' (1971:116).

Kirkby's *Grammar* is thus highly unusual. It provides a lot of original terminology, but it borders on the eccentric and contains some obscure explanations. Gibbon apart, it does not seem to have been very influential.

Benjamin Martin (1704-1782)
Benjamin Martin's *Institutions of Language* (1748; see Martin 1970) has the subtitle 'a Physico-Grammatical Essay on the Propriety and

Rationale of the English Tongue'. It is an ambitious undertaking, despite its comparative brevity (111 pages). It covers an impressive range of linguistic topics and illustrates these with reference to a number of languages, such as the classical tongues of Hebrew, Greek and Latin as well as some modern vernaculars like French, Italian, Spanish, Portuguese, German, Dutch and of course English, including 'Saxon', i.e. Anglo-Saxon or Old English. It is therefore, in a sense, a historical grammar that aims to trace many of the eighteenth-century features of English from their distant origins in different language families and can be seen as a precursor of the rise in philological interest in the nineteenth century. On the one hand, Martin considers grammar to be universal in essence, but on the other hand he is acutely aware of even the subtlest differences between related languages, and he both lists and explains many of those. He also informs the reader that '[e]very language has a Syntax peculiar to itself' (1970:92). The book provides a wealth of data for many aspects of human language, such as the need for communication, writing systems, the nature of the speech organs, etymology, language system and change, to mention but some of them. In 1754, Martin published a new title, *An Introduction to the English Language and Learning*, which builds on *Institutions*.[49]

The universal aspect is seen, for example, in his view on the parts of speech:[50] 'In every speech or language there are four principal sorts of words, viz. (1.) Nouns, or names of things, (2.) Verbs, or words which alter or predicate some one thing or another. (3.) Words which imply the quality and nature of things. (4.) Words which relate to the manner and circumstances of things' (1970:27). In other words, nouns, verbs, adjectives and particles, though the last two terms are only found later and not as part of any definitions. Martin is particularly reticent in his use of 'particle' – it appears, for example, to denote the Italian article *lo* (1970:67) – and does not seem to regard it as the umbrella term for the usual minor classes. In this connection one instance of terminology should be mentioned, though it is most likely a mistake. After having shown in a table the forms of the German and (Anglo-)Saxon (definite) articles-cum-demonstrative pronouns in both the singular and plural, and given the English equivalents of the genitive, dative, accusative and ablative as 'of the', 'to the', 'the' and 'from the', respectively, Martin explains that 'the English article continues unvaried through all the cases in each number, which are shown by other *particles*, of, to, and from; and not by different terminations, as in the German and Saxon...' (1970:75, my emphasis). 'Participles' is clearly an error (Martin uses this term in its traditional sense elsewhere), but for what? 'Particles', or prepositions? Neither term fits comfortably into the context and prepositions are nowhere else called 'particles'.

When he comes to deal with the fourth group, Martin says, 'We are now come to such kind of words as have no various inflexions or different terminations; and these we find ranged under the following classes', and goes on to mention adverbs, conjunctions, prepositions and interjections. Prepositions are more precisely described as 'little words placed before others, to shew the relation or circumstantial references they have to one another' (1970:90). A little later he adds that prepositions 'are used either simply or in composition'. He gives examples of both kinds and informs us that prepositions 'used in compounding words were many more among the Saxons than what we have borrowed' (1970:91).

Other comments about prepositions are scattered through the book and crop up under various languages; for example, he states how both Greek and Latin make 'great use' of prepositions in composition and exemplifies many of them. Referring to English, Martin explains an element of prepositional syntax in this way: 'The genitive case of a noun we denote by the preposition *of*, and place the said noun after the subject of the predication, or nominative case; as, *the Son of man*; *the flower of the field*' (1970:92; his emphasis), but he does mention the use of apostrophe, too.

In brief, it has to be said that despite a number of interesting points in Martin's book, his take on prepositions shows little out of the ordinary.

James Harris (1709-1780)

James Harris's principal work on grammar, *Hermes: or a Philosophical Inquiry Concerning Language and Universal Grammar* (1751; see Harris 1968), belongs, as the alternative title suggests, to the category of philosophical grammars, and was a very influential one at that.

Harris was a classical scholar and had made a particular study of Aristotle. This influenced his analysis of the parts of speech, which he himself sees as a return to their Aristotelian origins. Pointing to the authority of Chapter 20 of Aristotle's *Poetics*,[51] he sets up the same categories, viz. the 'principals': nouns and verbs (or, in Harris's terms, 'substantives' and 'attributives') and the 'accessories': articles and conjunctions (or 'definitives' and 'connectives') (1968:23-36). The term 'attributive', for example, includes verbs, participles and adjectives, and it is quite clear why Harris prefers the term 'connective' to 'conjunction', for as he says elsewhere, 'Connectives ... according as they connect either Sentences or Words, are called by the different Names of Conjunctions or Prepositions' (1968:237). Thus, for Harris, 'connective' is simply the superordinate category term for these two subclasses.

Harris has a separate chapter on prepositions (1968:261-74), where at the outset he gives the following quite original definition: 'A Preposition is a Part of Speech, devoid it self of Signification, but so formed as to unite two Words that are significant, and that refuse to co-alesce or unite of themselves' (1968:261).

This is not a very clear definition, and for that reason it has been attacked by other grammarians; most virulently by John Horne Tooke (see below), who complains that prepositions here are purely negatively defined and continues, 'It contains a Negation and an Accident; and nothing more. It tells us what a Preposition *is not*; and the purpose for which he supposes it to be employed.' He adds, rather facetiously, that 'it might serve as well for a definition of the East India Company, as of a Preposition' (Tooke 1968:306-7; his emphasis).

The harshness of his wording notwithstanding, the essence of Horne Tooke's criticism is not unjust, particularly when one compares this general definition (as Horne Tooke does) with Harris's later comments about prepositions used as prefixes. In such cases, we are told, 'the Prepositions commonly transfuse something of their own Meaning into the Word, with which they are compounded' (1968:271). There is clearly a contradiction here between being devoid of meaning, on the one hand, and transfusing something of this (non-existent) meaning, on the other.

The notion of coalescence (mentioned in the definition) plays a central role in Harris's concept of syntax (1968:262ff.). He takes the idea from natural phenomena, some of which 'co-alesce and unite *of themselves*', whereas 'others refuse to do so *without help*' (1968:262; his emphasis). By applying this observation to the level of words in a sentence, Harris confuses the level of reality with that of linguistic representation. Thus, we are told, just as 'qualities' and 'quantities' naturally coalesce with their 'substances', 'actions' with their 'agents', and 'passions' with their 'patients', so 'attributives' coalesce with 'substantives' in a sentence. At the category level, this is the relation we find, for instance, between adjectives and nouns and between adverbs and verbs, and at the functional level, between subject and verb, and verb and object. From these relations Harris draws the general conclusion that 'those Parts of Speech unite of themselves in Grammar, whose original Archetypes unite of themselves in Nature' (1968:263-4). Here the confusion of levels is complete.

Although the same confusion persists in the example chosen by Harris to illustrate this point, his argument is of obvious relevance to the role of prepositions. Thus in 'The splendid Sun genially warmeth the fertile Earth', there is coalescence between (to limit ourselves to the functional level) 'the splendid Sun' and 'warmeth' (subject-verb) and between 'warmeth' and 'the fertile Earth' (verb-object). In this sentence, then, all the relevant individual parts coalesce 'of themselves'. However, the problem arises, Harris argues, if we want to 'add other Substantives' with appropriate semantic roles, say, 'air' and 'beam', to the sentence. How can they be accommodated? Clearly not as subject or object, since these roles are already filled, and not as 'attributes' to them either, as these words 'by nature' are not 'attributes'.

The answer lies in the use of prepositions. Through prepositions, Harris says, 'we connect those Substantives to Sentences, which at the time are unable to co-alesce of themselves' (1968:265). In this way we can expand the sentence in the example above by incorporating these 'other Substantives', to produce the new sentence: 'The splendid Sun *with* his Beams genially warmeth *through* the Air the fertile Earth' (1968:266; his emphasis), while preserving the sentence 'intire and one'. Moreover, Harris thinks that, with the help of this and similar examples, he can explain 'the Rise and Use of Prepositions' (1968:265).

With the benefit of hindsight, Harris's argument is unconvincing. He does not allow for the possibility that syntactic function and semantic role do not necessarily coincide. For instance, in his example the instrumental role realised by a prepositional phrase ('with his Beams') may equally well be realised as the syntactic subject (e.g. 'the beams of the sun warm...' or 'the sunbeams warm...', or the same role may be represented as the agent PP, as in '...by the beams of the sun', etc. In modern times, such many-to-one relationships between semantic role and syntactic function (which apply both ways) have received special attention in various versions of case-grammar.

The most original part of the chapter is Harris's attempt to explain how prepositions from denoting (almost) exclusively 'Relations of Place' through metaphorical use eventually came to denote also abstract (or 'intellectual') relations (1968:266-9). Again, the rationale for the primacy of 'the Relations of Place' comes from natural phenomena, for he mentions 'that grand Relation, which Bodies or natural Substances maintain at all times one to another, whether they are contiguous or remote, whether in motion, or at rest' (1968:266).

Harris divides the prepositions denoting relations of place into the following three groups (1968:267; his emphasis):

(i) those that denote 'the contiguous Relation of Body', e.g. 'Caius walked *with* a Staff' and 'the Statue stood *upon* a Pedestal';
(ii) those used to show 'the detached Relation', as in 'he is going *to* Italy' and 'these Figs came *from* Turky';
(iii) those denoting 'Motion and Rest'.

Under (iii), Harris makes a distinction between (a) 'that Lamp hangs from the Ceiling' and (b) 'that Lamp is falling from the Ceiling'. He claims that 'the Preposition varies its character with the Verb'. Thus, in (a), we are told that *from* 'assumes a Character of Quiescence', whereas in (b) it 'assumes a Character of Motion'. In other words, *from* has two different meanings (denoting state and motion, respectively) in the two examples. It is still open to argument whether prepositions can be said to have multiple meanings or whether we should rather operate with one, or a few, core meaning(s) ('Grundbedeutung(en)'). Horne Tooke, who represents an extreme and rather peculiar version of the latter view, strongly attacks Harris on these grounds, arguing (rightly, in my opinion) that notions of rest and motion belong, not to the preposition 'from', but to the verb ('hang' and 'fall', respectively) (Tooke 1968:381).

Harris imagines that the original use of prepositions to denote purely spatial relations was gradually extended to figurative space. This change is illustrated by means of the prepositions *over* and *under*, which at first co-occurred with concrete nouns ('sensible objects') only and indicated spatial relations, but later came to be used figuratively about, for example, 'social position', as in 'He ruled over his People' (said of a king) and 'He served under such a General' (said of 'a common soldier') (1968:268). The third stage, according to Harris, was achieved by further extending the use of metaphor to include the co-occurrence of prepositions with abstract nouns ('intellectual Conceptions'). In this way we get prepositional phrases like '(thinking) over a subject', 'under Anxiety', 'from Fear', etc.

The notion of a basic meaning of locality is even extended to prepositions used as prefixes, whose 'imparted meaning' in most cases is said to be 'resolvable into some of the Relations of Place' either in a local or figurative sense (1968:271). This is true of some Latin prepositions used as prefixes, where for instance, given a certain locality, *ex-* signifies 'out of' it, *per-* 'through' it, *sub-* 'under' it, etc. Moreover, the development from spatial to abstract relations seems to support Harris's general belief that 'there is indeed no Method to express new Ideas, but either this of Metaphor, or that of Coining new Words' (1968:269).

Lastly, Harris mentions the relationship between prepositions and case. He maintains in general that 'there are in fact no such things [as] cases in modern Languages' (as opposed to Latin and Greek), except 'a few among the primitive pronouns ... and the English Genitive'. By 'modern Languages', Harris must (English apart) have thought chiefly of the Romance languages since, for example, Scandinavian languages use (as they also did in the eighteenth century) the genitive case-form much more widely than English, not to mention that German and Icelandic to this day have four distinct cases, including case variations with prepositions. But over-simplified as the statement is, it shows that Harris holds the view that any language should be analysed on its own terms and not by reference to the structure of 'dead' languages such as Latin and Greek.

In conclusion, it may be mentioned that there are certain similarities between Harris's two most fundamental conceptions of prepositional use and two modern syntactic theories. On the one hand, the idea of coalescence and semantic role-fillers realised as prepositional phrases (despite the shortcomings pointed out above) is not unlike the treatment of these concepts in case-grammar, as already suggested.[52] On the other hand, the premise that concrete spatial relations are historically (and, perhaps, theoretically) prior to other prepositional relations recurs in modern localist theories.[53] One must assume, however, that to Harris they were two sides of the same argument, namely that prepositions originally arose in order to 'connect the Substantives to Sentences, which at the time are unable to co-alesce of themselves' (1968:265), and that these early prepositions were at first exclusively used to signify spatial relations and were only gradually extended via figurative/metaphorical use to denote abstract relations. If so, this is a coherent and plausible theory, even from a modern viewpoint.[54]

Anne Fisher (1719-1778)

There is a lot of uncertainty surrounding Anne Fisher, the first woman to write an English grammar.[55] She was married to Thomas Slack, a printer in Newcastle-upon-Tyne (and hence sometimes listed as Ann(e) Slack). Her participation in *A New Grammar* (see Fisher 1968, but also 1754 and 1762) was announced in the *Newcastle Journal* in 1745, together with the opening of her school (cf. Alston in Fisher 1968:Note).

The publication history of her grammar is not straightforward either. No copy has survived of the first edition of *A New Grammar*, or to give it its full title, *A New Grammar: being the most Easy Guide to Speaking and Writing the English Language Properly and Correctly*, and to which has been added 'Exercises of Bad English' (cf. Fisher 1968:Note). The second edition is from 1750 (see Fisher 1968) and has, after the Preface, a short piece (dated 11 November 1749) by 'A.B.' ostensibly addressed 'to the Author' using an initial 'Sir'. In addition, on the title-page it is stated that the book is 'by the Author of The Child's Christian Education, and others', which points to Daniel Fisher (perhaps a relative). There is also a mention of *The Child's*

Christian Education in the initial 'Letter to the Author' (1968:6; note that page numbers start again from 1 in the text proper a little later). In a third edition from 1751, the author is down as 'D. Fisher' (Daniel again?), but from the fourth edition (see Fisher 1754) the name appears as 'A. Fisher' on the title-page, though the much extended Preface is dated 1749, rather bafflingly since it is not included in the 1750 edition.[56]

It is clearly a pedagogical grammar aimed at practical teaching and is, at the end of the Preface, recommended partly to 'those Gentlemen … who are honoured with the Care and Education of Youth' and partly to 'Young Ladies' who want to improve their English (1754:vi). Perhaps this concern led to a slight revision of the title in the seventh edition (and later ones) to *A Practical New Grammar*, followed by the rest of the full title to which is added 'The Seventh Edition Enlarged and much Improved' (Fisher 1762). It is clearly the 'same' book, and despite the 'Enlarged and much Improved' label it seems identical to the 1754 edition, apart from some minor changes to a few text extracts at the end of the book. Thus the Preface, for example, is exactly as in the earlier edition, except for one paragraph (about the author's 'principal Design in compiling this Grammar, intitled, A New Grammar' (1762:vi) – note that the new title is not reflected here!) having been moved backwards.

The *New Grammar* is composed around the principle of questions and answers, like several previous grammars for practical purposes. Here, too, 'Grammar' is divided into the four standard parts and we hear that syntax 'teaches the right joining of Words in a Sentence, or Sentences together' (*ibid.*) and is from the start of the actual text defined as 'the Art of expressing the Relation of Things in Construction, with due Accent in speaking, and Orthography in writing, according to the Custom of those whose Language we learn' (1968:1). If this sounds familiar, there is a reason for it since it is a faithful repetition of Richard Johnson's definition and as such it is open to the same attack for confusing 'things' and 'words' as Buchanan was to launch against Johnson (see R. Johnson above and Buchanan below). In the fourth edition, where this is repeated, there is also a somewhat different formulation at the beginning of the Preface, viz. as 'the Art of [conveying, denoting, or expressing the Ideas of one Person to another] by Rule, or in the Manner the best Speakers and Writers express their Sentiments' (1754:i). Moreover, grammar is here said to be 'truly accounted the Basis of Literature, being the Source from which all the other Sciences proceed' (*ibid.*). So not only is grammar a *science*, it is the foundation of all the others, although it has to be said that the notion of 'science' in those days differed somewhat from ours. Even so, few people would probably express themselves so boldly nowadays.

The question of the parts of speech is also addressed early in the extended Preface to the fourth edition, where we are told that '[t]he Parts of Speech, or Kinds of Words which constitute any one Language, are *the same* in *all* others' (*ibid.*; my emphasis). Consequently, a person might just as well learn the rules of English as of Latin. Part III ('Of Etymology or, the Kinds of Words') deals specifically with word classes (1968:65-115). Here 'Etymology' is defined as 'that Part of Grammar which treats of the several Kinds of Words, (or Parts of Speech) their Derivations, Ending, Change, and Likeness to one another' (1968:65). Words are either 'Primitive' or 'Derivative', a 'Primitive Word' being one 'which comes from no other Word in our Language' (*ibid.*). Words in English (and hence in all languages) are divided into four parts of speech: 'Names' (i.e. nouns), 'Qualities' (i.e. adjectives), 'Verbs' and 'Particles' (1968:66). Of the other traditional classes, 'Relative Names, or pronouns' (1968:67) come under 'Names'; participles are divided between 'Qualities' and 'Verbs', depending on their use (1968:79); whereas there seems to be some doubt about articles which have 'the Nature of Qualities … but they are commonly called Articles' (*ibid.*), although when 'articles' appear before 'Qualities', 'it is by reason of some Name expressed or understood', so on the whole we must assume that they are a kind of 'Qualities' (1968:81).

There is nothing about 'case' under 'Names' in the 1750 edition, but in a footnote in the fourth edition (and later) Fisher notes that since English has only one case (viz. the genitive), the language expresses 'the Circumstances, Properties, or Affections of Things to one another *by the Help of little Words called Prepositions*' (1754:70; my emphasis). However, this refers only to 'Names' since, unlike these, 'Relative Names' (i.e. pronouns) have both 'a leading and following State' (i.e. a nominative and an oblique – accusative – case) (1968:68; 1754:63). This fact, as regards nouns, is seen as a great advantage (again in Fisher 1754) as it relieves English from 'the great Trouble that is found in other Languages' of having 'twelve Cases, and five or six different Declensions'; here 'cases' must have been counted separately for singular and plural. What is noteworthy is that far from seeing this development (coupled with the conflation of genders) as deplorable and English as 'inferior' to the classical languages, Fisher hails it as a great advantage 'which no other Language antient or modern enjoys, except the Chinese' (1754:70). This may be an early view of what Jespersen later regards as 'progress in language' (Jespersen 1894 and elsewhere).

Chapter IV of Part III (1968:96-106) is called 'Of Particles'. Particles are defined as 'little words that express, or denote some Circumstance, Manner, or Quality of an Action, and join Sentences together', and there are four kinds of them: adverbs, conjunctions, prepositions and interjections (1968:96). In a footnote to 'Interjections' it is said that the particles 'are often used *interchangeably*, the one for the other … the same Word being now an *Adverb*, then a *Conjunction*, sometimes a *Preposition*, at others an *Interjection*, as is obvious to the Eye of every observant Reader' (1968:106). However 'obvious' it may have been, it would have been helpful to have had a few examples of this.

A preposition is said to be 'a Part of Speech, most commonly set separate or before other Parts, especially Noun-Substantives, to shew the Respect or Relation one Thing has to another' (1968:99); note again 'Thing' rather than 'Word'. But they also have another use, which is expressed in flowery terms, namely 'to be join'd in Composition with a vast Number of Words' and thus 'they create a great Variety, give a peculiar Beauty, Fluency, and Elegancy to our Language', and in what amounts to an 'aside' the reader is informed that in English '[w]e do all by the Help of Prepositions, which the Greeks and Latins did, *partly by Prepositions*, and partly by the Diversity or Difference of Cases' (*ibid.*; my emphasis). This is followed by a long list of separate prepositions and a shorter one of the 'Prepositions join'd, or set in Composition', i.e. used as prefixes: *a, be, for, fore, mis, over, out, un, up, with*. Once again, one may question the prepositional status of more than a few of them. There are even separate lists of Latin and Greek prepositions. The rest of the section is made up of three parts which need not concern us, as they are examples of the individual English prepositions, used in composition, and of Latin and Greek 'Prepositions, used in the Composition of English Words' (1968:99-105).

Part IV ('Of Syntax', 1968:116-32) defines syntax as '[t]he right joining of Words in a Sentence, or Sentences together' (1968:116) and consists of nine 'General Rules for English Concord'. In Rule VII we read: 'A Preposition has the following State [i.e. case] of a Relative [i.e. pronoun] after it', exemplified by: 'She abides with us, they came to me' (1754:116).[57] Fisher explains further that '[s]ometimes the leading State [i.e. nominative] is set after the Preposition; but then a Verb is understood', as in 'they came before *we*, i.e. before we came'. The most notable thing about this is that we are told that '*before* is turned into an adverb, and *we* belongs to the verb'. Most grammarians at the time (and later) might have thought that *before* in this use was not an adverb but a conjunction as traditionally conceived, but Fisher does make it clear that if the verb is not 'understood', the correct form is 'they came before *us*' (*ibid.*). For the benefit of young learners there is a later section (Chapter IV) with 'Examples of Bad English' related to each of the 'Rules', and 'Rule VIII' duly provides us with little grammatical horrors such as 'John is below I' and 'She abides with thou', i.e. using the nominative instead of the oblique form of the pronoun after a preposition (1968:128-9). It is therefore something of a mystery to find that the third example of 'Bad English' is 'They came to me'; what is wrong with that? and what else could it be? Since it was one of the few instances of demonstrating 'the following State' under 'Rule VII', perhaps it has just mistakenly been transferred from there without any change of case (the ungrammatical *I* for the correct *me*?). If so, it was not spotted in subsequent editions.

This is not quite the end of Anne Fisher, though. *A New (Practical) Grammar* was extremely popular and saw at least thirty-five editions before 1800 (cf. 1968:Note). A new title dealing with English grammar, *The New English Tutor*, probably appeared in 1763 and a third edition of it was printed in Newcastle in 1774 (cf. Michael 1970:562). Even more importantly, The Rev. J. Wilson brought out a 'new version' of *A New Grammar* in 1792, but for this see under J. Wilson below.

James and John Gough (1712-1780 and 1721-1791)
When *A Practical Grammar of the English Tongue* appeared in 1754 (see Gough 1967), it said on the title-page that it was 'First compiled by James Gough, of Mountmelick. Revised, digested and enlarged with sundry material Rules by John Gough, of Cole-Alley, Dublin'. A sixth edition from 1792 is known, as is a reprinted eighth edition in Dublin, 1801. The short Preface refers to 'the Authors' (1967:iii), while the longer section under it, called 'Some Observations On the Study of the English Language, and a regular Method of Education purely English' (1967:viii-xix), is by John Gough. The work is therefore an example of cooperation between the two, but to say more specifically who contributed what to it would be pure speculation. What one can say is that it is intended 'for the Use of Schools' (1967:title-page) and this is further emphasised in the short Preface. Here the authors declare themselves indebted especially to two previous grammars, viz. those by Gildon & Brightland and by Greenwood, respectively; indeed, they reveal that they have not only used these as guides but also 'in some few Places transcribed from them' (1967:Preface, p. v). However, they find that these two grammars 'seem to have been written for Men rather than Children' (1967:Preface, p. iv), and this is a balance that they want to redress. A school grammar 'must not be a Critical Grammar of the Language, but a Summary of the most material rules observed by good Writers in the Construction thereof' (1967:Preface, p. v).

It is clear why they see themselves in the tradition of these earlier grammarians (and further back of John Wallis and the Port-Royal grammarians, too), as their approach is quite uncompromising towards the often intrusive Latin influence. They consider any attempt to explain English in terms of Latin 'quite improper, because the Genius's of the two Languages are widely different', and add, 'We have properly nothing to do with genders, Declensions, or Moods'. They do not pull their punches when they state that to them Latin technical terms 'are perfectly useless in an English Grammar' and therefore 'not instructive' (1967:Preface, p. iv). This is as clear a statement about the desirability of analysing English (and any other vernacular) purely on its own terms as one could expect in the mid eighteenth century.

Grammar is defined simply as 'the Art of Speaking and Writing truly and properly' and is divided into five parts: the traditional four but in addition a fifth one that 'treats of ... the several Parts of Speech' (1967:1). These come under 'Etymology' where many previous writers also placed them. In Part II 'Analogy', the Goughs acknowledge that other grammarians usually operate with eight parts of speech, but they think it 'sufficient for our Purpose to say, There are four Parts of Speech', viz. (like Fisher) name, adjective, verb and particle (1967:40). The term 'name' was used by Lane and by Gildon & Brightland and some of their followers as well as by Fisher, so the Goughs would have known it from one or more of these. Of the usual classes not listed here, personal pronouns are called 'Personal Names' and placed under 'Names', while demonstratives, quantifiers and numerals all belong under adjectives, which are here a separate class. Participles are forms of verbs, and particles are 'divided into four Kinds', viz. adverbs, prepositions, conjunctions and a 'fourth Sort' with no name, but clearly interjections (1967:55-6).

It is said of prepositions that they 'are used to denote the State of Words, and their Reference or Relation to each other' and that their name derives from the fact that 'they are *put before* one of the Words whose Relation they shew to another', e.g. 'William went to Corke' and 'the Arrival of the King' (1967:55; their emphasis). This is a very compressed definition and hardly a model of clarity, bearing in mind the intended audience. To take the first part first, the meaning of 'State of Words' is not obvious; 'State', as we have seen, was a common term for case in those days, but the authors specifically repudiate the notion of case (a Latin term) except for personal pronouns and relative/interrogative *who*(*m*) or, in their vocabulary, 'Personal Names'. These have two cases: 'Antecedent' (i.e. the traditional nominative) and 'Consequent' (i.e. the oblique case) (1967:42-3). Readers may also be confused about 'Reference or Relation' as these terms (presumably) have different meanings, but no further explanation is offered. Finally, in the second part, 'put before' must mean appearing before but not as part of that word, i.e. functioning as prepositions as suggested by the examples, not as prefixes, but in view of the long tradition some readers may have wondered.

English particles and Latin and Greek prepositions as part of 'Compound Words' are given a separate chapter (Chapter III of 'Etymology', 1967:98-101), while in Part IV ('Syntax') it is mentioned that

'The Consequent Case cometh after the Verb, and after Prepositions', but the examples – in tune with the treatment of case – all contain personal pronouns in the oblique case. Nothing else is said of relevance for prepositions, which is a little disappointing, even in a school grammar, especially when one considers the many modern features of the Goughs' whole approach to grammar.

Samuel Johnson (1709-1784)

Dr Johnson hardly needs any introduction. His *Dictionary of the English Language* (1755; see S. Johnson 1967) in two huge volumes is arguably the most important work in the field of English language before the nineteenth century. In the dictionary (1967:II, 20H), a preposition is defined as 'a particle governing a case' and it 'signifies some relation, which the thing signified by the word following it, has to something going before in the discourse', exemplified by 'Cesar came *to* Rome'. In view of the impressive scale of the dictionary, it is perhaps unfair to expect too much detail for individual entries,[58] but considering Dr Johnson's stature and intellect it is nevertheless difficult not to feel disappointed with this sparse information, which given the mention of *Clarke's Latin Grammar* seems to derive from that work, where a reference to a prominent English grammar might have been expected.

However, Dr Johnson's contribution does not quite end there. Prefaced to the dictionary (apart from the Preface itself) are two other sections: (a) 'The History of the English Language', and (b) 'A Grammar of the English Tongue'. They are both relatively short; the second covering just over twelve (admittedly very large) pages, each divided into two columns, and it is clearly this second section that is of most relevance to us. At the beginning of it, grammar is defined (very succinctly indeed) as 'the art of using words properly' and is said to comprise the customary four parts (1967:I,E,a). Johnson freely admits that in this he is merely following 'the common grammarians', as he does in adopting 'the terms already received, and already understood' (*ibid*.). A slightly different definition is given in the dictionary entry under the word 'Grammar': 'The science of speaking correctly; the art which teaches the relations of words to each other' (1967:I,10,O).

Although 'Etymology' is the longest of the four parts, it must be said that this grammar is little more than a summary of already well-established presentations and quite inadequate for our purpose. For example, there is no overall mention of how many parts of speech there are, and which ones are recognised as such. 'Etymology', we hear, 'teaches the deduction of one word from another, and the various modifications by which the sense of the same word is diversified', offering 'horse/horses' and 'I love/loved' as examples. This definition seems to include, on the one hand, the modern sense of etymology, i.e. the origin and development of individual words, and on the other hand, the different inflectional and derivational forms of (certain types of) words, but there is nothing about the parts of speech *per se*.

Instead, Johnson leaps straight into the word classes without any introduction. First we find 'Of the Article', followed by 'Of Nouns Substantives', 'Of Adjectives' (for Johnson clearly a separate class), 'Of Pronouns' and 'Of the Verb', even – presumably intended as a sub-class – 'Of Irregular Verbs'. After this, one would have expected at least a few words about the 'minor' parts of speech, but the next (and, as it turns out, last) heading is 'Of Derivation', which among other things considers various aspects of the morphological composition of words (e.g. derivational affixes), as well as what we would call phonotactics ('extracted from Wallis', though not uncritically, cf. the end of the section) and the origin of some words derived from other languages. In this section, there are no headings for adverbs, prepositions, conjunctions or interjections as separate classes, or as members of a more general class.

There is, however, a mention of prepositions under 'Nouns Substantives' when Johnson deals with 'case'. Here he states that '[t]he relations of English nouns to words going before or following are not expressed by *cases*, or changes of termination, but as in most of the other European languages by prepositions, unless we may be said to have a genitive case' (1967:I,b,1).

Johnson's treatment of 'Syntax' is almost farcical, comprising eleven lines including examples (!); something for which Robert Lowth later chastised him, though without mentioning his name (see Lowth 1967:v). Johnson seems to be aware of this, for he introduces his ultra-brief comments with the following 'excuse', which deserves to be quoted in full:

> The established practice of grammarians requires that I should here treat of the Syntax; but our language has so little inflection, or variety of terminations, that its construction neither requires nor admits many rules. Wallis therefore has totally omitted it; and Johnson,[59] whose desire of following the writers upon the learned languages made him think a syntax indispensably necessary, has published such petty observations as were better omitted. (1967:I,c,3)

It is hard to know whether to laugh or cry. His previous critical remarks about Wallis are now replaced by implicit approval, and Ben Jonson is castigated for embracing syntax on the grounds that it is relevant for Greek and Latin (but apparently not for English). Johnson seems not to have contemplated the alternative position – that syntax may also be relevant for English – let alone to have considered any definition of what syntax might be. In the following few lines he does, however, make one comment about prepositions, namely that 'all prepositions require an oblique case' and proceeds to give four examples with different prepositions governing *me* ('*to* me', '*from* me', '*of* me', '*with* me'). There is no mention of this in the section 'Of Pronouns'.

Of course, Johnson's introductory grammar sketch cannot be compared with a full-scale grammar, but what *is* there, and in the dictionary entries, does not offer much assistance to any reader looking for information about prepositions.

Anselm Bayly (1719-1794)

Anselm Bayly was Canon of St. Paul's Cathedral and Sub-Dean of the Chapel Royal. His first venture into grammar, *An Introduction to Languages, Literary and Philosophical* from 1758 (see Bayly 1968), concentrates on English, Latin, Greek and Hebrew, i.e. the vernacular and the three sacred languages. It is in many ways an ambitious undertaking that has, in Alston's words, 'been unjustly neglected by historians of grammar' (1968:Note). It builds on the four traditional divisions of grammar (though using slightly different terms): Orthoepy, Orthography, Analogy (or Etymology) and Syntax and includes at the end four dissertations on topics of language. Bayly attempts to write a 'rational Grammar' (1968:Preface) and tries at every stage to give examples from the three classical languages. Unfortunately this is often done at the expense of English, at least of a proper definition and explanation of the phenomena in English. In its day, Bayly's *Introduction* was certainly much more useful for its treatment of phonetics than of the parts of speech in general.

Bayly refuses to accept the traditional eight parts of speech because he finds that 'a manifold Division may tend to burden the Memory rather than to inform the Judgement', therefore 'it will be better perhaps to make only *two* or *three Divisions* of *Words*' (1968:19; his emphasis). In fact, he makes three: nouns, verbs and particles. Nouns consist of noun substantives, noun adjectives and pronouns (articles form part of pronouns), verbs include participles, and 'particle' – as so often – is the general term for adverbs, prepositions, conjunctions and interjections.

Substantives may stand in 'certain Relations' to each other or to a verb, and these relations may be expressed either by 'certain Particles' (i.e. prepositions), or by 'Construction [i.e. word order, here defined as "the natural Order in Speech"] without varying its Termination'; in other words, without inflectional endings. Comments follow about the six Latin cases (without examples), although with the possible prepositions translated into English (1968:83). This is not an explanation for beginners, or for people interested in English for that matter.

There are many useful details under nouns and verbs for students of the classical languages, but Bayly shows scant interest in particles. The four pages that he devotes to this class consist mainly of lists of English words and their foreign equivalents and the chapter heading really says it all, 'Of Particles simple and compound in *Latin*, *Greek* and *Hebrew*' (1968:83). This is certainly the case with prepositions, where additionally we are told which Latin members of the group govern the accusative, the ablative, or both, while for Greek it is merely stated that '[i]n Greek Prepositions serve to the *Gen. Dat.* and *Accusative*' (*ibid.*; his emphasis).

After mentioning the particles (mostly prepositions) that are 'used in Composition', Bayly concedes that '[t]he above is only a general Explication of the *Particles*'. Any particular use is left for readers to deduce from the context, the excuse being that 'among all Nations the *Particles* are applied with so great Latitude, that they are not easily reducible under any Scheme of Explication' (1968:89).

To be fair, Bayly's *Introduction* does not deal specifically with English, unlike his much later work *A Plain and Complete Grammar* with *the English Accidence* from 1772 (see Bayly 1969), dedicated to the Prince of Wales, the later Prince Regent and, as King, George IV. Under the first mention of the parts of speech we hear that words are 'the substitutes of things, their *qualities, actions* and *relations*' (1969:19; his emphasis). Nouns substantive are 'words of the first order', adjectives are 'words of the second order', verbs 'of the third order', while the words 'of the fourth kind', called 'particles', comprise pronouns, articles, adverb, prepositions, conjunctions and interjections. At the same time, 'the substantive and verb are the principal parts of speech' (1969:20-21).

This deviates in some ways from his earlier presentation. According to Michael (1970:266), Bayly recognises four parts of speech in his much less important *A Practical Treatise on Singing and Playing* (1771), but argues that he 'is again following a threefold classification and keeping substantive and adjective in one category' in *A Plain and Complete Grammar*. However, things are more complicated than that. Admittedly, it looks at first glance as if he has preserved adjectives in the noun category and later he talks of the 'Noun Adjective' (1969:18, Part II).[60] On the other hand, in the section with questions and answers M. specifically asks, 'How many are the kinds of words, or parts of speech?', and S. answers, 'According to the preceding use of words there are four distinctions, or parts of speech' and goes on to mention 'noun substantives', adjectives, verbs and particles, and on the same page, having repeated the first three terms, he adds, 'These are the great or principal parts of speech, the others, which express the relations, are *particulæ*, the little' (1969:26; his emphasis). This seems clear evidence that Bayly here operates with four, not three, classes, though compared with a few pages earlier, some confusion remains and this is not confined to adjectives. Pronouns, which are at first said to come under particles, are later dealt with as 'The following nouns' (1969:21, Part II).

More space is devoted to prepositions in this work than in *An Introduction*, but the treatment is still rather feeble. When they are first mentioned, prepositions, which like the other particles express 'relations', 'stand before nouns, but prefix'd to verbs, as *withdraw, forego,* forming *compounds*' (1969:22; his emphasis). Later, in a section of their own with the title 'The Relations, or Particles, called Prepositions', there is a list of the most common members followed by a few lines about the use of a number of individual prepositions, after which we are told that '[t]hese prepositions, placed in separation before nouns, are also used in composition, sometimes prefixed, and sometimes affixed, to substantives, adjectives and verbs, bearing the same sense in both situations', i.e. they are either 'Privative' (negative, diminishing, etc.) or 'Intensive' (affirmative, augmenting, etc.) (1969:52, Part II). This is all that exists of any general 'discussion' of the class. It is not clear what the difference is between 'prefixed' and 'affixed' since every subsequent mention is to 'prefixed' (to nouns, verbs, etc.).

However, a little more light is thrown on (members of) this class in the chapter on syntax. Bayly's terse opening statement, 'Words are either literal or figurative; so is language' (1969:62, Part II), shows that he is well aware of this semantic complexity, but he does not apply it to prepositions. These appear in connection with two aspects of syntax: case and relative pronouns. Bayly continues to be under the influence of Latin when discussing case in English, and the Latin cases except for the vocative are applied to English one by one. We hear that '[e]very verb active must have after it an accusative case', but this is not true of any 'verb neuter' (i.e. copulas and other verbs without a passive form) which may instead have 'a dative or ablative'. However, '[w]hen two nouns come after a verb, only one can be said properly to follow the verb; the other is governed by a preposition understood' (1969:66, Part II). A preposition in such constructions can then either be expressed or be 'elliptical', compare 'he gave me money' with 'he gave money *to* me' (1969:66, Part II). Under the genitive case, Bayly surprisingly does not mention the *of*-construction, but he does list other meanings of *of* such as 'from' and 'concerning' and – this is clearly the point – he compares them with their Latin equivalents. He uses previous terminology when he talks about some prepositions in English being 'signs of the dative and ablative cases', though this is only to say that these are often omitted, compare 'woe is me' with 'it is woe *to* me' (1969:70, Part II). Later we are told that 'Prepositions in compound require the same case as in separation', which given that he is describing English sounds rather mysterious, even though he provides a few examples such as 'A good man *abstains* even *from the appearance* of evil' (1969:75, Part II; his emphasis), the implication being that *from* equates to the first element of *abstains*.

The last aspect relevant for prepositional usage concerns relative pronouns, but in fact some examples contain interrogatives instead. First we learn that '[t]he relative, when not the agent, is to be put into such case as its governing noun, verb, participle or prepositions shall require' (1969:83, Part II). At least *who* has an 'oblique case', viz. *whom* (Bayly does use this term), but *which* does not. Nevertheless this difference is not discussed and the use of case is taken to be the same for both in examples such as '*with which* I am delighted' and '*with whom* I have been long acquainted' (1969:84, Part II). Of course, Bayly is also aware that with relative pronouns 'the preposition is often placed from the pronoun at the end of the sentence, subjoined to the verb'. Such usage was frequently frowned on by grammarians, but Bayly is quite sanguine about it and finds that 'when done with judgement, [it] makes variety and gives a peculiar freedom and harmony to the period' (*ibid*.). It is thus acceptable to have examples of the type 'an author *whom* I am much delighted *with*'. Where he draws the line is when the relative is omitted from these constructions – and he points his finger at the writer Jonathan Swift, in particular, for indulging in this 'liberty' – deeming such practice 'highly improper', e.g. in 'these were some of the arguments (*which*) I often made use *of*' (1969:84-5, Part II). Here, according to Bayly, the relative must (or should) not be left out.

The fact that Bayly still bases English syntax squarely on the Latin case system makes him seem somewhat backward-looking after the middle of the eighteenth century, particularly in *A Plain and Complete Grammar*.

Joseph Priestley (1733-1804)

Joseph Priestley was a colourful and influential person in the second half of the century and in the most positive sense a child of the Enlightenment. He became proficient in a wide range of artistic and scientific subjects as well as in religion and politics. His early posts included being a Presbyterian minister and a teacher/educator, but above all he was a prolific writer of books, articles and pamphlets. His increasingly critical and radical attitudes to contemporary religion and politics made him a controversial figure and he emigrated to America in 1774. He knew several languages and in 1761 was appointed as tutor at Warrington Academy in Lancashire, the same year that he published *Rudiments of English Grammar* (adapted to the use of schools), which appeared in a number of editions up to the end of the century. In the following year he gave a series of lectures in that institution on the theory of language, which were published under the title *A Course of Lectures on the Theory of Language, and Universal Grammar* (1762; see Priestley 1970), and this is the book that we shall be concentrating on. In view of the later 'rivalry' between them, it is worth mentioning that Priestley's *Rudiments* predates Lowth's *A Short Introduction to English Grammar*, if only by a few months, which absolves him from any charge of plagiarism, as he seems to point out in the second edition of *Rudiments* (cf. Tieken-Boon van Ostade 2008:103-4 and 2011:81-2).[61] In contrast to Lowth, Priestley is viewed by many as the main representative of a descriptive approach to grammar.

He opens his Introduction to *A Course* by declaring that 'Language, whether spoken or written, is properly termed an *Art*; the rules of it being calculated to direct our practice' (1970:Introduction, iii; his emphasis) and goes on to stress its immense importance to mankind. Grammars, in turn, are 'books that contain the rules and precepts of this art' (*ibid.*). However, Priestley was not a polymath for nothing, so he further claims that 'All *Art* is founded on *Science*' and uses medicine as a rather complicated analogy (1970:Introduction, 4-6; his emphasis). This means that language is subject to proper scientific enquiry and, according to Alston, he is thus 'the first English writer to proclaim the study of language as a science' (1970:Note), but others, such as e.g. John Wilkins and James Harris, certainly worked along the same lines and Anne Fisher mentions it explicitly. His aim in this lecture course is, characteristically, to examine what he calls '[t]his *theory* or *rationale* of language' and the following quotation gives a flavour of his idealism and ultimate ambition for human language:

> it is only from a perfect knowledge of the theory of language in general that we can form any rational expectations of what some ingenious persons in the repub-

lick of letters have conjectured may be one of the last and greatest achievements of human genius, viz. a *philosophical* and *universal language*, which shall be the most natural and perfect expression of human ideas and sentiments, and much better adapted than any language now in use, to answer all the purposes of human life and science. (1970:Introduction, pp. 7-8; his emphasis)

In the fourth Lecture 'Of the General Distribution of Words into Classes', Priestley gives a brief survey of the parts of speech, and in the summary at the end he mentions substantives, adjectives, pronouns, verbs, prepositions, conjunctions and adverbs. He is uneasy about interjections as a class; he describes them in rather non-committal terms as '[t]he words usually known by the name of Interjections' and finds that they are 'more properly the inarticulate expressions of the passions of *joy, sorrow, anger, surprise*, and the like, than appropriated to any particular and determinate ideas'. They are therefore 'observed to resemble the inarticulate sounds of brute animals' (1970:65; his emphasis). It is this 'inhuman' aspect of interjections that gives Priestley pause for thought. Of the other classes, or subclasses, there is no clear distinction between the terms 'nouns' and 'substantives' (only once does he use the 'appellation of Nouns Substantive'), but he generally prefers the latter. There are vague hints that nouns may include both substantives and adjectives, as in many earlier grammars, but in all essentials adjectives are treated as a separate class. Participles come under verbs, while articles, interestingly, are seen as closest to adjectives (1970:86). It should be borne in mind that Priestley throughout the exposition is concerned with 'universal grammar', although he discusses English as well.

Prepositions are first defined as '[w]ords appropriated to denote the relations of nouns to a part, or the whole of the sentence', and the widespread use of them in 'all languages' is explained by the claim that 'it would create endless confusion to vary the determination of words for every relation', i.e. the endings of nouns, etc., which explains the existence and usage of prepositions, even in inflectional languages such as Greek and Latin (1970:60). Priestley continues along the same lines in the fifth Lecture on nouns. After mentioning the six Latin cases and the functions of their endings, he informs us that '[b]y the addition of prepositions to some particular cases of words, they express the remaining circumstances and relations'. His further point that 'very different relations are expressed promiscuously by the same case, and the same relation by different cases' could equally well have been made – but does not seem to be – about prepositional usage (1970:73-4). However, Priestley does not describe English in terms of the Latin system of cases: 'In English ... prepositions are used without any change of case' and this merely *corresponds* to the genitive, dative and ablative in Latin. The use of the accusative case in Greek and Latin, in particular, is paralleled in English 'by its place after the verb', i.e. by word order (1970:78).

The ninth Lecture includes a slightly extended presentation of prepositions. The definition here has a somewhat different slant when it is stated that they 'have been invented to express the relation or situation of one word to another; for the cases of nouns can express but few of those relations' (1970:126). Priestley also has a perceptive comment about the figurative and abstract use of prepositions, seeing it as an extension of 'their original acceptation' in which they 'relate to *local position*' (1970:126-7; his emphasis). Therefore 'when they are applied by analogy, to things that are not sensible, but intellectual, moral, etc.', one should consider what preposition would be used in a 'local' sense. Hence the occurrence of *on* in the example 'a paraphrase *on* the scriptures' is 'proper' because one is 'conceived to lie or rest ... upon the other' in a physical sense (1970:127).

Another detail demonstrates the care with which Priestley deals with his topic. Like so many others, he states that '[p]repositions admit of no inflections in any language', but adds 'unless some of them may be said to be compared' (*ibid.*). His example is '*near* him' versus '*nearer* him', but in such cases he contends that 'they are considered as *adjectives*' on the grounds that 'another preposition [viz. *to*] is understood', as in 'near(er) *to* him' (1970:127-8).

There are many other intriguing language topics in Priestley's Lectures (e.g. 'growth of languages', analogy of language, complex languages, revolutions of languages and of translation, and idioms, to mention but some of them) which, together with the scientific underpinning, makes this a fascinating venture, and even though his treatment of prepositions is limited in scope, it contains several perceptive insights.

James Buchanan (dates unknown)
James Buchanan was master of Loughbury House, Camberwell, Surrey, and thus another in the long line of schoolmasters who took to writing grammars. He had already produced a more elementary grammatical treatise *The Complete English Scholar* in 1753 before publishing (anonymously) his main grammatical work *The British Grammar* in 1762 (see Buchanan 1968). A third edition of the latter is recorded in London in 1779, and a later one in Boston in 1784. Its subtitle is 'an Essay, in Four Parts, towards Speaking and Writing the English Language Grammatically, and Inditing Elegantly' and its intended audience is not just schoolchildren since it is 'For the Use of Schools of Great Britain and Ireland, and of Private Young Gentlemen and Ladies'. This sets the tone of the book; throughout, there is emphasis on the pedagogical aspects and for Buchanan it is equally important to educate boys and girls whether it is in schools or in private homes. The rather unusual title is explained by a note on the first page of the Preface, saying that 'English has been long the Language of Ireland, as well as of Great-Britain'. Finally, it should be mentioned that there is a rather obsequious dedication to the young Queen Charlotte, wife of King George III and a keen patroness of the arts.

The Preface is extraordinarily long (36 pages) and covers much that one might expect to be reserved for the text proper. This includes a 'preview' of the parts of speech, several of which are rehearsed by means of the question-and-answer technique that is also employed widely in the rest of the book. We hear, for example, without great surprise that *above* is a separable preposition 'because it can be used alone', whereas *a, be, for* (does he mean *fore*?), *ad*, etc., are inseparable prepositions 'because they cannot be used unless in Composition' (1968:x-xi). In the Preface, Buchanan also deals with more general matters such as the importance of teaching 'the Grammar of their own Language' to 'the British Youth' and even brings in John Locke in support of this view (1968:xvii). This is apparently essential for 'a proper English Education' and he joins those who deplore the fact (and by 1762 it still seems to be a fact despite all the earlier objections to it) that 'the whole of a young Gentleman's Time [is] being engrossed and sacrificed to a dead Verbality' (i.e. Greek and Latin) (*ibid.*). That is not to say that Buchanan does not find it useful for some people to learn the classical languages, but a thorough knowledge of English is a prerequisite for doing so and is also something that helps citizens in many walks of life.

In the actual text, grammar is defined as 'the Art of expressing the Relations of Words in Construction, with due Quantity in Speaking, and Orthography in Writing' (1968:1). In the accompanying footnote (these are generally for the more advanced students), he boasts that this definition 'is certainly the best and most comprehensive that has yet been given' and even finds it 'an Improvement on the judicious Mr Johnson's', for whom 'Grammar is the Art of expressing the Relations of *Things* in Construction, with due *Accent* in Speaking' (*ibid.*; my emphasis). He is clearly referring to Richard Johnson (see above and discussion there) and takes issue with the latter's use of 'Things' rather than 'Words' and of 'Accent' instead of 'Quantity' in his definition. As mentioned before, it is fair to say that he has a point.

Against this background, it comes almost as a disappointment that Buchanan upholds the conventional eight parts of speech. He makes a point of stating that 'all the Words of a Language [are] comprised in these eight Sorts of Words, or Parts of Speech' and that 'the Parts of Speech [are] the same in the English as in other Languages' (1968:72-3). Elsewhere, he emphasises the importance of studying each language separately and claims that each has its own grammar, but the parts of speech remain in their canonised form and number. He does, however, introduce a historical perspective in a footnote, where he very briefly mentions Plato, Aristotle, the Stoics and 'the Latin Grammarians' (*ibid.*). At least it shows that he is aware that recognition of the parts of speech has developed over many centuries, not emerged ready-made.

Prepositions are discussed in greater detail in Chapter IX ('Of the Prepositions'). Here a 'Preposition is a Part of Speech, which being added to any other Parts of Speech serves to shew their State, Relation, or Reference to each other' (1968:148); 'State', as before, in the sense of 'case'. He then repeats what he said in the Preface about separable and inseparable prepositions and gives examples of both; indeed, he uses the rest of the chapter to explain, with examples, what each inseparable preposition signifies, not only the English ones but also those in Latin and Greek. This is no doubt pedagogically useful but adds little to any discussion of the role of prepositions.

However, he does to some extent make up for this in Part IV ('Of Syntax'), in which 'Section IV' is called 'Of the Construction of Adverbs, Conjunctions, and Prepositions'. First we hear that *from*, *for* and *to* are 'often understood', as in 'banished (from) England', 'bought (for) my brother' and 'give (to) me', as well as the *to* 'after the helping Verbs *can*, *let*, etc. and before the Infinitive Mood' (which is arguably not a preposition at all). Then he informs us that '[t]he Prepositions … are naturally placed betwixt the Words whose Relation and Dependance each is to express' (1968:181), but a further explanation would have been better than a few not very clear examples.

Buchanan also states that 'by the Prepositions we express the Cause, the Instrument by which, wherewith, or the Manner how a Thing is done' and illustrates this with these examples: 'I am pale *for* Fear; he was killed *with* a Sword; the Enemy advanced *in* three Columns', etc. (*ibid.*). This seems rather more informative.

In Chapter II of the syntax, Buchanan establishes some 'General Rules for English Concord' and supplies paragraphs of 'false Syntax' for each of the twelve 'Rules'. Here he introduces a wrong form of the kind of word he is focusing on and it is up to the reader/pupil to insert the right form. Thus in Rule VIII he is concerned with the 'State of a Pronoun' that follows a preposition and there are a host of examples with a nominative form of the type *'He begged an Apple of *I*' and *'I will write to *she*'. Again, though, no further information is provided.

It is difficult not to sympathise with Buchanan's aims or admire his pedagogical zeal, and much of his *Grammar* with its advanced footnote apparatus is quite laudable, but nevertheless his handling of prepositions and their syntax leaves something to be desired.

Robert Lowth (1710-1787)

Robert Lowth had a very distinguished career. He studied at Oxford and took holy orders there before being appointed Professor of Poetry at the University, a post that he held for eleven years. Later he served another eleven years as Bishop of Oxford, followed by his last ten years as Bishop of London where he was also made Dean of the Chapel Royal and a Privy Councillor. It was only health problems that prevented him from becoming Archbishop of Canterbury.

This was not a man to be ignored, and neither was his work on the English language, *A Short Introduction to English Grammar*, which was published in 1762 (see Lowth 1967) and quickly became one of the leading authoritative textbooks of its kind. Alston describes it as 'probably the most influential, and widely used text-book for the rudimentary instruction of English produced in the eighteenth century' and adds that it 'could claim a distinct authority which no other grammar had before Webster' (1967:Note). Nevertheless, it appeared anonymously and this was also true of the subsequent editions in his lifetime, except those printed outside Britain, i.e. in Ireland and America. It continued to appear in new editions and reprints until well into the nineteenth century and was twice translated into German.[62]

Despite its title, which Alston believes echoes the first part of Lily's Latin grammar, this is by no means a short presentation with its 186 pages and a number of additions already in the second edition. In the long and elegant Preface, Lowth touches on several aspects of English that have been mentioned earlier, such as the widespread inaccurate, i.e. ungrammatical, use of the language; the formal simplicity of English compared with both the ancient and other modern European languages; the need for all people to learn the basics of English grammar, even 'the Learner ... of the lowest class'; and the fact that insight into the forms and structure of the language will not only 'teach us to express ourselves with propriety' but is a prerequisite for learning Latin and other languages. It is precisely the simplicity of English that is the cause of this perceived neglect, for 'Were the Language less easy and simple, we should find ourselves under a necessity of studying it with more care and attention' (1967:Preface, p. v). His grammar is intended to address these issues and to do it in simple terms, or as he puts it, 'The chief end of it was to explain the general principles of Grammar as clearly and intelligibly as possible' (1967:Preface, pp. xiii-xiv).

It is striking how similar most of these aims, and the accompanying claims about the lack of interest in learning and teaching the language properly, are to those which we have seen expressed by a number of previous grammarians, and Lowth indeed heaps praise on two of his predecessors. First, he mentions how half a century earlier Jonathan Swift, whom he regards as 'perhaps our very best prose writer', wrote to the Earl of Oxford (who was then Lord Treasurer) to complain about 'the imperfect State of our Language' and how 'in many instances it offended against every part of Grammar' (1967:Preface, pp. i-ii). Secondly, he strongly recommends for further study Harris's *Hermes* (see above), which he praises as nothing less than 'the most beautiful and perfect example of Analysis that has been exhibited since the days of Aristotle' (1967:Preface, pp. i-ii).

Lowth defines grammar as 'the Art of rightly expressing our thoughts by Words' and distinguishes 'Universal Grammar', which 'explains the Principles which are common to all languages', from the 'Grammar of any particular Language' where these principles are applied 'according to the established usage and custom of it' (1967:1). Grammar itself consists of the well-known hierarchy of letters, syllables, words and sentences. As for word classes, Lowth states that '[t]here are in English nine Sorts of Words, or, as they are commonly called, Parts of Speech' (1967:7). These are the traditional eight, but with the adjective included at the expense of the participle, and in addition the article as a separate class. They are each very briefly defined at this point, the preposition being 'put before nouns and pronouns chiefly, to connect them with other words, and to shew their relation to them' (1967:8). A little later, the prepositions *of, to, on, by* and *for* are singled out. When they are 'placed before the substantives and pronouns' they 'connect them with other words, substantives, adjectives, and verbs … and shew the relation which they have to those words', thus *for* denotes the end, *by* the agent, *on* the object, and *to* and *of* possession, but there are no examples.

In the later, slightly expanded section on prepositions, much of this definition is repeated, but there are also a couple of additions. In one it is pointed out that an important use 'is to express those relations which in some languages are chiefly marked by Cases, or the different endings of the Noun' (1967:91-2). Again there are no examples, but Lowth seems to see the use of prepositions in English as an alternative to case endings and does not claim that English should be analysed in terms of Latin categories, though it turns out that this impression has to be modified. In another comment, Lowth indicates a historical development by stating that '[m]ost Prepositions originally denote the relation of Place, and have been thence transferred to denote by similitude other relations' (1967:92). In other words, (all?) meanings other than spatial ones are derived from spatial usage (cf. Harris above and again note 54).

Prepositions next come into the limelight in the syntax chapter called 'Sentences', where Lowth makes several points. First, he informs us that prepositions in English govern and are followed by 'the Objective Case', e.g. 'with him', 'from her', 'to me', etc. (1967:126-7). Lowth consistently uses the terms nominative and oblique case about pronouns and appears to deplore any influence from Latin terminology. Thus he takes issue with 'Dr. Bentley', i.e. Richard Bentley, who in *Dr. Bentley's emendations on the twelve books of Milton's Paradise lost* (1732) criticises Milton's construction 'He descending' (Milton, *Paradise Lost*, xii. 227), arguing that it should be 'Him descending' on analogy with the Latin ablative in 'Illo descendente'. But, as Lowth comments, '*him* is not the Ablative Case, for the English knows no such Case' and sees '*his* descending' as a better option. He even adds the scathing conclusion: 'This comes of forcing the English under the rules of a foreign Language, with which it has little concern' (1967:107). So far so consistent.

However, there soon seems to be a crack in this otherwise stout defence of English terms when Lowth mentions that the 'prepositions *to* and *for* are often understood; as, "give me the book; get me some paper"; that is, *to me*, *for me*' (1967:131-2). Here Lowth asks himself in a footnote: 'in these and the like Phrases, may not *me*, *thee*, *him*, *us*, which in Saxon [i.e. Anglo-Saxon] are the Dative Cases of their respective Pronouns, be considered as still continuing such in the English, and including in their very form the force of the Prepositions *to* and *for*?' (1967:132). 'There are certainly some other Phrases', he continues, 'which are to be resolved in this manner' and mentions as an example 'Wo is *me*', where *me* in the Anglo-Saxon equivalent 'wa is *me*!' is 'the Dative Case: in English with the Preposition *to me*' (*ibid*.). In this brief glimpse Lowth at least hints at a slightly more complex case system for English, which does not rule out the term 'Dative Case' despite what has gone before.

Another example of prepositional usage is preposition stranding with relative pronouns, or as Lowth expresses it: 'The Preposition is often separated from the Relative which it governs, and joined to the Verb at the end of the Sentence, or some member of it', illustrating this with the sentence 'Horace is an author, *whom* I am much delighted *with*' (1967:127; his emphasis). Lowth thinks that this is 'an Idiom which our language is strongly inclined to' (thus using this construction himself) and finds it both prevalent and acceptable 'in common conversation' and very suitable for 'the familiar style in writing'. Still, it is clearly a matter of style and preference, for 'the placing of the Preposition before the Relative is more graceful, as well as more perspicuous; and agrees much better with the solemn and elevated Style' (1967:127-8). What is notable about this statement is not so much that a 'solemn and elevated Style' ultimately is to be preferred, but that this is largely a descriptive assessment rather than a dogmatic assertion, albeit subject to stylistic considerations. However, although preposition stranding was often condemned at that time, we have already witnessed examples of writers with a (more) tolerant attitude to this kind of prepositional usage.

Another insight of Lowth's concerns verbs and prepositions. After briefly mentioning that these two classes can be joined in composition, which may at times result in 'a new sense to the Verb', as in 'to understand', 'to withdraw', etc., he explains that 'in English the Preposition is more frequently placed after the Verb, and separate from it, like an Adverb'. This, too, 'is no less apt to affect the sense of it, and to give it a new meaning', but it 'may still be considered as belonging to the Verb, and a part of it' (1967:128-9). For example, he says, '*to cast* is to throw; but *to cast up*, or to compute, *an account*, is quite a different thing'. In such examples ('to fall on', 'to bear out' and 'to give over' are others), 'the meaning of the Verb, and the propriety of the phrase, depend on the Preposition subjoined' (1967:129). This is quite a subtle analysis of the semantics of what we know as 'phrasal verbs', where 'the Preposition … hath the construction and nature of an Adverb' (Lowth does not claim that it *is* an adverb), just as 'the Adverbs *here*, *there*, *where*, with a Preposition subjoined … have the construction and nature of pronouns', though he does not say what kind of pronoun, cf. *hereof*, *therewith*, *whereupon*.

Lowth's treatment of prepositions is more extensive and insightful than most others in the eighteenth century and that is true of many other aspects of grammar, too. It is no wonder that this work was held in high regard for such a long time and appeared in so many editions both during Lowth's own lifetime and afterwards. It was referred to by many of his successors in the late eighteenth century, from Ash to Murray, and seen by them as a benchmark of grammar writing.

John Ash (1724-1779)
John Ash was a Baptist Minister at Pershore in Worcestershire. The first edition of his *Grammatical Institutes* was published in 1760 (see Ash 1967), but only an imperfect copy of it survives and none of the second or third edition. The text used here is therefore a copy of the fourth edition, the date of which is probably, but not certainly, 1763 (cf. 1967:Title-page and Note). This is the reason for placing it at this point in the chronological order of grammarians. To add to the confusion, this fourth edition has the subtitle 'or, an easy Introduction to Dr. *Lowth*'s English Grammar, designed for the Use of Schools'. Bishop Lowth's *Short Introduction* (see above) appeared in 1762 and therefore did not exist at the time of Ash's first edition, but the present edition is said to have been 'revised and corrected by the Author' (1967:Title-page), so one can only surmise that this was done with an eye on Lowth's grammar. Ash's book proved extraordinarily durable and reappeared in numerous editions and reprints right up to 1810, including two German translations (like Lowth's), as well as being, according to Alston, the first grammar 'produced in England to enjoy publication in America' (1967:Note).

In the Preface, Ash is clearly on the side of those who advocate a sound knowledge of the mother tongue and makes a case for general education 'not only for Ladies, but for young Gentlemen designed merely for Trade', for whom 'an intimate Acquaintance with the Properties, and Beauties of the English Tongue, would be a very desirable, and necessary Attainment; far preferable to a Smattering of the learned Languages' (1967:Preface, p. A2). But, like others before him, he finds most of the earlier attempts at providing a worthy English grammar wanting and charges the authors with having 'too inconsiderately adopted various Distinctions of the learned Languages, which have no Existence in our own', or they have been 'too general in their Definitions, and Rules' (1967:Preface, p. A3). The following 'Advertisement' claims that the early editions have 'been well received by the

Public', which has encouraged the author to revise the original version and (for some unknown reason) the publisher to change the title, at first to the longer *The Earliest Introduction to Dr. Lowth's English Grammar*. This makes Ash feel compelled to issue a partial apology for 'in some Instances' daring 'to differ from so great a Man', but he reassures the reader that such divergences have been due to 'Principles which to him [i.e. the author] appeared to be satisfactory' (1967:Advertisement, p. viii-ix).

After dealing with the alphabet and sounds, Ash states at the beginning of the section called 'Grammar' that '[i]n *English* there are *ten* Kinds of Words, or Parts of Speech' (1967:27; his emphasis). This shows some independence from Lowth, for although the article is one of these parts, as it is for Lowth, Ash diverges from the latter by also making the participle a separate class. Grammar itself, which is here said to be 'Adapted to the English Tongue', is 'the Art of expressing our Thoughts with propriety, either in Speaking or Writing' (*ibid.*). It is worth noting that nouns have two cases: the nominative and the genitive, and the latter 'is formed by adding *s*, with an *Apostrophe*, to the *Nominative*: as, Men, *Men's*; Ox, *Ox's*' (1967:33; his emphasis). There are two interesting things here: (i) there is no mention of the *of*-construction being a form of the genitive, as it is in most previous presentations; and (ii) in a long footnote Ash argues against the use of the apostrophe, in part on historical grounds, and he fully expects the use of the apostrophe as a genitive marker to be discontinued in the same way as the adoption of the Latin case system in English has been, at least in his opinion.[63]

The treatment of most of the other word classes in this section is very brief. A preposition is defined as 'a Word *set before Nouns*, or *Pronouns* to express the *Relation* of Persons, Places, or Things to each other: as, He came *to*, and stood *before* the City' (1967:67; his emphasis). However, in the chapter on syntax a few more details surrounding prepositions are highlighted. Thus we hear that '[t]he *accusative* Case of a pronoun is *always set after Prepositions*: as, "To *me*, for *them*"' (1967:79; his emphasis), where one notices that pronouns (but not nouns, as shown above) do have an accusative case. Later we are told that '[t]he Preposition, *to*, is *always* used *before* Nouns of *Place*, after Verbs and Participles of *Motion*: as, "I went *to London*; I am going *to*

Town"', but also that 'the Preposition, *at*, is *always* used when it *follows* the *neuter* Verb in the same Case: as, "I have been *at London*; I am *at* the Place appointed"' (1967:82-3; his emphasis).[64] Finally, Ash makes a distinction between the spatial use of *in* and *at*, to the effect that *in* precedes '*Countries*, *Cities* and *large* Towns, especially if they are in the *same* Nation' (hence 'He lives *in London, in France*'), whereas '*At* is set before *Villages*, *single* Houses, and *Cities*, if they are in *distant* Countries: as, "He lives *at Hackney*"' (1967:83; his emphasis). The last example may not illustrate the whole rule for *at*, but it is clear that Ash uses both size and distance as parameters for distinguishing these two prepositions when used spatially.

It is no exaggeration to say that in this small textbook, with its avowed aim of leading 'Young Gentlemen and Ladies in to the Knowledge of the first Principles of the English Language' (1967:title-page), the Latin influence has truly been broken and the focus is solely on English, which is seen most clearly in the description of case and in the decision not to preserve the Latin eight parts of speech. There are definitely signs of independent thinking at work here, despite Ash's obvious veneration for Lowth.

James Elphinston (1721-1809)

James Elphinston was master of an academy in Kensington. His main work on English grammar, *The Principles of the English Language Digested* with the subtitle 'or, English Grammar reduced to Analogy', is a very comprehensive account in two volumes from 1765 (see Elphinston 1765), though Michael (1970:559) cites John Nichols[65] for claiming that it was composed in 1753. An abridged version 'digested for the use of schools' appeared in 1766.

Elphinston shows himself to be on the 'philosophical' side of the approach to grammar and language studies in the opening paragraph of his Preface:

> In an age and a country, where the sciences and arts are analytically examined and philosophically cultivated, it appears unaccountable that language alone, the avenue of science, and the bond of society, should have so little drawn the attention of Reason, and far less the eye of Philosophy. (1765, I:iii)

With his emphasis on analogy, it is natural that he should be concerned with the features that (at least certain) languages have in common, but at the same time he acknowledges the differences. This is concisely expressed later in the Preface when he says of English, French, Latin and Greek that they are here 'all four reduced to one general, yet each to its separate system' (1765, I:xi). He claims that it is one of his aims to 'show our language as regular as it is rich' and furthermore to 'draw not only the English but the French tongue from the obscurity of Rote [i.e. custom] to the light of Reason, which has never yet beamed upon her in our horizon …' (*ibid*.). The phrase 'in our horizon' is the redeeming factor here; Elphinston does not apparently assert that this has not been done in France. It is therefore not surprising that in the closing paragraph of the Preface he states (with no false modesty) as his true goal in 'this first and fundamental work' that 'by occasionally exhibiting whatever is common … to all languages, it will be endeavoured to demonstrate the Theory of the English language in all its parts and principles; to evince by Reason, and ascertain by Authority, the harmony of Use in the economy of our tongue…' (1765, I:xii).

The grammar is divided into the four usual parts, though here cast in slightly different terms: I. Orthoepy (i.e. pronunciation) and Orthography, II. Etymology, III. Syntax, and IV. Prosody or Versification. Already at the beginning of Part I, Elphinston gives a kind of definition of grammar in the chapter entitled ('Of the Alphabet'), with heavy use of metaphors taken from painting:

> *Speech* is the picture of thought: *Writing* is that of speech. It is therefore the business of *Grammar*, first to ascertain the sounds of any tongue, and then to demonstrate the manner of painting them. Speech consists of *words*, as thought of idea's [*sic*];[66] and of words the constituent parts are letters. (1765, I:1; his emphasis)

In Part II, Elphinston argues that the composition of the parts of speech is contingent on 'the arrangement of the parts of thought', which suggests that he may be influenced by the Port-Royal grammarians a hundred years earlier and by Locke's philosophical stance. In his seven parts of speech (noun, verb, pronoun, adverb, preposition, conjunction and interjection), he excludes participles but is not prepared to include adjectives, which remain the traditional 'noun adjective' subclass. Indeed, he says specifically that '[s]ubstantive and adjective [are] naturally inseparable (for a thing can no more exist without a quality, than a quality without a thing) …' and even claims that they are 'like man and wife' (1765, II:2).

The whole of 'Etymology' is concerned with the composition of words, i.e. word formation, and Elphinston is extremely thorough in his analysis. Towards the end of it he addresses '[t]he composition of the invariable parts of speech', i.e. adverbs, prepositions, conjunctions and interjections. This, on the other hand, does not spark off a long debate, and as far as prepositions are concerned he merely lists a number of 'compound prepositions' with a few interspersed remarks about their current use (1765, I:369).

Part III 'Of Syntax, or the Construction of Words' is a very different matter and Elphinston devotes Chapter V, which runs to as much as thirty pages (1765, II:129-58), to a discussion of prepositions. (§1), the first (of four) paragraphs or subsections and called 'The division and distinctions of the prepositions', begins with a definition of this class that is highly unusual and deserves to be quoted in full:

> Prepositions are mere directives of motion or exhibitives of situation; and in their vast variety of literal and figurative service, they become happy instruments of the most delicate combinations, whether of noun and noun, verb and verb, or of noun and verb together. (1765, II:129)

Although this does not capture all aspects of prepositional use (definitions rarely do), at least it highlights part of their semantic properties (motion, rest, etc.) and some of their syntactic interaction with nouns (perhaps including pronouns) and verbs. He then divides prepositions into no fewer than 18 semantic categories along with the prepositions representing them, for instance – just to give a flavour of them – 'rest' (*in, within, without*), 'motion or tendency' (*to, into, towards, till*), 'property or partition' (*of*), 'nearness or restriction' (*beside(s)*), and so on, ending with two complementary types: 'priority in time or place' (*before*) or 'in time' only (*ere*), and 'posteriority in time' (*after, since*) and 'in place' (*behind*). What is remarkable is that the categories are set up in such a way that there is no overlap of prepositions at all; that is, no preposition appears in more than one category, though in practice it would not have been difficult, in the mid eighteenth century, to find examples of prepositions having a variety of uses and covering several possible semantic fields, especially when considering both their 'literal and figurative service'. Therefore, if this were all the information presented to the readers, we would be entitled to conclude that in devising the categories Elphinston had deliberately sacrificed his own 'most delicate combinations' at the altar of discrete neatness and a strong notion of symmetry. But that would be a great injustice to him, as he goes on to exemplify many of the complexities in use and meaning that prepositions give rise to.

In fact, Elphinston's analysis of syntactic variations and of semantic comparisons and distinctions is so detailed that to provide a full summary would be an onerous task and take us too far, but some examples may at least give an idea of the scope of his efforts. Take *on*, for instance, which is one of the most commonly used prepositions with both spatial and temporal meaning as well as frequently appearing with figurative and abstract sense. Elphinston compares and contrasts it with several other prepositions. Thus both *on* and *over* can contrast with *under*(*neath*), and when we add to them *above*, *below* and *beneath*, a complex semantic field of vertical space emerges (1765, II:132). *On*, we are told, is often identical in use and meaning with *upon* (e.g. 'the book is (*up*)*on* the table'), but in other environments it is not. Among others, these include constructions when *on* is the 'adverbial opposite of *off*', denoting 'continuance' by replacing *forward*, as in 'go/say/read/write/so *on*', and when it forms part of 'some situative idioms', such as '*on* shore/foot/horseback/high/one hand' (*ibid.*). He even makes the diachronic observation that in some of these idioms *on* 'familiarly runs into the inseparable *a*', as in *aboard*, *ashore*, etc., in what we might call an instance of grammaticalisation.[67] And so on.

However, Elphinston mentions that prepositions 'may be divided according to their structure' as well as to their sense, and he uses formal criteria by distinguishing 'the thirteen monosyllables' from 'the eighteen dissyllables'. These are all listed, though one is always sceptical about precise numbers of this nature, and Elphinston himself partly justifies this doubt by pointing out that there are 'equivalents' (or expanded versions) of some of them, e.g. *to* > *unto*, *till* > *until*, *through* > *throughout*, etc. Some elements are classified as 'prepositional adverbs', viz. *abroad* and *aboard* as well as (less convincingly) *along* and *across*, the latter two being prepositions (certainly in some of their uses) in most people's estimation. Finally, he singles out some 'participial prepositives' in the shape of the present participle forms *seeing, considering, concerning*, etc., which together with 'the compound *notwithstanding*' and 'the simple *except*' are also acknowledged to be used as prepositions.

The second paragraph (§2) deals with '[t]he various use and interchange of the prepositions'. Here, if anything, Elphinston goes further in his enthusiasm for the seemingly endless intricacies of this word class, as shown in his opening sentences:

> To digest the numberless elegancies of which every particular preposition must in its various senses and substitutions be susceptible; or the various prepositions, which in different relations, or the same, may vary or affect one idea preceding or following; however desirable to a plan which includes every variation of syntax, seems no more to be either promised or expected than all the possible applications of every noun or verb. Yet their original employments being already ascertained, it may not be impossible to elucidate farther at once their variety and interchange. (1765, II:139)

And this is what Elphinston attempts to do on the following pages where he handles a string of constructions, often involving a past participle or an adjective, that can combine with different prepositions. To take a few examples: 'hard *of* heart, hard *at* hand, hard *by*'; 'glad *of* (or *at*) and sorry *for* (or *at*) a thing'; 'surprised *with-by-in-at*'; 'concerned *with-in-for-at-about*' (1765, II:140). But for Elphinston, '[t]he greatest must ... doubtless be the variety of verbal direction, according to the infinity of ways in which existence as well as action may be pointed', and he spends over a page on examples with verbs, such as: 'to be *at, in*, or *out of* a situation'; 'to run *at* full gallop, *with* full speed'; 'to weep *for* or *through* joy, to dy[68] *of* or *with* grief'; and a fairly complex one: 'a thing is done *in-*[out] *of-for-from-by-through-with* wisdom, folly, etc., as state, source, end, means or manner are respectively intended' (1765, II:140-41).

This almost bewildering variation in prepositional use means, in Elphinston's view, that we can 'better account for the idioms', such as 'take *to* wife', 'bring *to* nought', 'as well as the multitude of directions'

225

that are found with 'every general verb' and expressed by 'adverbial prepositions', by which he means the particles of phrasal verbs like 'go *on*', though he is careful to add that 'though they seem adverbs, as without regimen, [they] are nothing the less real prepositions' (1765, II:142). In other words, what he seems to say here is that these 'adverbial prepositions' may function as adverbs when they have no complement ('regimen'), but in word class terms they really are prepositions. This is a subtle deviation from many earlier, contemporary and, for that matter, later grammarians for whom they are adverbs in such circumstances. However, a note of caution is in order since Elphinston a little later talks about 'cases … in which a preposition may, nay must, cease to be such, and become a directive adverb', though he is quick to add that in such cases 'the ellipse supplied restores the preposition' (1765, II:147), so a certain ambiguity seems to be at work. But of all the prepositions, one stands out, for 'none can boast so various and general application as *of*, which appropriates in every relation', and Elphinston provides numerous examples of that, including quotations from the New Testament.

The third paragraph (§3) has the heading, 'The regimen and place of the prepositions'. Here Elphinston wants to 'explore their regimen and place, as they situate or direct things, persons, actions, or circumstances; in grammatical stile, as they govern noun, pronoun, verb, or adverb' (1765, II:146). Again, we see him separate notional from grammatical terminology and he discusses at length the preposed and postposed positions of the prepositions. For example, he contrasts the 'common (or familiar) stile' of questions like '*what* does it amount *to?*', '*whom* do you aim *at?*' and '*what* is he proud *of?*' with what he calls 'the precise' variants '*to what* does it amount?', '*at whom* do you aim?' and '*of what* is he proud?' without seemingly taking sides, but he points out that examples such as '*what* it amounts *to* is …' and 'the person I aim *at* is …' can 'become precise only by resolution or suppletion', that is, a prepositional complement must be inserted, as in 'that *to which* it amounts is …' and 'the person *at whom* I aim is …'. But there are extreme cases, such as '*what* are you *for?*', where, according to Elphinston, 'the natural question … loses all its nativeness and almost its nature' (as well as its meaning) if it is transformed into the formal equivalent: '*for what* are you?' From this it appears that he finds the examples with the preposition postposed (or stranded) more natural and hence, one assumes, to be preferred (1765, II:146-7).

However, Elphinston stresses that it is chiefly the monosyllabic prepositions that can 'become … postpositive … in the familiar', while 'the dissyllables claim the power of subjunction only in the sublime', by which he means in poetry and quotes some lines from Edward Young's *Night Thoughts* as well as from Milton, Pope and the Bible with examples of a preposition in an unusual postposed position (1765, II:148).[69]

In relation to verbs, Elphinston makes the point that prepositions are 'truly prepositional', i.e. they appear before them, e.g. with infinitives like '*to* be' (where *to* is regarded as a preposition, though later (1765, II:155) he suggests as an alternative term 'the infinitive article') and gerunds (here called the 'participial') like '*after* being', but he claims that they 'govern only the nominal part of verb, that is, its action, whether expressed, as commonly, in the participial, or elegantly in the theme itself', though not all prepositions can 'govern verbs' (1765, II:150-51). This was not a common argument in prepositional syntax. Some prepositions, we are told, can also 'specify' adverbs, e.g. *by* followed by 'far, much, little' and the '[n]umberless … examples of *from*'s situative regimen' (1765, II:152). Nevertheless, he rejects the notion that *from*, *to* or *by* 'can govern any adverb', since in the case of the first two '*a* or *the place* or *situation*' is 'understood', as is '*a* or *the quantity*' with *by* and they constitute 'their respective regimen' (1765, II:152-3; his emphasis). So government (or regimen) can depend on ellipted elements and is not just related to the 'surface' construction.

'Ellipse of preposition' is in fact the topic of the fourth paragraph (§4). This may happen with *to* when marking an indirect object; compare 'Give the person the thing; give it him' with 'Give the thing *to* the person; give it *to* him' (with word order change of the direct and indirect object in the first example) (1765, II:153). But most of the examples of constructions with or without prepositions relate to 'verb + preposition', that is, whether the verb 'governs' a direct object or a prepositional phrase (i.e. what some refer to as a 'prepositional object'). A few instances will suffice as illustration, with the preposition(s) in square brackets indicating the alternative construction. Thus we can have: 'to ask-seek-wish-hope-hunt [*for* or *after*] a thing'; 'to enter [*into*]

227

a place, a thing'; 'to fly-escape [*from* or *out of*] a place, a danger – [*from*] a person, a pursuit', etc., where the meaning is more or less the same in both cases. However, there are many other examples where the meaning differs according to the presence or absence of the preposition, e.g. 'to call a person, and to call *on* or *upon* him'; 'to reach a thing, and to reach *at* or *to* it'; 'to hit a thing, and to hit *on* or *upon* it', etc.

The fact that this lengthy summary could only deal with certain aspects of Elphinston's analysis of prepositions shows how detailed it is and how different from many of his contemporaries who take this word class far less seriously. However, that it was not a unique occurrence at the time to pay such close attention to prepositions may be seen from the next work to be discussed, published in the same year.

William Ward (1708-1772)
William Ward became Master of Beverley Grammar School in 1751 and published *An Essay on Grammar* in 1765 (see Ward 1967). It consists of two 'treatises': a 'speculative grammar' and a 'practical grammar'. Since there is considerable overlap between the treatment of prepositions in the two treatises, the main points of both parts will be presented as an integrated account.

Ward knew and admired Harris's *Hermes* (cf. 1967:xiii, 52), but his grammar is by no means derivative; his treatment of prepositions is as original as Harris's and far more comprehensive. He does not share Harris's classification of the parts of speech, in which prepositions are listed as a subcategory of 'connectives' (see Harris above). Rather, he preserves the conventional Latin type of classification with eight categories (with the possible addition of articles), for although nouns and verbs are said to be 'the principal parts of speech' (1967:11), the four traditionally 'minor' categories, i.e. adverbs, conjunctions, prepositions and interjections, are each referred to as 'this part of speech' in the relevant sections, and at the beginning of the practical grammar he explains why he sees no benefit in altering the time-honoured division (1967:320).

As far as prepositions are concerned, Ward makes the subdivision between 'signs of cases' and 'other' prepositions (e.g. 1967:70, 245). In the chapter on 'signs of cases' (1967:53-72), *by, of, for, to, from, with, in* as well as *than* are all said to be such 'signs' and are in some instances compared with the equivalent cases in Latin. For example, *by*, when used in an agent PP in a passive sentence, may be compared with the Latin ablative case (1967:63), and *of*, among other things, with the genitive case, or it may be 'substituting' for a transitive verb form (cp. 'a horse of strength', 'a horse having strength' and 'a horse which has strength') (1967:64).

There is a list of 45 English prepositions in the speculative grammar (1967:246) and a virtually identical list in the practical grammar (1967:441). In both, *of, by, for* and *than* are contrasted with the rest as being the only ones 'not particularly applicable to relations of place' (1967:246).

The status of *than* is somewhat ambiguous. In some places Ward explicitly denies that it is a preposition (e.g. 1967:242); nevertheless, not only is it mentioned together with some prepositions as one of the 'signs of cases' (1967:66), it is also closely linked with *of, by* and *for* (1967:246, 441) and even included in the list of prepositions in the practical grammar (1967:441). It is easy to see why Ward seems to be in two minds about it, for *than* shares several of the general characteristics of the prepositions. Like the other case signs, and the other prepositions in certain uses, it specifies a relation between two entities; it is 'a mere mark, or notice, which supposes a certain mode of estimation of the mind of man' (1967:66). It 'always depends upon some word that requires the act of comparison', linking this to a word denoting 'a degree of some quality', and thus expressing 'the comparative mode of construction'. Hence it is closely associated with several of the spatial prepositions, since examples like 'to stand above-below-before-behind a man' can be paraphrased as 'to stand higher than-lower than-more forward than-less forward than a man', just as 'to advance beyond the wood' is 'to advance farther than the wood' (1967:66-7). In short, a notion of comparison is embedded in the relational associations of some spatial prepositions.

Ward does not really provide a clear definition of prepositions, although there is a half-hearted attempt at this in the practical grammar (1967:439), where – as happens elsewhere too – he waxes lyrical and defines each part of speech in the form of a poem. Instead he turns his attention to some of the central and complex problems involved in an analysis of prepositions. The keyword here is 'relation'; it is obvious to Ward that all prepositions are 'expressions of relation', but it is not obvious 'how such various kinds of relations amongst objects themselves, can be expressed by one and the same preposition without confusion'. Nor is it clear why, conversely, 'one and the same relation may be expressed, on many occasions, by the help of different signs or prepositions' (1967:243).[70] To illustrate the second point, Ward uses an example of distance (which elsewhere he discusses in greater detail, see 1967:70). According to that argument, the following three constructions express one and the same distance:

(a) the distance of London from York[71]
(b) the distance from London to York
(c) the distance between London and York

(Note that in each construction, 'London' and 'York' may be reversed, to give us a total of six equivalent expressions.)

Ward's explanation of this is that we are here faced with 'three different modes of estimating one and the same quantity', and he proceeds to give a detailed account of the differences between the three expressions. Because different modes are involved, 'different signs of connexion are used', even though 'the result of all the expressions amounts to the same thing' (1967:244). Ward sees a parallel between language phenomena such as these and algebraic processes where we may also 'proceed several different ways', but still arrive at a result which is the same as it would have been, had we followed 'any other way of proceeding'. This, in fact, comes close to calling prepositions (in this use) variables or operators, and that may well be what Ward means.

The opposite possibility (i.e. that the same preposition can express different relations) is explained, somewhat circularly it seems, by the fact that relations which are 'different in themselves may be apprehended and applied by the same mode of proceeding' and therefore frequently, though not invariably, 'denoted by the same preposition' (1967:440). That, Ward maintains, is the case in the two expressions 'to be *at* a place' and 'to be *at* cards'. But although this observation is claimed to hold for languages in general (Ward must here be thinking, above all, of the Germanic and Romance languages), he acknowledges that there is no way that we can tell what relations are expressed by any one preposition in a particular language, for example the various relations denoted by *at*, *on*, etc., in English. The actual choice of preposition to establish different relations is therefore language-specific.

Since the primary function of prepositions (with the exception of *of*, *by*, *for* and *than*) is to express spatial relations between 'objects', it follows that such relations cannot exist between 'abstract objects' because they are 'incapable of external place, or local motion' (1967:244). But although this is logically true, it is not, according to Ward, how we experience the world, and that brings us to another crucial factor in Ward's analysis of prepositions: the operation of the mind.

An important difference between the data of the external, spatio-temporal world and our mental processes is that the mind often operates by means of analogy (though Ward does not use that term). Therefore, whatever their status in the outside world, 'the mind perceives, that abstract objects have connexions with each other' and, furthermore, that these 'require nearly the same modes of estimation which the relations of local situation do' (1967:244). Consequently, both kinds of 'connexion', as perceived by the mind, 'require the same mode of attention in order to estimate it', which makes it natural that they should be 'denoted by one and the same sign'. (Ward expands this explanation considerably, but to follow that would take us too far afield.) So where Harris explains the development from concrete to abstract relations in terms of metaphor, Ward offers a psychological explanation.

Ward's appeal to the mind is relevant for at least two more aspects of prepositional analysis. The first one concerns the syntactic and semantic relationship between a prepositional phrase and the constituent(s) it enters into construction with. In any ordinary relation, whether concrete or abstract, there must be present 'two objects at least, or a verbal state and an object', otherwise it will not be possible for the mind to 'form any conception of it' (1967:248). This does not, however, mean that the 'two objects' necessarily remain separate at the end of the mental process. On the contrary, it appears that a kind of fusion typically takes place in the mind. The main function of a preposition is therefore to denote a particular 'mode of thought', which in the mind unites the two parts that until then existed there 'separate and distinct' (1967:439). As a result, prepositions are 'not mere marks of relations amongst objects and states, but directions to the mind to apply its discursive powers in certain manners'. (Some might be tempted to take the uncharitable view that Ward is here attempting to show that 1+1=1, but that would be unfair since it would imply that the preposition functions as a sign of addition, which Ward does not claim.) As examples of this, he mentions that 'the Creator of the universe' only denotes one object, though two are involved in the expression. Similarly, 'to preside over the universe' denotes 'but one verbal state' (*ibid*.). In other words, 'the compound expression', as Ward puts it, is 'no ways encreased in number', or to quote the last two lines of his definition in verse:

'That sev'ral things unite in diff'rent views,
And no encrease of number thence ensues'. (*ibid*.)

This must mean that Ward is committed to the view that in examples with a clearly locative or directional preposition such as, say, 'the shed behind the house' and 'the man walked across the bridge', this kind of unity is always achieved. Assuming this to be true, the reference of the prepositional phrase might then be said to provide the 'background setting' of the (material) object referred to by the noun, or of the action or state denoted by the verb, which, as we saw earlier, can be extended by analogy to cover also the equivalent mental image of abstract relations. So when Ward talks about uniting the two objects in the mind, a painting might be a helpful analogy since it offers a *simultaneous* presentation of a 'view' that in language can only be represented *successively*, whether in speech or writing.

The second aspect of Ward's view of mental processes to be mentioned here concerns the alleged existence of a natural order of processing spatial relations. In Ward's example, 'to stand before-against-beside-in-out of-behind-beyond-on the house', each preposition 'directs the mind to apply the state to the house under a different mode of estimation' (1967:246). The interesting question is, however, in what way we mentally estimate each of the relations. Ward's answer seems to be that there is indeed a natural order of doing it, according to which 'the attention proceeds from the fore part, to a closer approach to some part of it [i.e. the house]' and so on, until it reaches 'the top part of it' (1967:247). The fact that Ward talks of this proceeding as 'a kind of ideal view' suggests that the prepositions in the example do not appear in random order, but rather reflect the natural (or, as we might say, unmarked) order of processing spatial relations. If that is indeed Ward's claim, it seems very dubious. It is presumably open to experimental evidence but, to my knowledge, none exists.

Like most of his predecessors, Ward mentions the fact that prepositions occur as the first element of compound nouns, verbs, adjectives and adverbs (1967:249-50, 441-2), thereby becoming 'a constituent part of the conception that is denoted by any of these words' (1967:249). The vast majority of these prefixes are 'not the original English or Saxon prepositions', but rather 'the French, Latin and Greek prepositions' (1967:250). As far as their function in these compound words is concerned, Ward makes an interesting distinction. When they are prefixed to nouns, adjectives and adverbs, the usual ability of prepositions to coalesce[72] with two syntactic constituents is confined to one constituent (we might say that their valency is reduced by one), which means that a noun like 'pre-eminence', despite having 'the force of the preposition *above* in it', does not 'unite with another substantive', in contrast with the expression 'eminence *above* others', where '*eminence* unites with *others* by means of *above*' (1967:249; his emphasis). Similarly, the adjective 'pre-eminent' can only coalesce with one noun, for example 'station' in 'a pre-eminent station', but not 'unite two substantives so together as *above* does', just as an adverb like 'previously' can only unite with a verb. There is, however, an exception to this since, according to Ward, 'a preposition, when united with a verb intransitive, frequently has the effect of a separate preposition' (*ibid.*). Thus, for instance, 'to precede' is said to be 'of the same import' as 'to go before', as is 'to succeed' when compared with 'to come behind', and equally, 'a man preceding or succeeding another' is an expression 'much of the same import with "a man coming before or behind another"'. Therefore 'the same kind of correspondence' exists between the relations of the two 'objects' in constructions with 'precede-succeed' and those with 'before-behind', 'only the correspondences of the verbal states are conceived to be estimated by a different kind of proceeding from those which are used when the prepositions are mentioned' (1967:249-50). Ward does not say that the prefixes often, as in this case, turn the verb into a transitive one, so that the correspondence may be more correctly stated as one between a transitive verb and an intransitive verb + a PP. A finite, transitive verb (with an overt object) coalesces with (we might say, governs) both its subject and its object, and this relationship is precisely what Ward claims for spatial prepositions (cf. the examples above where the 'case-sign' *of* alternates with the transitive verb 'have').

Ward examines the link between intransitive verbs and prepositions in more detail by drawing attention to the fact that some 'original English prepositions' co-occur with intransitive verbs in the passive voice, to form a construction that Ward takes to be peculiar to English (1967:250, 442). It is noteworthy that all the five prepositions which Ward claims are able to enter into this kind of construction (*of, from, to, with, for*) also function as 'case-signs' (see above), though Ward does not make this connection clear. Thus we have the following examples (a)-(e):

(a) to be heard of
(b) to be heard from
(c) to be talked to
(d) to be talked with
(e) to be bargained for[73]

Such 'compound verbs' often differ in meaning from simple verbs; for instance, Ward glosses 'to dispense' as 'to distribute', but 'to dispense with' as 'to execute or disannul' (1967:442). What happens syntactically in this construction is explained by Ward in the following way:

> Here the substantive which should be the nominative case to the verb, is considered as known of course from the nature of the verb; and the substantives which should depend on the prepositions, 'of-from-to-with-for', become of the nominative case on which the verb ... is made to depend. (1967:250)

Ward correlates his passive examples with the corresponding active sentences and notes that these prepositions 'depend' so closely on the intransitive verb in the passive form 'as to make a part of the verb itself' (*ibid*.). He does not pursue this analysis any further, but what is probably implied is that a reanalysis may have taken place in constituent structure, in examples such as 'they sent for the doctor', from S-V-PP (i.e. they – sent – for the doctor) to S-V-O (i.e. they – sent for – the doctor), with the result that verb + preposition form a unit, i.e. a prepositional verb (cf. the passive equivalent, 'the doctor was sent for (by them)' where the prepositional complement in the active sentence (i.e. 'the doctor') is the subject, and note that verb + preposition may together be replaced by a transitive verb, e.g. 'summoned').[74] In view of these theoretical issues, it comes as something of an anti-climax when Ward meekly concludes that 'this mode of construction is used merely to save words' (*ibid*.), especially since Ward appears to be right that this construction is peculiar to English. At least it is not found either in the other Germanic or in the Romance languages.

Ward's analysis is of interest to a modern reader mainly for his demonstration that prepositions fundamentally express relations, whether spatial or abstract ones, and for the way in which he explains these relations in terms of operations of the human mind. Furthermore, by suggesting that the specific meaning of prepositions in abstract relations – the most extreme example of which is their role as 'case-signs' – may be compared to an algebraic sign, he seems to pre-empt the use of variables in some modern linguistic theories and analyses.

Daniel Fenning (1714/5-1767)

Daniel Fenning was a schoolmaster at Bures, Suffolk. He wrote several school textbooks on the English language, but for our purpose the most relevant one is *A New Grammar of the English Language* from 1771 (see Fenning 1967), which was published posthumously and by 1800 had been reprinted no fewer than eight times (cf. 1967:Note). On the title-page it is said to be 'an Easy Introduction … calculated for the use, not only of schools, but of private gentlemen' (no women mentioned), though the Preface states that it is 'intended chiefly for the use of English Schools' (1967:Preface, p. ix).

The first sentence of the Preface could easily have been written by many of the previous grammarians in this study – and for that matter by all subsequent ones: 'Considering the great number of English Grammars that have already been offered to the Public, it will naturally be expected, that I should explain the motives that induced me to trouble the world with another treatise on the same subject' (1967:Preface, p. iii). The answer, in Fenning's case, is that after he had used his own grammatical material with his pupils for a while and seen some of it finding its way into the public domain, 'many of the most eminent School-masters in the kingdom strongly importuned' him to publish his *New Grammar* – and he was persuaded to do so.

He informs the reader that in it he has 'strictly adhered to the old terms and the old divisions' (1967:Preface, p. iv), and this is borne out by his division of grammar into the traditional four parts, though he admits that some include Orthoepy as well. On the other hand, his definition of grammar as 'the *Art* of communicating our thoughts by words in the plainest and most intelligible manner' is at the same time both broader and narrower than most previous ones, and he justifies the use of 'Art' by saying that 'it consists of certain rules' (1967:1). In Part II ('Etymology') he also deviates from most of his predecessors when he establishes nine parts of speech by including both the article and the participle, though he excludes the adjective which is, once again, a 'noun adjective' (1967:16-18).[75] His take on case is 'modern' rather than traditional, contrasting the two cases in English (nominative and genitive) with the six cases in Greek and Latin (which is a little over-generous to Greek). He further explains that English supplies 'the want of these cases ... by means of [certain] prepositions' (1967:22-3). Thus, although he accepts that an English noun can in theory be declined in the same six cases partly by using the right prepositions, he basically upholds the separation of English from the classical languages.

The whole grammar is composed as a question-and-answer session (with the entries Q and A), presumably to make the content simpler and more easily intelligible for the intended audience. Fenning goes through the nine classes and devotes a 10-page-long chapter to prepositions (Chapter VIII). With some repetition from earlier, his initial definition sees a preposition as 'a word that expresses the relation which one word hath to another, and performs in English what in Latin is effected by cases, or the different terminations of nouns' (1967:79-80). Unsurprisingly, we hear that prepositions are so called 'because they are commonly *placed before* the words, to which they refer', but he also provides an example of them being placed *after* these words, viz. 'How much did you buy it for?'. It is more interesting that Fenning enumerates (with examples) five 'kinds of words' that prepositions can be 'joined to'. These are: (a) 'substantive nouns' ('He came to England'); (b) pronouns ('He spoke to me'); (c) 'verbs in the infinitive mood' ('He promised to write'), which we would (no longer) accept as a preposition; (d) the 'compound perfect participle', i.e. a present participle followed by a past participle ('after having dined'); and (e) 'sometimes to adverbs' ('from hence') (1967:80). One can quibble about a few details, but there is no denying that this is a fairly detailed explanation and illustration of prepositional syntax, and it is not even in the chapter on syntax.

Fenning's eye for distinctions is also revealed when he deals with the meanings of prepositions. Having already said that it is no more reasonable to explain these in general than it is for any other words and that such explanations belong to a dictionary rather than a grammar, he relents when it comes to prepositions 'used in composition'. The rest of the chapter is thus dedicated to an elucidation of the meanings, first of those English prepositions that appear as the first element of compound words (including *a*), and secondly of those from Latin (but not Greek) with a similar function.

In Part III (Syntax), Fenning moves on to 'the construction' of the various classes and in Chapter IV of it to that of adverbs, prepositions, interjections and conjunctions. Here we are told that 'the construction of Prepositions' is that they 'take the oblique case after them' and that although they are usually placed before the oblique case, this may not be so when a preposition 'governs the relative', as in 'That is the man, *whom* I spoke *to* yesterday' (1967:110-11). A little later (in Chapter V 'Additional Remarks', which are intended for more advanced students), Fenning explains that in fact a preposition 'does not always govern the oblique case', e.g. in 'Who is this for?' and 'Who did you give it to?' (i.e. *who* rather than the oblique form *whom*). Again this shows Fenning's descriptive rather than dogmatic approach to grammar, for one cannot help wondering how many eighteenth (or even nineteenth or early twentieth) century grammarians would have accepted the form *who* in these examples.

Fenning may have seen himself as a traditionalist, but he shows that he can think independently and he is by no means a slavish follower of the more conservative practices that we have witnessed often enough before. There is therefore every reason to believe that his pupils (and readers at the time) were well served by his presentation and explanations.

John Fell (1737-1797)

An Essay towards an English Grammar was published anonymously in 1784, but has for some time been attributed to John Fell (see Fell 1967), who was a minister at Thaxsted, Essex, and a tutor at Homerton, which was then located in London (cf. 1967:Note).[76] The Preface is thought to be by one of Fell's pupils, Richard Sharp, writing in the guise of 'the Editor'. Most of the Preface is taken up by a criticism of the language in English literature 'during the last thirty or forty years'. The main complaint is that these writers are said not to have 'expressed themselves in a pure and genuine strain of English' and are charged with 'adulterating our language with foreign mixtures', especially Latin (1967:Preface, pp. vi-vii). Although this complaint is not a new one, it is said to have 'become more frequent, and more extensive than ever' and to encompass 'not only Latin words, but Latin idioms', resulting in 'a sort of angliciz'd Latin' (1967:Preface, p. vii). No names are given, but this trend is contrasted with the writers at the beginning of the century, such as Dryden, Swift, Pope and Addison, not to mention Shakespeare's 'immortal wit'. The answer is to concentrate on teaching children English (grammar) before other languages are introduced and both Lowth and (though unnamed) Dr Johnson are quoted with approval.

It is at this point that Fell's approach to language is presented and it is a remarkably modern one. On the one hand, it is alleged that he believes that a grammar should be descriptive, not – like so many others – prescriptive: 'It is certainly the business of a grammarian to find out, and not to make, the laws of a language' (1967:Preface, p. xii). (Substitute 'rules' for 'laws' and we have a statement that most current linguists can endorse.) The grammarian thus becomes 'a faithful compiler' rather than 'a legislator'. But it goes further than that.

What is correct is not what the grammarians preach but what the language community practise. To quote again from the Preface: 'He [the Author] does not presume to regulate the customs and fashions of our speech, but only notes and collects them', and it continues: 'It matters not what causes these customs and fashions owe their birth to; the moment they become general, they are laws of the language; and a grammarian can only remonstrate, how much soever he disapprove'. The 'tribunal of use', i.e. common usage, is 'the supreme authority and last resort' and hence the final arbiter, for – we are told – 'all language is merely arbitrary' (1967:Preface, pp. xii-xiii). This is a far cry from the insistence on certain types of correctness in many other grammars, in the face of widespread 'deplorable' usage, but at first sight it is at odds with the criticism of the use of language in the then recent literature, unless the latter is seen as an affected minority practice compared with the 'actual' use found among ordinary native speakers. Whether Fell lives up to these expectations is another matter.

Certainly, his definition of (English) grammar seems a little awkward against this background because it is for him 'the Art of Speaking and Writing the English Language, agreeably to the established usage of the best and most approved Speakers and Writers' (1967:1). But this is precisely the problem – and Fell is by no means alone in this – for who decides who these 'models' are? And is 'established usage' the best guide if the usage changes? If Fell did not write the Preface, as suggested above, perhaps that helps explain such apparent discrepancies.

Unlike most earlier grammarians, Fell announces that it is 'no part of the present design' to deal with orthography (including syllables) or matters of pronunciation, so he moves straight into the parts of speech followed by syntax. Fell claims that 'English Grammarians have generally considered the Language as consisting of nine parts of speech' (1967:2) but, as we have seen, that is not strictly speaking correct. His own nine classes include the article and the adjective, but not the participle. As such, it would therefore not look out of place in many traditionally inclined present-day grammars of English. Somewhat bizarrely, declension of nouns appears under the heading 'Article' and there are examples both with and without prepositions. Those without prepositions are confined to the 'nominative and objective cases' and the genitive so that 'king' is the form of both the two former cases. With prepositions, the scheme is expanded to include the dative ('to a king / to kings') and the vocative ('O king(s)!'), *O* being treated as a preposition. No ablative case is mentioned, but the cases with preposition contradict the Preface, where it is argued that English should be analysed independently of Latin and other foreign languages (1967:9-11).

Prepositions are given a section of their own. Their name is explained by the fact that 'they are terms set before other words' and 'serve to point out the situation, or relation, which one thing bears towards another'. It is further mentioned that in English 'they also denote those relations, which, in some other languages, are marked out by cases', and they are said to appear before 'substantives, pronouns, and participles of the present tense'. Finally, there is a reference to the observation by Lowth that most prepositions 'denote the relation of place' and that this use has been expanded ('transferred') to other areas (1967:61). As definitions in the eighteenth century go, this is a fairly detailed one, and quite a lot more is added in the chapter on syntax. The rest of the section is made up by an alphabetical list of individual prepositions and what they relate to (but without examples). At the end Fell mentions a few compounded items (*into, out of, toward(s), upon, within, without*) and explains in each case their origin and coalescence into one word (except for *out of*). Thus he claims that '[m]ost of the prepositions are likewise frequently used as adverbs' and 'some of them, as adverbs, assist other prepositions, and thus coalesce into one word, so as to form a distinct preposition'. In fact, some of them 'will, in this manner, take to themselves adverbs', e.g. '*in*, as an adverb, assists the preposition *to*; hence the preposition *into*'. Similarly, *out*, which 'is no preposition, but only an adverb ... frequently accompanies and modifies the preposition *of* (1967:65). The suggested process is thus: adv. + prep. = prep., whether in one or two words. Again, this is an analysis that will appeal to many modern grammar writers.

There are another six pages on prepositions under syntax, summed up in 21 short paragraphs, some of which are worth mentioning. As in many previous treatments, the terminology used is often not what we would employ today, but the meaning is usually clear. Fell asserts that all prepositions govern 'an objective case' (no exceptions as with Fenning) in both nouns and pronouns, e.g. 'through the field', 'to me'

(1967:125). He stresses that the preposition also precedes a noun or pronoun in the genitive ('the possessive case') governed by 'the substantive, which the preposition belongs to', i.e. the prepositional complement, as in 'on Paul's neck', 'in his hand', 'by whose care' (*ibid.*). In much of the rest of the treatment, Fell is at pains to show where in the clause 'the preposition with its attendant case' (i.e. the PP) can occur, especially in relation to the subject ('the nominative case') and the (finite) verb. Thus we are shown examples of the PP positioned initially in the clause, after the subject, between the auxiliary and the main verb, and of course after the main verb (including verbs in the passive voice), which may or may not be in the final position in the clause (1967:126).

A few types of verb are singled out for special mention, such as '[a]ll neutral verbs of gesture, and many of those which express, or intimate the passions'; examples include 'sit/stand on', 'long/wait for' and 'rejoice/laugh/wonder at'. It is merely said that these are often followed by a PP, but the underlying implication is that in each case there is a strong selectional link (i.e. collocation) between the verb and the preposition. 'Many transitive verbs', too, can be used 'in the above form', i.e. followed by a preposition (PP) rather than by a direct object, e.g. 'know/hear of these things', 'testify of me', 'taste of his bounty', etc. Later it is said that this also applies when such verbs are in their passive form, e.g. 'those, who are looked upon as …', 'he was pointed at', and in connection with 'participial and verbal substantives, derived from verbs of [this] kind', as in 'a looker on' and 'being stared at' (1967:127-8).

Another use of prepositions is 'after verbs of all kinds' when prepositions are 'put in an adverbial sense', i.e. in 'phrasal verbs' such as 'sit/fall/lie down', 'stand/get up', but also some with a direct object (which are not distinguished in the text), as seen from examples like 'he laid down the book' and 'they lifted up their eyes to heaven'. Such usage is said to be 'purely idiomatic'. A related function is the use of *on* 'in this sense' to 'denote the progress and continuance of an event, state, gesture, or action', e.g. 'say/sleep/walk/write on' and even (less convincingly) 'we will bring you on your way' (*ibid.*).

There are also examples where two prepositions occur side by side. In one case, according to Fell, the first item is not actually a preposition but rather 'an adverbial addition to the verb', such as *up* in 'He came up to us' and *off* in 'they went off from us', and as such this is an extension of the comments on 'phrasal verbs'. The other case is simply where two prepositions 'each [with] its own attendant case somewhere or other in the sentence' happen to be next to each other (here italicised), e.g. '…which I was never inclined *to at* any period of my life' and 'whomsoever I may meet *with in* that business' (1967:129).

Fell finds that there is sometimes 'improper use' of *that* instead of *which* when the preposition is separated from 'its attendant case', e.g. in (a) 'the knight left the money with her, *that* he had crossed her hand *with*', and in (b) 'Quickset her cousin, *that* her mother wished her to be married *to*' (1967:130; his emphasis). In (a), it is no doubt the addition of 'with her' that worries Fell; without it, *that* would have followed its correlative and almost certainly have been acceptable to him. (b) is different since the alternative to the allegedly incorrect *that* is not, as implied, *which* but *who*(*m*), which raises some other issues about the use of *that*.

Unlike some of his predecessors, Fell does not object to the separation of the preposition from its complement *per se* or from the verb it is linked to (with or without a complement). He states that this happens frequently, e.g. ('with a verb of gesture') 'for, *at* your *grief*, see how my wretched sister *weeps*' and when governing a relative/interrogative or a 'substantive', as in 'he brought the nation into those distresses, *which* it has, at this time, to contend *with*', 'but *what* will not ambition and revenge descend *to*', and 'for *all these things* do the nations of the world seek *after*' (1967:228; his emphasis). He also echoes Lowth in claiming that this is 'an Idiom which our language is strongly inclined to'. In fact he goes further, for whereas Lowth clearly prefers the preposition to precede the complement in anything but colloquial style, Fell (in a long note) finds 'this idiom … perfectly consistent with the greatest simplicity of arrangement'. Indeed, he thinks that the postposed position of the preposition 'is more suitable to the genius of the language, than to place it next to the word governed'. He even emphasises that the fact that 'the contrary custom is followed in the learned languages … can never be urged as a rule in English grammar' (1967:129). Here Fell is certainly true to the descriptive principles put forward in the Preface.

Fell's *Essay* may not have enjoyed the popular acclaim that was accorded to some of the other grammars we have looked at, as it does not seem to have been reprinted or to have generated later editions (cf. 1967:Note), but despite the fact that it is greatly influenced by Lowth, it is sufficiently independent to deserve attention and praise for its insistence on a descriptive analysis that in several areas pre-empts later studies, and his treatment of prepositions is certainly a very thorough and interesting one.

George Neville Ussher (dates unknown)
George Neville Ussher is another author of whom we know very little. The grammar for which he is remembered, *The Elements of English Grammar*, first appeared in 1785 (see Ussher 1967) and enjoyed a number of reprints, though interestingly more in America than in England. It is also unusual in being 'designed particularly for the use of Ladies' Boarding Schools' (1967:title-page) and for that reason it is dedicated to 'Lady Guise of Highnam Court in the County of Glocester'.

It is clearly Ussher's intention to write a basic introduction to English grammar since he finds previous works even 'of our ablest grammarians ... too voluminous and abstruse for the capacities of children, and more adapted to finish the scholar than to initiate and instruct the young beginner'. On the other hand, 'smaller abstracts' of these works are seen to be 'upon too contracted a plan to furnish an useful knowledge of grammar, particularly to those who do not learn the ancient languages' (1967:Preface, p. v), so the author wants to steer a middle course between these two extremes. This is probably where Ladies' Boarding Schools come into the picture as it was not the custom to teach girls the classical languages that many boys learnt at school or privately. It does not come without a touch of condescension, though, when Ussher goes out of his way to emphasise that he has rejected 'all abstract terms that could be dispensed with', omitted 'all reference to the learned languages' and delivered 'the rules in the plainest manner possible' so that the presentation will not be too taxing 'for the comprehension of the young beginner [read: girl]' (1967:Preface, p. vii).

Ussher makes it plain that he disapproves of the common device of structuring grammatical information in the form of questions and answers (as we have seen it used by a number of grammarians). Such dialogues may be in order for 'the beauties of taste or of the imagination' but they are 'totally foreign to the purpose in a treatise of abstract science' (*ibid*.). This is not the only place where Ussher refers to grammar as a 'science', which was not unheard of at the time but nevertheless still rather unusual. He tries to argue that English, and English grammar in particular due to its 'peculiar structure and genius', can match Latin and Greek in status, despite having been 'thought incapable of grammatical accuracy' about a century earlier (an exaggeration on Ussher's part), but he concedes that this is not true in all respects since even 'in its present improved state we may not find in it the majesty and force of the learned languages'. On the positive side, he finds that 'its simplicity is remarkable', and here prepositions seem to be cast both as villains and as heroes, for this simplicity is achieved 'notwithstanding the number of prepositions that encumber it, though we must own at the same time they contribute to its variety and precision' (1967:Preface, p. vi). That this 'swings and roundabouts' view of the role of prepositions appears as early as in the Preface says something about the importance of this word class in Ussher's overall assessment of the language.

There is nothing unexpected in his division of grammar into the four usual parts, nor in the by now familiar division of words into the same nine classes that was made by Fell and others (1967:1-2). Although substantives have only two cases (nominative and genitive), Ussher finds it 'convenient to mention the Objective Case' and describes it a little later as 'that Case which follows Verbs and Prepositions' (1967:8). If we take 'follows' literally, that is clearly inadequate, but he has a good deal more to say about this and other matters in the chapter 'Of Prepositions'. Here the class is defined as 'words prefixed to Nouns and Pronouns, and sometimes to Participles, in order to connect them in a sentence' and their use is said to establish a connection between a word of one of these classes and 'the former part of the sentence' (1967:77-8). In some cases, viz. 'when the Preposition is joined to a Verb merely to express a circumstance belonging to the Verb', it [the preposition] 'becomes an Adverb', whether it stands next to the verb or 'at a distance from it' (cf. Fell's wording above: 'an adverbial addition to the verb'). But Ussher immediately complicates matters by saying that *on* and *up* in the following examples 'are Prepositions used as Adverbs': 'They drive *on* at a great rate' and '*Up* into the clouds he flew' (1967:78; my emphasis). So are they prepositions or adverbs here?

The rest of the treatment of prepositions is more fragmented. He mentions, for example, uses and meanings of *at* and *in*, and shows how the meaning of the governing verb or particle can change when combined with different prepositions. Ussher remarks, quite interestingly, that when a preposition follows a verb (to become a phrasal or prepositional verb), this construction can be considered as much a 'compound Verb' as when the preposition is 'prefixed the Verb, making but one words with it', compare 'overdo', 'undergo' with 'give over', 'pass by' (1967:79-80). This claim was not common coinage in grammars.

However, this positive view of Ussher quickly gives way to concern, for in the next paragraph, which deals with prepositions and relative pronouns, he not only echoes Fell's general view but copies Fell's long note word for word (see above) without the slightest acknowledgement or any mention of Fell in the Preface or elsewhere. Admittedly, it was common practice to be 'influenced' by earlier grammarians (we have seen previous examples of it), but this seems to be an extreme case and one cannot help wondering how much else has been directly or indirectly 'borrowed' from Fell or others. Fell's *Essay* appeared the year before Ussher's *Elements*, so it is not surprising that Ussher should be familiar with it, albeit rather 'over-familiar' when it comes to the passage mentioned. The rest of the chapter consists of a list of verbs and the prepositions that can collocate with them.

John Horne Tooke (1736-1812)

John Horne Tooke[77] was a very colourful figure in the late eighteenth and early nineteenth century. He took part in many aspects of the political life of the day, which among other things earned him a spell both in Parliament and in prison. His principal work on language, *The Diversions of Purley*, was published in 1786. A second edition (Part 1 of which is the relevant part in this context) appeared in 1798 (see Tooke 1968), but in terms of chronology Horne Tooke is entered according to the date of the first edition.

The Diversions of Purley is a highly eccentric work in many ways and takes the form of a dialogue between Horne Tooke's friend Richard Beadon, master of Jesus College, Cambridge, (in the text referred to as (B)) and the author himself (H).[78] It is the function of (B) to ask seemingly awkward and challenging questions, only to be 'put right' by the well-informed scholar (H). It is also a very polemic work, in which Horne Tooke often goes out of his way to pour scorn on previous approaches and analyses that differ from his own, and in this respect Harris's *Hermes* is one of his favourite targets.

According to Horne Tooke, all problems concerning divisions into parts of speech can be solved by reference to the etymology of the word, or words, in question (and here etymology is used in its modern sense). Thus he claims that when words are traced back to their origins, it turns out that there are only two parts of speech: nouns and verbs. Words that on the surface appear to belong to other word classes are really just later corruptions of nouns or verbs. Consequently he rejects all categorisations that result in more than these two parts; for example, he attacks Harris's four-class system and his reliance on ancient authorities (in this case, chiefly Aristotle), and he is contemptuous of the tendency towards further subdivisions and more and more refined distinctions.

Against this background, it may seem almost a contradiction in terms to discuss Horne Tooke's treatment of prepositions, but he does offer an account of the traditional parts of speech, even if he does not agree with their category labels. For example, he gives a summary of previous attempts to establish the exact number of prepositions (1968:306-14), but concludes that to do so is not possible 'since their number in every language depends merely upon how many of the most common words shall become obsolete or corrupted' (1968:311). His obsession with etymology causes him 'to lay it down as a rule, that, of different languages, the least corrupt will have the fewest Prepositions: and in the same language, the best etymologists will acknowledge the fewest' (1968:299).

Prepositions and conjunctions are often mentioned together (after all, for Horne Tooke they are not really separate parts of speech), since the only difference between them is 'the apparently different application', namely that conjunctions are 'applied to sentences' and prepositions 'to words' (1968:352). On this point Horne Tooke sides with the Stoics and criticises Priscian and later writers for dividing them into two classes. They should be treated alike as they were both originally nouns or verbs, for 'the same sort of corruption, from the same cause, has disguised both' (1968:307).

In attacking the distinction traditionally made between prepositions and conjunctions, Horne Tooke does not deny that it has its practical uses, especially in the teaching of grammar to schoolchildren. But although it 'may be useful enough' (1968:327) in that context, this does not excuse the adoption of the distinction by philosophers and grammarians who have wrongly 'taken them for real differences in *nature*, or in the *operations of the human mind*' (1968:328; his emphasis).

Because of his preoccupation with etymology, Horne Tooke (unlike e.g. Ward) shows little interest in the ability of prepositions to express relations. He does, however, touch upon the subject when he puts forward his belief 'that the names of all abstract relation ... are taken either from the adjectived common names of objects, or from the participles of common verbs' (1968:453). For example, the words 'Head' and 'Heaven', he says, are 'evidently the past participles "Heaved" and "Heaven" of the verb to Heave', and he derives *upon* and *up* from the same source as 'Top' or 'Head' and with the same meaning (1968:452). The relations of place, in particular, are said to be 'commonly from the names of some parts of our body' (1968:453). At this point he acknowledges Wilkins's 'ingenious attempt to explain the local prepositions by the help of a man's figure' (1968:454, and see Fig 1. under Wilkins), but he criticises Wilkins for 'confining his attention to ideas', and thus overlooking 'the etymology of words, which are their signs, and in which the secret lay' (*ibid.*).

The application of etymology is not only Horne Tooke's chief source of explanation, it is in many respects his only one. Hence, just as a word's etymology can provide the answer to what part of speech it originally was (and therefore, in Horne Tooke's view, really is), so the meanings of prepositions, as of conjunctions, can be deduced by tracing them back to their origins, for it is Horne Tooke's (almost Platonic) claim that the meaning of any word is identical to the meaning of the original word, of which the present one is merely a corruption. Bearing this in mind, it is no wonder that he completely rejects Harris's view that prepositions have no independent meaning; on the contrary, they are 'the names of real objects' (1968:318).

Let us look at a few examples since, to his credit, Horne Tooke usually provides ample exemplification. For instance, the French preposition *chez* has allegedly no exact counterpart in any language, not because French minds operate differently from others, but simply because 'there happens not to be in any other language a similar corruption of some word corresponding precisely with CHEZ', it being 'merely a corruption of the Italian substantive CASA' (1968:300), though of course both languages are descended from Latin. Indeed, Horne Tooke goes one step further by maintaining that because of this etymological relationship 'CHEZ ... has all the same meaning in French, which CASA has in Italian' (1968:302).[79]

Equally, we are told, 'SANS' is really 'a *substantive*: and it means simply *Absence*' (1968:328). Though 'sometimes used instead of WITHOUT',[80] it is 'not an English but a French Preposition' (*ibid.*), corrupted from 'the Italian preposition *Senza* (formerly spelt *Sanza*) as in *SENZA di te*, i.e. *ASSENZA di te*' (1968:330), which in French (after omission of the case sign) becomes '*SANS toi*'. Again, Horne Tooke derives a French word from Italian and looks no further.

As far as English prepositions are concerned, Horne Tooke's method is exactly the same. Thus, for example, 'the English Preposition THOROUGH, *Thourough*, *Thorow*, *Through*, or *Thro*' [is] no other than ... the Teutonic substantive *Thuruh*' or its Gothic equivalent 'and, like them, means *Door, gate, passage*' (1968:334-5). Horne Tooke goes on to apply this observation to one of Harris's examples (i.e. 'The splendid Sun with his Beams genially warmeth through the Air the fertile Earth' – mentioned under Harris above), which he re-analyses in the following way: 'The splendid sun – JOIN his beams – genially warmeth – PASSAGE the air – the fertile earth' (1968:335). Harris's two prepositions *with*[81] and *through* are here analysed in terms of their 'underlying' (not Horne Tooke's expression) verb and noun, respectively. In another previously mentioned example, Harris distinguishes three different meanings of *from* in the sentences (a)-(c):

(a) these Figs came FROM Turky[82]
(b) that Lamp hangs FROM the Ceiling
(c) that Lamp is falling FROM the Ceiling

Horne Tooke rejects this distinction, claiming that 'FROM means merely BEGINNING', as 'it is simply the Anglo-saxon and Gothic noun' with that meaning (1968:342). Any difference in the sentence meaning of (a), (b) and (c) stems not from the preposition but from the verbs, which Horne Tooke analyses as follows (his emphasis):

'*Came* is a complex term for one species of motion.'
'*Falls* is a complex term for another species of motion.'
'*Hangs* is a complex term for a species of attachment.'

And he continues, 'It is impossible to have complex terms for each occasion of this sort. What more natural then, or more simple, than to add the signs of those ideas, viz. the word BEGINNING (which will remain always the same) and the name of the *place* (which will perpetually vary)?' (1968:343; his emphasis). In this way Horne Tooke is able to give a unified analysis of the three examples:

(a) Figs came - BEGINNING Turkey
(b) Lamp falls - BEGINNING Cieling[83]
(c) Lamp hangs - BEGINNING Cieling

and he makes the following parallel:

Turkey the *Place* of BEGINNING to come
Cieling the *Place* of BEGINNING to fall
Cieling the *Place* of BEGINNING to hang

Moreover, we are told that the same analysis applies when the reference is to 'time' rather than 'place' (1968:344-5).

In order to give a full demonstration of his unitary analysis of prepositions, Horne Tooke engages in a major *tour de force* by taking 17 examples of the preposition *for* from Greenwood and 42 from Dr Johnson (plus four as conjunction) and reducing them all to a noun with the basic meaning 'CAUSE' (1968:366-92). Needless to say, many of the 'explanations' offered are extremely subjective.

The fact that prepositions have no independent status in Horne Tooke's system enables him to be more 'generous' than some of his predecessors in assigning members to this 'class'. For example, a number of present participle forms, such as *touching*, *concerning*, *respecting*, etc., are called prepositions (1968:455). This could quite easily be justified on syntactic grounds, but Horne Tooke sees no need for any justification and simply presents it as a fact that requires no further comment.

The limitations of his method are put in perspective when he is defeated by some of the commonest simple prepositions. He admits that he cannot offer any satisfactory 'explanation and etymology of these words', i.e. *in, out, on, off, at* (1968:456). Nor does he think that such shortcomings jeopardise his theory as a whole, but as far as prepositions are concerned, one is surely entitled to have serious misgivings about any theory that purports to explain the grammar of this class in terms of one single parameter (etymology) and then fails when faced with some of its most widely used members. Horne Tooke, like other writers, must be judged on his intentions, especially since he overtly claims, in this very chapter, to be 'laying the foundation for a new theory of language' (1968:401).

It is worth noticing that a theory, such as Horne Tooke's, which treats all language development as evidence of increasing corruption, must, to be consistent, see so-called 'primitive' languages in a more favourable light than was usually done. That Horne Tooke does so is clear from the following passage, which attempts to combine this view with an explanation of the origins of prepositions (and conjunctions):

> As far as relates to ... prepositions and conjunctions, I hope it is ... pretty evident that, instead of *invention*, the *classes* of them spring from *corruption*; and that, in this respect, the Savage languages are upon an equal footing with the languages (as they are called) of *art*, except that the former are less corrupted... (1968:399; his emphasis)

It is difficult not to have very mixed feelings about Horne Tooke's achievement. On the one hand, he is a keen observer and critic of others' work, and his criticism (e.g. of Harris) is quite often justified. Furthermore, some of his integrated analyses of prepositions and their relations to verbs seem strikingly modern and are echoed in some localist theories,[84] and that he exerted considerable influence on the linguistic climate in late eighteenth and early nineteenth century England is well documented.[85]

On the other hand, his dogmatic belief in etymology as the ultimate explanation of language phenomena blinded him to other possible, and perhaps complementary, analyses, in particular to the importance of syntax, and his views on (lexical) semantics seem totally misguided. His claim that word meaning at any stage of language development (even the most recent one) is solely dependent on the meaning of the original form of a given word, is not easy to take seriously. It is also a grave flaw, in terms of his own theory, that many of his derivations are completely wrong,[86] and he never fully addresses the question of how far back in time one should go when establishing the 'origin' of a word. We have already looked at examples where Horne Tooke derives French words from Italian ones and English words from Anglo-Saxon or Gothic. But does it really stop there? After all (though we understand this better now), those languages each represent one stage of a development that stretches much further back so that any end-point must be arbitrary and decided on practical grounds, e.g. the existence of written records, or (reasonable) confidence in particular reconstructions.

Horne Tooke forms a strong contrast to most of the treatments of prepositions we have looked at so far, and his new theory (as he called it), despite its extremism and its many questionable claims, became influential in early nineteenth-century England. But by deliberately limiting his outlook to etymology (to the exclusion of other explanations) and by making numerous blunders in the actual derivations he undertakes, he falls well short of his own avowed aim of founding a new theory of language. During the decades when his 'new theory' held some sway over language studies in England, these shortcomings were often ignored (note, for instance, his profound influence on John Dalton below), but when the more solid foundations of the new Continental philological movement in the nineteenth century began to be appreciated in England, the flimsiness of Horne Tooke's system was quickly exposed and his 'theory' collapsed, leaving little trace on subsequent linguistic studies (cf. Aarsleff 1983, especially Chapters II and III).

J. Wilson (dates unknown)

J. Wilson's publication of *Fisher's Grammar Improved* (full title: *Fisher's Grammar Improved; or, an English Grammar in which Fisher's Plan is Preserved, and the Work made more perfect by Various Amendments*) in 1792 is a curious one. It is based on Anne Fisher's *A New Grammar* (later *A New Practical Grammar*) from 1750 and subsequent editions, which we examined above, and appeared fourteen years after Anne Fisher's death in 1778. The version used here is the second edition ('much improved') from 1797 (see Wilson 1797), but Wilson is placed here in accordance with the date of the first edition. Little is known of the Rev. J. Wilson other than, as stated on the title-page, he was 'Vicar of Biddulph and Master of the free grammar school in Congleton'. The reproduced Preface to the first edition is nothing more than a condensed version of Anne Fisher's Preface to *A New (Practical) Grammar*, but the Preface to the second edition is more informative and here Wilson explains some of the circumstances surrounding this grammar. For example, using the imagery of a building in need of some repair, he relates how he was almost reluctantly sucked into making more and more changes, having intended 'just to correct a few glaring Mistakes', including some points about pronunciation (1797:v). However, he also thought he ought to 'restore to Etymology such Names for the Parts of Speech, and other Terms of Art, as are generally used in other Grammars …', and not just for English (*ibid.*). This refers to Anne Fisher's rather eccentric terminology, and Wilson decides, in order to avoid confusion in learners, to use the traditional (Latin) nomenclature, e.g. 'substantives' for 'Names', 'adjectives' for 'Qualities', etc., and not to introduce anything alien to 'the Simplicity of the English Language' (1797:v-vi). Similarly, the 'Nominative Case' replaces Fisher's 'leading State'. Like others before him (cf. e.g. Ussher above), he expresses qualms about the 'Propriety of publishing a Grammar by Way of Question and Answer', but solves this through a compromise by which he keeps most of the questions, whereas 'scarce half a Dozen Answers remain unaltered in the whole Book' (1797:vii). Nevertheless, he strongly defends the view 'that it was better to correct an old Grammar, than to introduce a new one', on the grounds that 'the Number of Grammars is *already sufficiently large*; and an old one, properly corrected and kindly received, would be diminishing the Propagation of Errors, at the same Time that it was disseminating Truths' (1797:vii-viii; my emphasis). There is a good deal of humility and, perhaps, realism in this view, which is not evident in many of the previous grammars.

So what changes from Anne Fisher's *A New (Practical) Grammar* are there of relevance to us? The definition and the divisions of grammar are the same, but when it comes to the parts of speech the adjustments are striking. Not only is the terminology different; instead of four parts there are now no fewer than ten, viz. the eight from the Latin tradition plus articles and adjectives (the latter were also a separate class ('Qualities') in Fisher). However, it should be mentioned that the changes are not all due to Wilson; the title-page makes it clear that whereas the sections on Orthography and Prosody have been amended with the help of 'Walker, Sheridan, and others', those of Etymology and Syntax have benefited 'principally from Lowth'. So in a way, Wilson has blended Fisher and Lowth into a third version, but not completely uncritically since Lowth does not include participles among his (nine) word classes.

In view of the proliferation of the parts of speech from four to ten, one notices that the concept of 'particle' as a general term (for adverbs, conjunctions, prepositions and interjections) has disappeared. There are also important changes to the notion of 'case', which is now the term used universally. Where Fisher (1754 and 1762), with some satisfaction, notes that there is only one case in English nouns ('Names'), though two in pronouns ('Relative Names'), Wilson takes the – some may think retrograde – step of bringing nouns in line with pronouns in this respect. He is aware, though, that it is controversial to have both nominative *book* and accusative *book*, as well as genitive *book's* (1797:54), for in a footnote on the same page he admits that '[a]dopting an Accusative Case among the Substantives may perhaps be censured as superfluous', but defends his decision by pointing out that 'its Use, when we come to governing Words, is so distinct from the Nominative, that it seems worth while to *assume* it here, as it must be used in the Pronouns' (my emphasis). This may be explained by Wilson opting for function rather than form in an attempt to treat 'substantives' and pronouns equally in terms of case, but his uneasiness also shows how far mainstream English grammar had come from being automatically described in the same terms as Latin, and it is a departure from Lowth's *Short Introduction*, which Wilson by his own admission is indebted to.

The actual section on prepositions under 'Etymology' is a faithful copy of Fisher's previous treatment, with the one addition that when prepositions are 'subjoined to Verbs ... having no other Word depending upon them [i.e. being governed by them] they become Adverbs' (1797:82). The two examples provided – 'to make over, to set in' – show that Wilson is talking about prepositions as part of (present-day) phrasal verbs. Fisher's 'Rule VII' (or VIII in the 1754 and later editions) is here 'Rule IX', but only the first two lines are reproduced stating that '[p]repositions will have an Accusative Case after them' (with the afore-mentioned change in the name of the case), not those where she deals with the alternation between the function of adverb and preposition (see under Fisher above). Like most others, Wilson sees *to* as a preposition when used in front of an infinitive (1797:101, 106). We may also note that Wilson seems to have scrutinised Fisher's examples of 'Bad English', which he has partly increased and partly changed, so that the mysteriously 'wrong' sentence, 'They came to me', has disappeared, the nearest equivalent being the now truly incorrect 'He came with I' (1797:116-17).

Wilson's 'Improvement' shows, in the first place, the lengthy popularity of Fisher's grammar, but also that he cannot have been very impressed with the English grammars that appeared in the intervening decades, although he does admit to using Lowth for some of his amendments. As we saw, Wilson's original intention 'just to correct a few glaring Mistakes' soon gave way to the need for more extensive amendments, but one cannot help feeling that the outcome is an uneasy compromise between simply copy-editing Fisher's grammar and presenting something new. For that reason, Wilson's contribution to English grammar must be said to be limited, but the fact that he thought this particular grammar worthy of an update as well as the changes that he made to it are nevertheless points of some interest at the threshold of the nineteenth century.

Lindley Murray (1745-1826)
With Lindley Murray we have reached one of the true heavyweights of English grammar writing, as his *English Grammar* from 1795 (see Murray 1968) was not only one of the last English grammars of the eighteenth century but also by far the most influential one for several decades of the nineteenth. Born in America, Murray moved to England in 1784 and his *Grammar*, including an abridgment of it first published in 1797, became widely regarded as the model of a grammar for many years to come. In 1808 it was expanded into a two-volume work, and all three texts are found in more than three hundred editions (cf. 1968:Note). It says something both about Murray's perceived exemplary character and the long-standing fame of his *Grammar* that, long after his death, he should still be considered the soul of respectability in Dickens's *The Old Curiosity Shop* (1841) and his work, by implication, recommended reading. This is seen in the novel when the waxworks proprietor, Mrs Jarley, needs to set a good example for young ladies from boarding-schools:

> And these audiences were of a very superior description, including a great many young ladies' boarding-schools, whose favour Mrs. Jarley had been at great pains to conciliate, by altering the face and costume of Mr. Grimaldi as clown *to represent Mr. Lindley Murray as he appeared when engaged in the composition of his English Grammar* … (Dickens 1997:225; my emphasis)[87]

The longevity of Murray's *Grammar* is not a result of it being particularly original or innovative in its content. On the contrary, it is heavily influenced by previous presentations, not least by Lowth's *Short Introduction* more than thirty years earlier (cf. 1968:Note). That Murray was well aware of this fact is evident from his Introduction where he states that precisely because of the works of all his predecessors, all that can be 'expected from a new compilation' is 'a careful selection of the most useful matter, and some degree of improvement in the mode of adapting it to the understanding, and the gradual progress of learners' (1968:iii). This pedagogical aim pervades Murray's writing, and the clarity with which he presents his material is almost certainly the reason for the immense and prolonged popularity of the work, on both sides of the Atlantic Ocean.

Murray's traditional approach begins with the definition of grammar as 'the art of speaking and writing the English language with propriety' and the division into the customary four parts (1968:1). Of these, 'Etymology' deals with 'the sorts of words, or, as they are commonly called, Parts of Speech', and Murray lists the nine classes that are still found in many modern grammars, viz. 'the Article, the Substantive or Noun, the Pronoun, the Adjective, the Verb, the Adverb, the Preposition, the Conjunction, and the Interjection' (1968:19). There can be no doubt that Murray's ever increasing authority, due to the popularity of his *Grammar*, did much to 'canonise' these classes so that from this time onwards it is rare to find participles included and adjectives and articles excluded, which are really the only changes from the traditional Latin categories.

The list is followed by very short preliminary definitions of each part of speech. Of the preposition it is said that it 'is set chiefly before nouns and pronouns, to connect them with other words, and to shew their relation to those words', with the addition that a 'preposition may be known by its admitting after it a personal pronoun, in the objective case', e.g. 'with *him*', 'for *her*', 'to *them*' (1968:20-21). Indeed, when it comes to case, Murray shows his 'modern' credentials by arguing that English has two cases in nouns (nominative and possessive, or genitive) and three in pronouns (1968:27, 31). He rejects the argument made by many of his predecessors that prepositions in English can govern different cases (as in Greek and Latin) and states confidently that case means 'only the variation of a noun or pronoun, by termination or within itself' (1968:28). However, this confidence rests on the authority of three learned doctors, i.e. Lowth, Johnson and Priestley, to whom Murray clearly defers and whose names he believes 'are sufficient to decide this point' (*ibid.*). This is a good demonstration of Murray's acute awareness of the tradition which he is happy to be part of, but also of the somewhat derivative nature of his *Grammar*.

Later there is a longer section on prepositions (1968:77-9), where Murray repeats his definition from earlier and then looks at different aspects of prepositional use. First, he distinguishes separable from inseparable prepositions. The former are simply 'those which may be used separate from other words'; he mentions *above, about, over, under, at, after, with* as examples, but adds that 'some of these are sometimes conjoined with other words, as in 'overtake, undertake, afterward' (1968:77). The inseparable prepositions, on the other hand, 'are used only in the composition of words' and they are exemplified by *be, fore, mis*; in other words, prefixes, hardly prepositions.

Concerning prepositions and case he merely refers the reader back to his previous statement. He mentions in passing that '[t]he generality of [prepositions] originally denoted the relation of place, but they are now used to express other relations' (1968:77-8) and lists thirty examples. It is not difficult to guess where he got the idea from for this statement; both Priestley and Lowth have a lot more to say about the same development. He makes some semantic comments about a few of these prepositions; for instance, he observes the asymmetry between *within* and *without*. Thus *within* is said to relate 'to something comprehended in any place or time' (1968:79), and although at first he claims that '[t]he signification of *without* is opposite to that of *within*', he acknowledges that 'it is more frequently opposed to *with*', e.g. in 'You may go *without* me' (*ibid.*).

On the same page of this short section, Murray makes two further, related points about prepositions. He notes that '[s]ome of the prepositions have the appearance of conjunctions', as in '*After* their prisons were thrown open,' and '*Before* I die,' but adds that 'if the noun *time*, which is understood, be added, they will lose their conjunctive form', e.g. 'After [the time when] their prisons …'. Surely he means function rather than 'form'.

A similar point is raised concerning prepositions and adverbs, and in almost identical words: 'The prepositions *after, before, above, beneath*, and several others, sometimes appear to be adverbs', e.g. in 'They had their reward soon *after*' and 'He died not long *before*'. But this, too, comes with a rider, viz. 'if the nouns *time* and *place* be added, they will lose their adverbial form', as seen in 'He died not long *before that time*'. Here the same comment about 'form' applies as above.

Like some of his predecessors, Murray does not claim that the relevant words *are* conjunctions or adverbs, respectively; they merely 'have the appearance' or 'appear to be' one or the other. It is also significant that when a noun (phrase) is inserted, they will 'lose their conjunctive [or adverbial] form' (for 'form' again read function). It is therefore not clear whether Murray wants to contend that an actual shift of class has taken place in his examples, or whether it just has the semblance of it. His wording seems to suggest the latter.

However, the interconnection between conjunctions and prepositions appears to be stronger than the one between adverbs and prepositions, and it does not end there. In the section on 'Conjunctions', Murray suddenly changes tack by suggesting that these two parts of speech may be elements of a higher class, namely as 'Connectives'. This argument is related to the notion of 'discourse', which shows that Murray is prepared to look beyond the narrow word class boundaries in setting up what he must regard as a new functional class. The passage is important enough to quote in full:

> Conjunctions and prepositions are words essential to discourse, and more so than the greatest part of adverbs. They form *that class of words called Connectives*, without which there could be no language; and serve to express the relations which things bear to one another, their mutual influence, dependencies, and coherence; thereby joining words together into intelligible and significant propositions. (1968:81; my emphasis)

Before we get carried away, it should be pointed out that this is not an original idea, but nor is it commonplace terminology. As it stands, it is very similar to the proposal made by James Harris (see above) for these two classes, but Murray was not forced to accept it. That he does so, at least suggests that Murray is not a traditionalist in all respects.[88]

The chapter on syntax is a long one (1968:86-145). It is divided into 'Rules', and 'Rule XVII' deals with prepositions (1968:121-6). The 'Rules' themselves are printed in 'normal' font size and the following exemplification in 'smaller letters', as explained in Murray's 'Introduction' (1968:iv). As a consequence, the whole of 'Rule XVII', apart from the first five lines, is written in small font size. The 'Rule' itself is very simple: 'Prepositions govern the objective case', and some examples are provided. In view of Murray's previous statement about prepositions and case, it is only natural that all but one of these show the preposition governing a personal pronoun (in the 'objective case'); what is less expected is that there is also an example of a noun as prepositional complement, namely the second prepositional phrase in his last example, which is italicised just like all the others: 'Strength of mind is *with them* that are pure *in heart*' (1968:122). It carries no explanation, but from a pedagogical viewpoint it is an unfortunate example.

In the rest of this section Murray deals with a number of constructions relevant for prepositions. First, he revisits the case issue by mentioning that 'the nominative case' is sometimes 'used instead of the objective' (1968:122), all the examples being of interrogative clauses (direct or indirect questions) with the preposition placed at the end (i.e. stranded), e.g. 'Who servest thou under?' and 'We are still much at a loss who civil power belongs to'. But for Murray this is clearly going too far since he comments: 'In all these places it ought to be *whom*' (*ibid.*; his emphasis). He thus stops short of Fell's purely descriptive approach in this area.

Afterwards Murray seems to comment on the same construction but with the pronoun in the objective case, as he recommends, and compares it with examples where the preposition precedes the interrogative, such as 'Whom wilt thou give it to?' versus '*To whom* wilt thou give it?' (*ibid.*; his emphasis). However, both this entire paragraph and the following one on verbs and prepositions, as well as the second one after that, are lifted verbatim from Lowth's account in *A Short Introduction*. There are only two minor changes: (a) 'Horace' is changed to 'He' in one of the examples, thus making it more general; and (b), far more interestingly, in the first clause of explanation after these examples Murray changes Lowth's statement, 'This is an Idiom which our language is strongly inclined to' (see Lowth above), to the more formal, 'This is an Idiom *to which* our language is strongly inclined' (*ibid.*; my emphasis), which in view of his stated preference is at least consistent.

We have previously seen examples of blatant plagiarism of this kind with little or no acknowledgement (e.g. in Wharton, Fisher and Ussher, but also Kirkby, Martin and even Dr Johnson committed this offence), and it is certainly uncomfortable in this day and age to observe as important a person as Murray engaging in it, despite general references to Lowth and others elsewhere in the *Grammar*, but times and attitudes have changed since then, so perhaps we should not judge it too severely. However, it would have been interesting to hear Murray's own individual view on these issues (if he had one). We can only surmise that when writing this account Murray must have had Lowth's book lying open next to him, just as Gibbon had Kirkby's works on his desk.[89]

The rest of Murray's points about prepositions can be summed up briefly. He has a prescriptive streak and condemns the construction when the preposition is separated 'from its noun, in order to connect different prepositions with the same noun', as in 'To suppose the zodiac and planets to be efficient *of*, and antecedent *to*, themselves', in all but legal language 'where fullness and exactness or expression must take place of every other consideration', but anywhere else this is said to be 'always inelegant, and should never be admitted' (1968:123).

When Murray says that '[d]ifferent relations, and different senses, must be expressed by different prepositions, though in conjunction with the same verb or adjective' (*ibid.*), it is far less obvious than it sounds. One example that illustrates this is, 'To converse *with* a person, *upon* a subject, *in* a house', but he also makes the subtle observation that we say '"We are disappointed *of* a thing" when we cannot get it, and "disappointed *in* it" when we have it but find that it does not come up to our expectations' (*ibid.*; his emphasis). This was a useful contribution to the semantics of prepositions at the time, and more helpful than when he adds that 'two prepositions must be improper in the same construction, and in the same sentence', offering as an example, 'The combat *between* thirty Britons *against* twenty English' (*ibid.*; his emphasis). It is unclear what Murray is getting at here, since the same sentence can easily contain several prepositions. If he wants to exclude, for instance, time and place or other types of PPs, he should have said so.

On the other hand, we are told, there are situations where 'it is impossible to say to which of two prepositions the preference is to be given, as both are used promiscuously, and custom has not decided in favour of either of them'. This is apparently the case with the alternative options in 'expert *at/in* a thing' and 'disapproved *of/by* a person' (*ibid.*; my emphasis).

Murray's last general point is that the same preposition is often used when 'subjoined' to a verb and to the noun derived from the verb, as in 'John shewing the same disposition *to* tyranny over his subjects' compared with '… *to* tyrannise over his subjects' (*ibid.*; his emphasis). Unfortunately, *to* is not the best preposition to use for such an illustration since it is identical with the infinitive marker *to* and thus subject to ambiguity. (Nowadays, we distinguish between the use of the preposition *to* before a gerund (in *-ing*) (e.g. 'I look forward *to meeting* you') and *to* as an infinitive marker but, as we have seen in a number of cases, that distinction was not generally made in the eighteenth century.) In the last three pages of his discussion Murray focuses on particular uses of certain prepositions.

The long-lasting success of Murray's *Grammar* was probably due to the fact that it was *not* innovative but represented a practice of grammar writing that gradually crystallised into an accepted system towards the end of the eighteenth century and which was respectful of traditional views and yet prepared to analyse the English language on its own terms. Seen in this light, his occasional over-reliance on some of his predecessors only helped to establish and reinforce a view on the parts of speech (and, indeed, on English grammar in general) that lasted for quite a long time.

(iv) *One Nineteenth-Century Grammar*

John Dalton (1766-1844)
John Dalton was above all an eminent scientist whose main fields were meteorology and chemistry. It was not least his work with weather conditions that led to his ground-breaking theory of atoms and the establishment of the first table of atomic weights. But he also dappled in studies of the English language. His *Elements of English Grammar* from 1801 (see Dalton 1801) has the subtitle, 'or A New System of Grammatical Instruction for the Use of Schools & Academies', and on the title-page he is presented as 'Teacher of the Mathematics and Natural Philosophy, and Secretary to the Literary and Philosophical Society, Manchester'. The book is dedicated to 'John Horne Tooke, M.P., Author of … The Diversions of Purley', whom Dalton clearly admired very much, but it appears from his 'Preliminary Observations' that although he has 'drawn a great deal from *one source* [i.e.

Horne Tooke] … I have not rested satisfied with the *ipse dixit* of the Author of *The Diversions of Purley*, when the time and opportunity afforded me means of confirmation and enquiry' (1801:xii; his emphasis). Here Dalton also introduces some fundamental ideas about the major word classes and concludes his introductory section with the observation that 'as language is the medium through which instruction in every science, and knowledge in general, must chiefly be communicated, an attention to its principles is of primary importance in every system of education' (1801:xiii). If this is his justification for writing a new grammar, his decision is only strengthened by having 'long thought that elementary books on Grammar were more remarkably defective than others' (*ibid.*). He mentions no names, but ends by declaring that he would welcome 'good natured criticism' for his own efforts in the field.

After a fairly brief 'Introduction' that discusses 'the Origins of Ideas; and their Relation to Language', clearly influenced by Locke, he turns immediately to 'Etymology', which he understands as the changes and derivations of the parts of speech, while grammar itself is given the following, very general definition: 'the art of expressing a person's thoughts in a Language according to approved custom' (1801:5). This statement also has clear Lockean overtones, and even at the time few can have found it very illuminating. For Dalton, and with more than a nod to Horne Tooke, only two parts of speech are 'essentially *necessary* to communicate our thoughts', viz. nouns and verbs, though he does accept that 'most Languages in time acquire words by composition, abbreviation, and other means' and that these can be considered to form separate classes, but not without stressing 'their derivation from the primitive parts of speech [i.e. nouns and verbs]' (*ibid.*). He therefore concludes that words can be divided into the following 'sorts':

1. Nouns, subdivided into: substantive, adjective and interjective [i.e. interjections];
2. Pronouns, subdivided into: substantive and adjective;
3. Verbs, including the verb substantive *to be* and participles;
4. Adverbs;
5. Conjunctions;
6. Prepositions.

Murray's long-lasting influence on later grammarians, not least in consolidating the acceptance of nine word classes, was mentioned above, but his division apparently had no effect on Dalton. By this time, it was a fairly outdated minority view still to include adjectives under nouns, but to place interjections there as well was highly unusual. Any thoughts of regarding the articles as a separate part are dismissed, mainly on the grounds that *a(n)* and *the* are too similar to *one* and *that*, respectively, to make any clear distinction. Consequently, if they were given the status of an independent class, so too should *one* (*two*, *three*, etc.) and *this*, *that*, etc. Instead, Dalton places them under adjectives and even suggests a subgroup of 'Definitives' (1801:i-ii) which is not far removed from present-day 'determiners'. Not surprisingly, Dalton's division into word classes had no great impact.

Dalton's early, brief definition of prepositions owes much to Horne Tooke's claim that nouns and verbs are the only two principal parts of speech, for after saying that prepositions 'are words considered as *connecting words to sentences*' (which sounds very dubious), he adds that they 'are [note the existential verb!] *substantives, adjectives, verbs* or *participles*, mostly abbreviated or corrupted by time, so as to have lost some of the regular forms of construction of such parts of speech, which has caused them to be considered as *indeclinable*' (1801:9; his emphasis). It is difficult to see what relevance this has for English grammar around 1800, even if it were true, but many of the most basic and simple prepositions cannot, with any confidence, be traced back to words of the classes mentioned.

Chapter VI of Part I is devoted to prepositions and here Dalton's 'definition' is no less unusual. He begins by re-stating his former pronouncement in slightly different terms: 'The character of Prepositions is, to be placed before other words, which they connect with sentences' (1801:82), but he then goes on to argue that prepositions are very similar to conjunctions and that the only difference between them is that prepositions 'connect one or more *words* to a sentence', while conjunctions 'connect one *sentence* to another' (1801:84; his emphasis). The first definition sounds rather vague, but is exemplified a little later. The rest of Chapter VI consists of an alphabetical list of prepositions, in most cases with some basic etymological information taken from H.T. (i.e. Horne Tooke) about their – quite often – (Anglo-)

Saxon or Gothic origins, which again shows how obsessed Dalton, like his 'master', is with etymology at the expense of modern usage. His term 'corrupt', e.g. used about *since* ('a very corrupt abbreviation', 1801:87), is symptomatic in this respect.

Under the section 'Rules for the Position of words', 'Rule VIII' reiterates the common observation that prepositions are 'placed *before* the nouns they govern' (1801:99); no other word classes are mentioned. He does point out, though, that '[t]he definitives *this, that, which, what*, and the pronoun *who* frequently precede their prepositions', as in 'I know not *whom* you are speaking *of*' and '*What* is he waiting *for?*'. Since these constructions are 'common with the best writers', they are grammatical, but placing the preposition before its complement would in these cases 'be equally eligible' (*ibid.*). This is another example of the increasing tolerance towards preposition stranding in interrogative and relative clauses.

Finally, in continuation of the point above, Dalton has a short section called 'Words that are both Conjunctions and Prepositions' and lists as members of this group: *and, but* (*be-out*), *else, for, since, till, without, yet* (1801:106-7). Some of these are uncontroversial, but a few do not seem much like prepositions, so it is worth looking at the examples given for them as prepositions.

In 'John *and* [add] Jane are a handsome couple', '[add]' is part of Dalton's example, presumably intended as an explanation. However, it is difficult to reconcile this (or most examples with prepositions) with his 'rule' that prepositions 'connect one or more *words* to a sentence'. We would normally say that, as a conjunction, *and* can combine clauses of the same type (or sentences, to use the then terminology) as well as combine words/phrases of the same kind within a clause. It is quite outlandish to claim that *and* is a preposition in the latter usage (and it did not catch on either).

Another example involves *else* as a preposition: 'He would have Sarah and none *else* [i.e. none *dismiss* Sarah, or *except* S.]'. Again the square bracket is included as an explanation and it shows how, like Horne Tooke, Dalton focuses on the (perceived) etymology of the word, for on the syntactic evidence it is very hard to see *else* as a preposition.

A third example concerns *yet* as a preposition: '*Yet* a little while; that is, "*Get* a little time"'. This is mystifying. The implication seems to be that (due to their similar word form?) *yet* and *get* are somehow synonyms and thus interchangeable, or that they derive from the same word.

Added to our previous observations, examples like these three make it difficult to take Dalton seriously as a grammarian. However, he can also be quite perceptive in his observations, for example when he informs us that *without* as a conjunction is obsolete, except in vulgar speech in Scotland and the North of England. Despite the derogative label, this sounds rather plausible as a late stage in the syntactic development and use of this word.

Although, at first glance, it may look as if Dalton is attempting something new, he proves to be virtually in thrall to the views of Horne Tooke which, although fashionable for a while in some circles, left no trace on grammar writing in the later part of the nineteenth century. Dalton was a brilliant scientist, but it was Murray's type of grammar, not Dalton's, and the tradition that Murray represented that came to dominate the field of English grammar up to, and even into, the twentieth century.

V. Summary

This study began with the earliest Greek divisions into sentence elements, as found in Plato and Aristotle. The emerging interest in the parts of speech was further developed by the Stoics, who among other things seem to have been the first to recognise prepositions as a separate category. By the time of the first century BC, the Alexandrians had established a system of eight classes (though there were individual variations), which was generally adopted by the Romans, except that they substituted the interjection for the article since the latter was non-existent in Latin. There is some overlap between the Greek and Roman tradition, with Varro representing an early, highly original if somewhat idiosyncratic, version of Roman linguistics and Apollonius Dyscolus (two centuries later) expressing the summation of the Greek contribution to the classical period. Among the later Roman grammarians, Donatus and Priscian stood out and became the supreme authorities in Western European grammatical studies throughout the Middle Ages (though from our perspective Apollonius Dyscolus is arguably more interesting). Their respective definitions of the parts of speech, including prepositions, generated many commentaries and modifications, and from the eleventh century onwards also alternative proposals, especially those devised by the group of 'Speculative Grammarians' known as the Modistae, but at no stage could the Roman masters be ignored. Even so, the Modistae presented their own treatments of the parts of speech, including prepositions, set within a highly elaborate and theoretical scheme that crumbled before the middle of the fourteenth century.

If the Modistae had shown the way by challenging the long tradition of the late Roman grammarians, the Renaissance witnessed an even more radical departure from the system handed down from antiquity. Several of the most original contributors to the discussion of the parts of speech and to the analysis of language in general now turned their attention to the hitherto ignored and often despised vernacular languages and, in a complete break with tradition, some of them even wrote their studies *in* these vernaculars. Grammarians such as Peter Ramus, Sanctius and Robert Estienne, together with a number of Italians throughout the sixteenth century, introduced ideas and practices into language analysis which became very influential and offered new and refreshing approaches to the examination of the parts of speech and in some cases to prepositions in particular. But not all work was innovative. Some expositions faithfully followed the established Latin tradition, and for the history of English grammatical writing none was more significant because of the long shadow that it cast than Lily's grammar, which received royal approval and thus became compulsory teaching material to generations of schoolboys learning Latin in the new grammar schools. And not only that; the whole concept of grammar was for many, even in the post-Renaissance period, synonymous with Latin grammar. Even when grammars of the vernaculars – in our case, the English language – began to appear, the Latin categories (including the case system) remained the model for many, and only gradually did the pendulum swing in favour of more independent presentations. Many of these early presentations are therefore good examples of what Jespersen calls 'squinting grammar', defined as 'grammar squinting at translations in other languages or at other constructions in the same language – instead of looking straight before one, as one should always try to do' (Jespersen 1933(b):46; reprinted in Jespersen 1933(c):345).[1] There was certainly a lot of 'squinting' at Latin in seventeenth and eighteenth century English grammars.

Although there had been previous examples of writings about language in English, notably Aelfric's instruction on Latin in Old English, it was not until the end of the sixteenth century that what is now recognised as the first genuinely English grammar (i.e. a description of the English language and in this case also written in English) emerged, in the shape of Bullokar's *Bref Grammar for English* from 1586. This, therefore, marks the beginning of our examination of fifty texts on English grammar (in a wide sense) over a period of more than two centuries from Bullokar to Dalton (1801). They do not by any means constitute a linear development, but it is nevertheless possible to deduce some trends.

At the beginning of Chapter IV, we looked at Michael's (1970) division into the following four different types of word-class system of the 273 English grammars up to 1801 that he operates with. It is reproduced here for convenience:

(i)   Latin systems
(ii) modified systems before 1700
(iii) vernacular systems
(iv) modified systems after 1700

Michael discusses and elaborates on these distinctions in Chapter 8 of his book (1970: 201-80) and we can summarise his characterisation of each of them in (a)-(d) below (cf. Michael 1970:210):

(a) Latin systems (as exemplified by Lily) may have 'minor variations', but these are 'often unwitting' and show no wish to change or reform the system. (b) The modified systems before 1700 can 'vary greatly' and include systems as different from the canonical Latin system as those by Wilkins and Dalgarno (the latter having only one recognised part of speech). Yet they differ from (c) the vernacular systems partly by preceding them, and partly by not containing the 'four primary parts of speech' (substantive, adjective, verb, particle) that mark these later systems. Finally, (d) the modified systems after 1700 display modifications introduced after the vernacular systems began to appear but without using 'their distinctive fourfold classification'.

Before I comment on the accuracy of this division, let us first see how the fifty 'grammars' in our study fit into the four systems. (Only systems exemplified in our material are mentioned; in each case the following bracket contains the number of separate parts of speech recognised in the scheme followed by the abbreviated names of these parts; note that Part. = Participle.) Michael's numbering is consecutive with regard to the four major types of system. The list below is divided into centuries, and authors' names are given in chronological order:

I. *Latin Systems*

Latin System 1 (8: N (Adj., Art.), Pron., V, Part., Adv., Conj., Prep., Int.)
16th C.: Bullokar
17th C.: Poole, Wharton, Lye, Lewis, Miege, Clare, Aickin
18th C.: Sheridan, Dilworth

Latin System 3 (7: N (Adj., Art., Pron.), V, Part., Adv., Conj., Prep., Int.)
17th C.: Hewes

Latin System 4 (9: N (Adj.), Pron., Art., V, Part., Adv., Conj., Prep., Int.)
17th C.: Jonson
18th C.: Ward, Fenning

Latin System 7 (8: N (Adj. (incl. Art.)), Pron., V, Part., Adv., Conj., Prep., Int.)
(Note that compared with Latin System 1, it is the Adj. here that includes the Art.)
18th C.: Greenwood, Duncan, Buchanan

Latin System 8 (8: N (Adj.), Pron., Art., V, Part., Adv. (incl. Int.), Conj., Prep.)
18th C.: Maittaire

Latin System 9 (10: Subst., Adj., Pron., Art., V, Part., Adv., Conj., Prep., Int.)
18th C.: Ash, Wilson

Latin System 10 (9: Subst., Adj., Pron., Art., V (Part.), Adv., Conj., Prep., Int.)
18th C.: Dr Johnson, Lowth, Fell, Ussher, Murray

Latin System 11 (8: Subst., Adj. (Art., Part.), Pron., V, Adv., Conj., Prep., Int.)
18th C.: Collyer

Latin System 15 (8: Subst., Adj. (Art.), Pron., V (Part.), Adv., Conj., Prep., Int.)
18th C.: Priestley, Elphinston

Latin System 20 (6: N (Int., Adj. (incl. Art.)), Pron., V (Part.), Adv., Conj., Prep.)
19th C.: Dalton

II. *Modified Systems before 1700*

Modified System (bef. 1700) 21 (5: N (Adj., incl. Art.), Pron., V (Part.), Adv. (incl. Prep., Int.), Conj.)
16th C.: Greaves

Modified System (bef. 1700) 22 (3: N (Pron.), V (Part.), Particle (Adv., Conj., Prep., Int., Art.)
17th C.: Gill

Modified System (bef. 1700) 23 (4: N (Art. w/Subst.; Pron.), V (Part.), Adv. (Conj., Int.), Prep.)
17th C.: Butler

Modified System (bef. 1700) 24 (3: Words of Action, of Help, of Quality)
17th C.: Lodowyck

Modified System (bef. 1700) 25 (9: Subst., Adj., Pron., Art., V (Part.), Adv., Conj., Prep., Int. – the last four as particle?)
17th C.: Wallis

Modified System (bef. 1700) 26 (1: N – as the only part of speech)
17th C.: Dalgarno

Modified System (bef. 1700) 27 (3 major categories: Integral (N (Adj., incl. Part.), V (derived Adv.); Grammatical Particle (Copula, Substitutive Particle (Pron., Int.), Connective Particle (Prep., Art.), Other Particles (underived Adv., Conj.)); Cross-categories)
17th C.: Wilkins

Modified System (bef. 1700) 28 (5: N (Art., Prep. and Pron. w/ Subst., Adj. (incl. Part.)), V, Adv., Conj., Int.)
17th C.: Cooper

III. *Vernacular Systems*

Vernacular System 31 (4: Subst. (1st/2nd pers. Pron.), Adj. (3rd pers. Pron.), V (Part.), Particle (Adv., Conj., Prep.))
17th C.: Lane

Vernacular System 33 (4: Subst. (Pron.), Adj. (Art., Part.), V, Particle (Adv. (incl. Conj., Prep., Int.)))
18th C.: Gildon & Brightland

Vernacular System 35 (4: Subst. (Art. (incl. Pron.), Adj., V (Part.), Particle (Adv., Conj., Prep., Int.))
18th C.: Gough

Vernacular System 36 (4: Subst. (Pron.), Adj. (Art.), V (Part.), Particle (Adv., Conj., Prep., Int.))
18th C.: Fisher

IV. *Modified Systems after 1700*

Modified System (after 1700) 42 (3: N (Pron., Part.), V, Particle[2] (Art., Adv., Conj., Prep., Int.))
18th C.: Jones

Modified System (after 1700) 43 (3: Subst. (Pron.), Adjunctive (Adj. (incl. Art.), V (incl. Part.)), Particle (Adv., Conj., Prep., Int.))
18th C.: Kirkby

Modified System (after 1700) 44 (4: Subst. (Pron.), Attributive (V, Adj., Part., Adv. (incl. Int.)), Definitive (Art.), Conjunctive (Conj., Prep.))
18th C.: Harris

Modified System (after 1700) 45 (4: N (Pron.), V (Part.), Adv., Particle (Conj., Prep. (incl. Art.), Int.))
18th C.: Martin

Modified System (after 1700) 46 (3: N (Pron. (incl. Art.)), V (Part.), Particle (Adv., Conj., Prep., Int.))
18th C.: Bayly

Modified System (after 1700) 51 (2: Subst., V)
18th C.: Horne Tooke

(This survey comprises 47 of the 50 authors analysed in Chapter IV; the last three – Walker, Locke and Richard Johnson – do not figure in Michael (1970) for various reasons.)

Such an overview has the advantage that it can establish at a glance at least the superficial status of prepositions as a part of speech during this period. The survey shows that out of the 47 of our grammatical texts appearing in Michael (1970), 31 recognise prepositions as a primary part of speech, namely all the writers deemed to follow one of the Latin systems plus Butler and Wallis (though the latter's system is not entirely clear). To these we should add R. Johnson (not in Michael's survey), while Walker is difficult to categorise, due to the nature of his work, and so is Locke. The individual treatments display some variety in their categorisation. Eight of them (Gill, Lane, Kirkby, Martin, Fisher, Jones, Gough and Bayly) make prepositions part of 'particles', though Martin is far from clear on this point, but Butler and Locke also use this term, as does Walker, of course, given the title of his work, even if his definition leaves much to be desired. Greaves includes prepositions under adverbs; Cooper places them under 'noun substantives' as a kind of 'adnomen', without using the term; Lodowyck has them as 'Words of Help', and Gildon & Brightland as part of 'Manner of Words', whereas Dalgarno and Horne Tooke only recognise one and two word classes, respectively. There is also some variation in the terminology used about this word class. Thus for Wilkins a preposition is a 'connexive particle', for Gildon & Brightland (and, following them, Collyer) it is a 'fore-plac'd word', and for Harris (together with conjunctions) a 'connective' (not 'conjunctive', as Michael (1970:264) writes), while Murray partly emulates Harris in this.

Nevertheless, Michael's division raises some questions about his groupings, above all about how one defines a vernacular system or, to phrase it differently, how much does a system have to deviate from the canonical Latin system in order to be considered vernacular? Michael sees vernacular systems as 'deliberate modifications of the Latin systems, which they profess to reform' and claims that 'they are closely associated with the reforming movement which sought to give English a grammar in its own right' (1970:210). In practice, the vernacular systems are said to 'agree in proposing four primary parts of speech (substantive, adjective, verb, particle)', but to 'vary in their distribution of the secondary parts' (*ibid.*) and the 'reforming movement' is further pursued in his Chapter 17 ('Protest and Acceptance', 1970:490-518).

But here is a snag. If a system is devised purely based on a consideration of English grammar, which happens with increasing frequency in the eighteenth century, it is quite easy to justify making adjectives (which in Latin-inspired systems are invariably a sub-category of nouns) an independent class and perhaps articles, too, while there seem to be no valid arguments for keeping participles as a class in their own right. But what about a class of particles? Is it really more natural to create such a class for English than it is for Latin, and what items should it include? Why cannot a system that substitutes adjectives for participles and even adds articles – leaving all other classes as they were in the Latin-based system – be considered a vernacular system (i.e. one set up on the basis of a close analysis of English)? It seems to have as much right to be called a vernacular system as one that includes a general class of particles (and perhaps even no articles). As usual with such definitions, the devil is in the detail. After all, the system just referred to (with adjectives instead of participles, and with or without articles; with articles, for example, in Murray's influential 9-part scheme from 1795) did indeed become the standard system, at least until quite recently, and is still widely taught in schools. Is it therefore reasonable to argue that technically this is *not* a vernacular system? It may of course be a question of terms; a modified 'traditional' system at least seems a better choice than a modified 'Latin' system, but why can it not be regarded as a vernacular system? As far as I can see, Michael has no answers to these questions, and the usefulness of the schemes set out above should be judged against this background.

Returning to our examination of English grammars, a large percentage of the writers were either teachers or had some kind of attachments to schools, academies, universities, etc., and many of the grammars analysed in Chapter IV are therefore first and foremost pedagogical works, written for teaching purposes and often for use in the very schools where the authors were employed, or in private education.[3] Many of these institutions are boys' grammar schools, but writers from Lane to Ussher increasingly mention that their grammars are also intended for the education of girls; indeed, in Ussher's case it is the primary aim, as it is for some of the women writers mentioned below. A number of these grammars for use in teaching, from Clare onwards, employ a question-and-answer structure which can help enhance the didactic purpose, but which may also provoke the scathing sarcasm and disdain for dissenting views that we find in Horne Tooke's presentation. However, a school attachment is not necessary for a pedagogical slant, as demonstrated by Wallis and some of the later writers inspired by him. On the other hand, some of the examined works display very different approaches to the analysis of language, notably the philosophical, universal grammars, such as those by Lodowyck, Dalgarno, Wilkins, Harris, Priestley, Horne Tooke and others (cf. Göbels 1999). In some respects, the latter types follow in the footsteps of the Speculative Grammarians of the late Middle Ages. These two contrasting strains of grammar writing existed and developed side by side during the more than two centuries that our time-frame spans.

Another dichotomy represented in our selection is that of a prescriptive versus a descriptive attitude to grammar writing. In general, the eighteenth century is associated with the rise of prescriptivism (and even proscriptive practices) and Lowth, in particular, has long been seen as the instigator and lynchpin (for some, the 'villain') of this approach to English grammar (cf. the most recent study of Lowth and prescriptivism in Tieken-Boon van Ostade 2011 and see Chapter IV note 62 above). According to this view, there is a direct line from Lowth to Murray since the latter (who borrowed extensively from Lowth and others) is also regarded by many as a prescriptivist (cf. Tieken-Boon van Ostade 1996). However, as we have seen, Lowth is not especially prescriptive when it comes to, for instance, preposition stranding – one of the classic bastions of prescriptivism – as he expresses preferences rather than 'laying down the law'. At the other end of the scale we find Priestley and especially Fell as representatives of descriptivism, though they do not practice what they preach in every instance. The 'battle' between prescriptive and descriptive grammars is therefore not always as clear-cut as some will have us believe, so a number of grammars that are generally regarded as embracing one or the other approach may present a more balanced picture in their dealing with specific issues.

It is undeniable that some of the texts under consideration contribute more – and in some cases, infinitely more – than others to the view on prepositions and prepositional use; one need only compare the richness of data in writers such as Wallis, Wilkins, Harris, Lowth, Elphinston and Ward, to name but the most obvious examples, compared with the comparative lack of information in the works of e.g. Poole, Wharton, Lye, Sheridan and Jones. Nevertheless, the latter authors are representative of a certain branch of the grammatical tradition and have therefore been included, not least for the sake of balance and breadth of coverage.

Of female writers, only Anne Fisher's grammar (in different versions) has been found substantial (and influential) enough for inclusion here, and being the first one written by a woman it has a special place in the history of eighteenth-century grammars, but Michael's list (1970:Appendix VI, pp. 547-87) reveals six other women writers, and these have been studied in some detail in recent years (see e.g. Cajka 2008).[4]

Finally, let us summarise some of the many functions and uses that prepositions are associated with in the grammars studied here. As early as in the works of the Roman grammarians, prepositions were seen to express *relations*; the obvious one was with the prepositional complement (usually a noun or pronoun) but often with another element as well, whether this was the verb or another noun, thus 'combining' or 'bringing the two together'. Such relations are widely emphasised in the English grammars and are dealt with in some detail especially by Wallis, Wilkins, Lane and Ward.

Another aspect of prepositions with roots in the classical tradition is their interaction with, or government of, *case* in the prepositional complement. This is mentioned by virtually every English grammarian, though many of them impose the Latin six-case system on English. It is mainly during the eighteenth century – and then only gradually – that the differences in case form and use between Latin and English are fully understood and distinguished. Bound up with the issue of case is the practice of some grammarians (e.g. Gill, Hewes, Poole and Mattaire) to regard certain prepositions as 'case signs'; a tradition which, as we saw in Chapter III, originates in the discussions among the Italian grammarians of the sixteenth century. A reasonably multifaceted account of case relations is found in Priestley.

A long-standing issue, again going back to the Romans, is the distinction between separable and inseparable prepositions, which is upheld by most of the early English grammarians, often with examples from Latin as much as from English. It was only during the eighteenth century that the realisation slowly began to emerge that some of the elements used as 'prefixes' (though the term was not used) might not be prepositions at all, according to the various definitions of this class. Greenwood's discussion of this topic is one of the most illuminating ones.

The position of prepositions is addressed in many of the grammars, beginning with Bullokar who mentions the stranded position (if not the term) in relative clauses, as do Cooper and Miege (among others) in the seventeenth century. This aspect of prepositional syntax is widely discussed by many eighteenth-century writers, but with varying degrees of sympathy for that construction.[5] There is far less preoccupation with the position of prepositional phrases within the clause, quite simply because the notion of phrases was not properly understood at the time, but even so Fell makes some comments about the issue.

Some of the other points picked up by certain writers (also) have relevance for modern linguists. One of these is the awareness of the difference between certain meanings expressed by prepositions – for some grammarians, in conjunction with the finite verb – such as motion versus rest, cause, etc., not to mention the 'casual' functions of possessor, beneficiary, agent and others that are more often than not described in case terms, at least to begin with usually with reference to Latin. Although many of these arguments are derived from the Roman tradition, they also point ahead to, for example, modern localist analyses, on the one hand, and case grammar, on the other. Another issue concerns the now widely accepted view that, historically, prepositions were mainly or exclusively used with concrete, spatial sense and only gradually acquired figurative/metaphorical and ultimately (in some uses) abstract meaning. This aspect is considered chiefly by Harris, Priestley and – from a psychological viewpoint – Ward. Harris also employs the term 'coalescence', which may be seen as a form of valency, while Ward talks of prepositions in terms reminiscent of present-day notions of variables and operators. Elphinston is on the trail of the modern concept of grammaticalisation in some of his historical explanations, which may have something in common with Duncan's claim that the use of prepositions is a form of linguistic economy.

Since it is impossible to sum up all the details that occur in so many grammars over a long period, the general points presented here merely reflect some of the predominant features. For more details, the discussions under the individual authors need to be consulted.

In conclusion, I can only repeat my previous disclaimer that this study is by no means intended to be a complete, all-encompassing study of English grammars before the nineteenth century since only a certain (though not insignificant) number of grammars and grammatical treatises have been included. Nevertheless, I believe that this selection is broadly representative of the total number of publications on English grammar from this period, and I hope that the discussions of the individual texts will have thrown some new light on the treatment of prepositions and may perhaps even inspire others to delve further into the intricacies of this often neglected, but in my view fascinating, word class.

Notes

Notes to Introduction:

1. There are four authors: Randolph Quirk, Sidney Greenbaum, Geoffrey Leech and Jan Svartvik.
2. The term 'word-class' was first used by Bloomfield (1914:108).
3. There are in fact a number of other contributors to this massive work, but the chapter on prepositions is written by these two authors, albeit listed there in reverse order, so I shall generally refer to H&P as the authors.
4. There is only one reference to Jespersen in the 'conceptual index' of the grammar, and that concerns the term 'content clause'. However, in a paper entitled 'The Part-of-Speech Classifications in English Dictionaries: Critiques, Criteria, and Proposals', delivered to the Philological Society in 2009, Geoffrey Pullum specifically referred to Jespersen's category of 'particles' and, before him, to a similar category in Dyche and Pardon's *A New General English Dictionary* (1735) as inspiration for the enlarged class of prepositions in H&P (2002). As we shall see in Chapter IV, such a categorisation was in fact quite common in the eighteenth century and earlier; Dyche and Pardon were by no means the first to operate with it, but I do not believe that Pullum intended to claim that.
5. Even *else* is said to be a 'borderline case' preposition in certain uses and an adverb in others (2002:615).

Notes to Chapter I:

1. For detailed information about the origins and development of the Greek language see for example Horrocks (1997) or, for a more concise survey, Moleas (2004).
2. The Index of Aristotle (1984) misleadingly lists the above places in the *Rhetoric* under 'conjunction' and refers to 1407b7 instead of 1407b13.
3. The concept of 'the Stoics' is a wide one. Here is meant specifically the 'early' Stoic period, stretching roughly from 300-100 BC.
4. For an exposition of the development of the parts of speech see Matthews (1994:29-38).
5. For comments on Dionysius's treatment of the parts of speech see Schenkeveld (1983).
6. Theodectes (c. 375-334 BC) was a literary figure and a pupil of Plato and Aristotle, who composed rhetorical works and speeches, and also wrote plays.
7. For an English translation of the *Tekhnē grammatikē* see A. Kemp (1987) whose introduction (pp. 169-72) also summarises the arguments surrounding the authenticity. More detailed discussion about the *Tekhnē* and its provenance can be found in Law & Sluiter (eds.) 1998 [1995], which contains the proceedings from a symposium on Dionysius Thrax held in Cambridge in 1993. For a concise list of arguments for rejecting Dionysius Thrax as the author of parts of *Tekhnē* see Law (2003:56).

8   It appears in Greek transcription with commentary in Wouters (1979:49-56) and is quoted in English translation in Law (2003:55-7).
9   This is repeated almost verbatim in Book XII, 17 (see Taylor 1996:65).
10 It was the Stoics who, by restricting Aristotle's general term *ptōsis* (fall) to something like morphological case, established what has been an important grammatical term ever since, cf. Robins (1997:33-5).
11 All references to the *Syntax* are to Householder's (1981) translation, listing Book and Section.
12 For the differences between *Schulgrammatik* and *regulae* grammars as well as their interrelations see Law (2003:83-91).

Notes to Chapter II:

1   Smaragdus (1986:217-30) does have a section on prepositions, but this is essentially a repetition of Donatus's treatment.
2   The translation of these passages is taken from Law (2003:121).
3   See Law (2003:118-24) for further (to us, baffling) examples of arguments taken from natural phenomena or the Bible and applied to grammatical rules.
4   No one has contributed more towards supplying and promoting knowledge of the early parts of this historical period than Vivien Law in a number of publications, in particular Law (1982, 1997 and, in textbook form, the relevant chapters of 2003). Her premature death in 2002 was a great loss to scholarship in this field.
5   Bursill-Hall (1975:179) compares this new impetus in linguistic analysis with the kind of paradigm shift discussed in Kuhn (1962).
6   In *Scholae grammaticae* (1559).
7   See also the French translation of Sanctius: 'D'autres divisent la grammaire en « letter », « syllable », « mot » et « discourse », ou, ce qui revient au même en « orthographe », « prosodie », « étymologie » et « syntaxe ». Mais le discourse ou la syntaxe est *la fin de la grammaire et non pas une partie d'elle ...*' (1982:107; my emphasis) (Others divide grammar into 'letter', 'syllable', 'word' and 'discourse', or, what amounts to the same thing, into 'orthography', 'prosody', 'etymology' and 'syntax'. But discourse or syntax is the end (i.e. main purpose) of grammar and not just one part of it ...)
8   Michael (1970:30), but cf. also Law (2003:172-3).
9   Both Kilwardby and Roger Bacon taught in Paris in the years before the middle of the thirteenth century and thus just prior to the early works of the Modistae (cf. Maierù 1994:288).
10 As Law (2003:171) points out, the Latin-based term 'speculative' corresponds to the Greek-based term 'theoretical'.
11 For a historical overview of the notion 'universal language' see Salus (1976).
12 Accounts of the *modi* are found, for example, in Pinborg (1967:109-23), Michael (1970:14-22), Thomas of Erfurt (1972:28-36), Siger de Courtrai (1977:xviff.), Covington (1984:22-35), Maierù (1994:288-315), Robins (1997:88-104) and Law (2003:172-7). The first, though non-technical, mention of the term *modus significandi* goes back as far as to Boethius (cf. Pinborg 1967:30, citing Thurot).
13 *Grammatica Speculativa*, ed. G.L. Bursill-Hall, Longman (1972:135).

14 Not, of course, to be confused with the Roman philosopher Boethius from the early sixth century, mentioned above.
15 See e.g. Bursill-Hall's detailed article (1976), in which he echoes Pinborg's assertion that 'subsequent to Boethius no new thesis in grammar appeared in the work of the later Modistae that Boethius had not already put forward' (1976:167, note 10).
16 There is overall agreement among linguistic scholars of the scholastic period that the epithet 'of Dacia' (Lat. *de Dacia*) indicates that this group of Modistae came from Denmark rather than from the old Roman province of Dacia, approximately present-day Romania. At the time, Dacia was often used as a Latin term for Denmark (perhaps even 'Scandinavia' more generally), and Pinborg (1967:67), following Heinrich Roos, finds it established that Martin of Dacia served as Chancellor to the Danish King Erik VI Menved around 1288.
17 The text used here is Godfrey of Fontaine's abridgement, edited and introduced by A. Charlene Senape McDermott, with a parallel English translation (see Boethius 1980).
18 For a more detailed exposition of this topic see Bursill-Hall (1976:168ff.).
19 Already Fridugisus of Tours (late eighth to early ninth century) discussed the abstract meaning of *nihil* and *tenebrae* (darkness) and their relation to reality (cf. Maierù 1994:273).
20 This wording is very reminiscent of Donatus's general definition of prepositions (see Ch. I): ... *aut mutat aut complet aut minuit* (completes [their meaning] or alters it or diminishes it).
21 This edition has a parallel English translation and an introduction by G.L. Bursill-Hall. All references are to this edition and cover both the Latin original and the translation.
22 Until well into the twentieth century, *Grammatica Speculativa* was believed to be a work by Duns Scotus (1265/6-1308), a Scottish philosopher and theologian, who studied in Oxford and later taught in Paris.
23 Thomas's term for 'govern' is *deservire*.
24 A list of the most central constructional dependencies is provided in Thomas of Erfurt (1972:107), Covington (1984:49), Robins (1997:97) and Law (2003:166-8).
25 The notion of transitivity may go back as far as to the Stoics. It is mentioned by Apollonius Dyscolus and further developed by Priscian (cf. Law 2003:90).
26 See Thomas of Erfurt (1972:286-9) and Bursill-Hall's summary on pp. 107-10 of the same.
27 There are other examples of 'oblique case subjects' on the same page.
28 Often spelt *anulus*.
29 For more detailed information on the fall of modistic grammar see e.g. Pinborg (1967:167-212), Covington (1984:120-26), Maierù (1994:302-6) and Law (2003:178-9).

Notes to Chapter III:
1 See, for example, the account of this event in J.E. Sandys (1921:676-8).
2 In the English translation of the Latin grammar (*Grammatica*, originally from 1572; see Ramus 1971), 'Rudiments of the Latine Grammar' (a translation of *Rudimenta grammaticae latinae*, 1595) is placed at the end and has separate pagination. Incidentally, Ra-

	mus had a sad end to his life as he became embroiled in the religious conflicts in France and ended his days as a victim of the St. Bartholemew Day massacre in 1572.
3	The author of *Minerva, seu de causis linguae Latinae commentarius*, 1587.
4	The poet Ercole Strozzi (1473-1508) from Ferrara, one of Bembo's many correspondents and among his interlocutors in *Prose*.
5	Cf. Bembo (2001:122).
6	Cited from Kukenheim (1932:108).
7	The last example is a quotation of part of a sentence from Boccaccio's *Decameron*, see Boccaccio (1989:14).
8	This is true, for instance, of Albanian, Basque, Croatian, Danish, Finnish, (modern) Greek, Hungarian, (modern) Icelandic, Irish, Latvian, Lithuanian, Polish, Russian, Sami, Slovene and Swedish (cf. Law 2003:234-5).
9	For this and some of intricacies of how Lily's grammar came into being see Alston's Note in Lily (1970).
10	Lily (1970) is partly unnumbered, but a few initial missing (numbered) pages are copied from a 1557 edition and reproduced in Lily (1970) as Appendix I.

Notes to Chapter IV:

1	Following Michael (1970), I have in one case gone beyond the year 1800 and included Dalton's grammar (1801) because in a sense it marks the end of a particular way of conceiving grammar.
2	Michael (1970:3) notes that only 167 of them were written as distinct English grammars; the rest appear as parts of universal grammars, dictionaries, encyclopedias, spelling books or other more general works.
3	The minor discrepancy between the total of these four groups (275) and the number of grammars (273) arises partly because only 259 grammars are considered relevant and partly because some writers advocate different systems in different works and are consequently listed under both. Cf. Michael (1970:208).
4	These systems are examined in greater detail in Chapter V.
5	For the following statistics see Michael (1970:Appendix II, 530-35).
6	The two Bullokar texts in this edition have separate page numbering; *Bref Grammar* appears as the second text.
7	Bullokar strove to reform English spelling by bringing it closer to the pronunciation. He therefore devised his own alphabet with more than the 24 letter symbols in current use at his time, though he is far from consistent in his use of them (for discussion see Bullokar 1977:v-x). For this reason I have at times modernised the spelling of some of the quotations.
8	There is no consistency in Greaves's use of Arabic and Roman numerals.
9	Gill is the spelling of most commentators, but on the title-page of his book it is spelt 'Alexandro Gil'. I follow the majority spelling.
10	There are only six surviving copies of the first edition from 1619. I have used the reproduction of the second edition from 1621 found in Gill (1968).
11	Like Bullokar, Gill was a proponent of spelling reform, which he demonstrates in his book.

12 References are to a reprint of the 2nd edition from 1634 (Butler 1910).
13 These verses are quoted in numerous places. The reference here is to Shakespeare (1988:xlv-xlvi).
14 Examples are legion. Take, for example, Macbeth's famous lines, 'I am in blood / stepp'd in so far, that, should I wade no more, / returning were as tedious as go o'er' (*Macbeth*, III.iv.135-7, cf. Shakespeare 1988:989).
15 Notably the 'relegation' of prepositions to the status of 'k-markers' in the earliest version of Case Grammar; see the Introduction above.
16 For a wider view of 'universal grammar' see Salus (1976), and for a full study of the 'universal grammar' tradition in England in the seventeenth and eighteenth centuries see Göbels (1999). For the seventeenth century see also Maat (2004).
17 The edition used here has parallel Latin and English text. References are to the English translation.
18 In Latin, usually *regere*, but not always; for example, Thomas of Erfurt uses *deservire*.
19 See e.g. Constantinescu (1974) and, for some critical comments to this, Padley (1985:195, note 305).
20 For a brief overview of Wallis's place in the English grammar tradition up to the middle of the seventeenth century see Subbiondo (1992b).
21 An important source for Dalgarno's life and work is found in the manuscript tract 'The Autobiographical Treatise' that was among the papers he left to his wife on his death. It was first published in Dalgarno 2001:353-90.
22 For Dalgarno's view of particles see also Maat (2004 and 2009).
23 A whole volume of articles dedicated to Wilkins and his position within English seventeenth-century linguistics is found in Subbiondo (1992a).
24 The table of contents has 'Philosophical Grammar' here, but the term 'Natural Grammar' is employed throughout Part III, so I shall use the latter term.
25 Francis Bacon (1561-1626), who was Baron of Verulam (and the First Viscount St. Albans). It is said to be among his *Desiderata*.
26 Wilkins refers to Duns Scotus's *Grammatica Speculativa*, but, as we saw earlier, this was later discovered to be a work by Thomas of Erfurt (see Chapter II, note 22).
27 Juan Caramuel y Lobkowitz (1606-82), a Spanish philosopher, ecclesiastic and writer, in his *Grammatica Audax*.
28 Tommaso Campanella (i.e. Giovanni Domenico Campanella) (1568-1639), an Italian philosopher, theologian and poet, in his *Grammatica Philosophica*.
29 Julius Caesar Scaliger (1484-1558), an Italian scholar and physician, in his *De causis linguae latinae*.
30 Gerardus Vossius (1577-1649), a Dutch classical scholar and theologian, in his *Aristarchus* (*sive de arte grammatica*).
31 By derived adverbs are meant adverbs derived from another part of speech, usually from adjectives by means of the suffix *-ly*, such as *nicely* from *nice*.
32 This point is partly missed by Michael (1970:247), even though he cites Wilkins's definition (1970:248, 250), but it is noted by Robins (1997:138).
33 Possibly a mistake for *below*, which appears in the list but not in the diagram, though clearly both are prepositions.
34 As mentioned above, the last pair can hardly be called prepositions in the traditional sense and hence in terms of Wilkins's own framework.
35 Cf., for example, Bennett 1975, though he makes other distinctions as well.

36 Michael (1970:570-71) mentions the existence of two versions of the text; an early one (1670?) in the British Library without a title-page, and a second version found in the Bodleian Library, Oxford, and in Wisconsin University library. I should therefore record that the text used here is based on the second version (what Michael calls 'Lewis, *Essay*, 1674') but in a copy held in Cambridge University Library, at the end of a book whose main part consists of the completely unrelated 'D. IVNII, *IVVENALIS Satyrarum Libri V*, M.D. LXV'. As Michael says, this version is in two parts with separate pagination, in which the section on pp. 17-23 is an address 'To the Reader' that seems to summarise the earlier *Essay*, while the actual text of the *Essay* runs from pp. 1-60. As with the copies in the Bodleian and in Wisconsin, this *Essay* does not include the 'Critical or Idiomatical Grammar' promised on the title-page.

37 'Syncrisis' means 'comparison'; it is an indication of how unusual the word was at the time that one of the few examples in the *Oxford English Dictionary* (X:378) is this one from Lewis.

38 As so often at the time, spelt 'Lilly' and 'Lillie's Grammar'.

39 There is some dispute about Cooper's year of birth; Alston gives it as '1646?' (Cooper 1968:Note), while Michael (1970:556) has '*c*. 1655'. *The Dictionary of National Biography* agrees with Michael, so this (approximate) date is followed here.

40 Note that the title is identical to that of Wallis's grammar.

41 Clare's spelling alternates between 'Præpositions' and 'Prepositions'.

42 Note that the Second Part is re-numbered, beginning with p. 1, and that both Arabic and Roman numbers are used for chapters.

43 Prince William Henry, Duke of Gloucester (1689-1700), was the only surviving child (beyond infancy) of the later Queen Anne and her consort, Prince George of Denmark and Norway. Anne (1665-1714), the daughter of King James II, became Queen of England, Scotland, and Ireland in 1702, which was after her son's death, and of Great Britain and Ireland in 1707 after the Act of Settlement. On Prince William's birth, King William III allowed him to call himself 'Duke of Gloucester' (but did not actually create him a duke) and, in January 1696, awarded him the Order of the Garter. He died in 1700 aged only 11. Lane's dedication, like Clare's, clearly preceded this sad event.

44 Note the use of the authorial 'I', which also occurs in other places. Michael (1970) is not in doubt about Gildon's authorship, while 'Brightland's role was certainly that of sponsor and it is probable that he was, with others, associated with the writing of the grammar' (1970:563-4; see also references there). The use of forms of the authorial 'I' at the very least suggests that some parts were written by one person only.

45 This is no doubt a reference to George Hickes's *Institutiones grammaticae Anglo-Saxonicae, et Moeso-Goticae*, 1689. Hickes lived from 1642-1715 and an excerpt of this work appeared in 1711, the year of Greenwood's *Essay*.

46 This is debatable. All the old Germanic languages possess a cognate form of *at* which is related to Latin *ad* rather than derived from it.

47 Jones's spelling.

48 Kirkby has been accused of plagiarism, e.g. of copying from Fisher's (now lost) first edition (see below) (cf. Tieken-Boon van Ostade 1996:84-7).

49 Like Kirkby, though even more blatantly, Martin seems to have turned plagiarism into something of an art form, though the charge brought against him concerns his dictionary *Lingua Britannica Reformata* rather than *Institutions* (cf. Tieken-Boon van Ostade 1996:83-7).

50 Alston (Martin 1970:Note) suggests that Martin may have derived his system of categories from Dyche and Pardon's *New general English Dictionary* from 1735, which includes a brief grammar.
51 In fact, the authorship of this chapter is uncertain, as mentioned in Chapter I (under Aristotle).
52 See again Fillmore (1968) for an early version of the theory.
53 See e.g. Miller (1985) and Herskovits (1986).
54 For a detailed illustration of this general development of prepositions in Old and Middle English see Lundskær-Nielsen (1993), and for a similar view regarding Greek see Bortone (2010) who concludes that 'the history of Greek prepositions, if analysed in its entirety, is largely congruent with the "localistic hypothesis" that concrete spatial meanings are the earliest ones, and entirely congruent with the "unidirectional hypothesis" that spatial meanings evolve into non-spatial ones but not vice-versa' (2010:xii).
55 There is not even agreement on the spelling of her first name. Alston, in the facsimile reprint of the second edition (Fisher 1968), as mentioned published anonymously, uses 'Ann' Fisher, whereas Michael (1970) has 'Anne' Fisher throughout. I have adopted Michael's practice, which seems to be the more general one.
56 For a more detailed study of Fisher's authorship see Rodríguez-Gil (2008).
57 In the 1754 edition there are ten 'Rules', and what follows here about the 'States' is there relegated to a footnote (1754:116).
58 A conjunction, for example, fares little better, being defined as 'a word made use of to connect the clauses of a period together, and to signify the relation they have to one another' (1967:I, 5I), without any examples, but with a reference to *Clarke's Latin Grammar*, i.e. John Clarke, *New Grammar of the Latin Tongue* (1733).
59 I.e. Ben Jonson, whose name Johnson consistently spells with an 'h', like his own.
60 There is separate page numbering in the two Parts: 'The English Accidence' and 'The English Grammar'. If not specified, references are to the First Part.
61 For a comparison of the first and second edition (1761 and 1768) of *Rudiments* see Hodson (2008).
62 For a very recent full-length study of Lowth's grammar see Tieken-Boon van Ostade (2011), in which the author refutes the allegations frequently levelled at Lowth of being the origin of extreme prescriptivism in English grammar, e.g. by Aitchison (2001:9-13). As shown below, his treatment of prepositions does not support such an allegation.
63 If he were alive today, Ash might have been delighted to observe the widespread dropping of apostrophes in everyday written English.
64 Ash has previously assigned the term 'neuter' to a verb that 'signifies *merely Being*', which applies above all, of course, to the verb *be* (1967:40), but traditionally the term often referred to verbs that were without a passive form and hence not 'truly' active verbs.
65 John Nichols, *Literary Anecdotes of the Eighteenth Century*, 9 vols. London, 1812-15, vol. III:32 note.
66 This spelling is apparently not a misprint, as it recurs elsewhere, e.g. at the start of 'Etymology' (1765:218).
67 For the term and notion of grammaticalisation see Hopper & Traugott (2003), and for a brief discussion of grammaticalisation involving prepositions in the development of English see Lundskær-Nielsen (1993:183-9).
68 This spelling is used in several places.
69 The full title of Young's work is *The Complaint: or Night-Thoughts on Life, Death, & Im-*

mortality, first published in 1743. This was an important contribution to the growing eighteenth-century fascination with the night side of life and the notion of the 'sublime'. It is well known that poetry allows more flexible word order, including the position of prepositions, than ordinary prose does. Consequently, one should be wary of attaching too much importance to such examples.

70   Cf. Locke (1975), who mentions only the first of these two complementary problems.
71   To modern speakers, the grammaticality of (a) is questionable, but it must have been acceptable to Ward in the mid eighteenth century.
72   Both the term and the notion of 'coalescence' here and elsewhere in Ward's *Essay* are almost certainly influenced by Harris.
73   These examples point to a change in the use of some combinations of verb + preposition in the passive voice over the last two centuries. Compared with modern English, (b) and (d) now seem distinctly odd; (c) (in the now normal sense of 'scold, admonish') is more commonly found with 'spoken' (e.g. 'the goalkeeper was spoken to by the referee'); (e) nowadays typically occur in active constructions (e.g. 'he got more than he had bargained for'); and even (a) which, given a suitable context, is quite frequently used (e.g. 'she was never heard of again'), is, on its own, more usual in the negated form in the idiom 'it was unheard of'.
74   For recent discussions of this type of analysis see Huddleston (1984:200-203), and Huddleston and Pullum (2002:274-80).
75   The system deviates a little from the one found in Fenning's *Royal English Dictionary* (1761 and later editions), where the article belongs under the noun, but, as Alston points out, his later *New Grammar* presumably represents his 'authoritative' scheme (1967:Note). Cf. also Michael (1970:214, 218).
76   Tracing its history back to 1695 in East London, Homerton moved to Cambridge as a teacher-training college in 1894. As Homerton College, it became an Approved Society of the University in 1976 and received its Royal Charter in 2010.
77   I follow other writers in using 'Horne Tooke' to refer to the person, but in the bibliography he is entered alphabetically as 'Tooke'.
78   Horne Tooke's close friend William Tooke, owner of the country estate of Purley near Croydon, Sussex, where the dialogue is set, and whose name John Horne adopted out of respect in 1783, appears as (T) in the introduction to Part I, but not in Part I itself.
79   For a treatment of this relationship in terms of historical reconstruction see Vincent (1980:53, 61).
80   *Sans* in this use was made famous by Shakespeare (as quoted by Horne Tooke) in the last line of Jaques's soliloquy, 'Sans teeth, sans eyes, sans taste, sans everything' (*As You Like It*, II.VII.166, cf. Shakespeare 1988:638).
81   For *with* see also (Horne) Tooke (1968:320-24).
82   Harris's spelling.
83   Horne Tooke's spelling.
84   See again Miller (1985) and Herskovits (1986).
85   See e.g. Aarsleff (1983).
86   A few examples of such mistakes are given in Robins (1997:162), but many more can be found.
87   For other references in nineteenth-century literature, and even in James Joyce's *Ulysses*, see Tieken-Boon van Ostade (1996:18).
88   As we have seen, Murray is not the first grammarian to wrestle with this problem, and

it is still a hotly debated issue in grammar writing, cf. the discussion in the Introduction above.

89 Plagiarism in the eighteenth century, and in the case of Lindley Murray in particular, is explored in some detail in Tieken-Boon van Ostade (1996:81-96), though Vorlat (1959) had previously examined Murray's 'sources'. The term as well as the concept of plagiarism seems to have arisen in earnest in the seventeenth century and the first British law on copyright was the Copyright Act of 1709, under Queen Anne. Murray does acknowledge some of his sources in the second edition of the *Grammar* (1810), after some less than complimentary reviews had pointed out this glaring omission from the first edition (cf. Tieken-Boon van Ostade (1996:87-8)), but it was a somewhat murky area throughout the eighteenth century and there are clearly different grades of plagiarising; e.g. 'borrowing' examples from earlier writers was certainly widespread practice.

Notes to Chapter V:

1 I owe these references to Knud Sørensen.
2 Michael (1970:262) has 'Participle' here, which is obviously an error.
3 But there were also people from other, sometimes overlapping, professions, such as two bishops (Wilkins and Lowth), other clerics (e.g. Bayly, Kirkby, Fell and Wilson), some scientists or other academics (e.g. Wallis, Jones and Dalton) including a philosopher (Locke), etc.
4 The other six are: Mrs Edwards (Michael 1970:558), Mrs Eves (Michael 1970:560), Jane Gardiner (Michael 1970:563), Mrs Lovechild – a pen-name for Lady Eleanor Fenn – (Michael 1970:572), Blanch Mercy (Michael 1970:575) and Mrs Taylor (Michael 1970:582). Of these, the last four wrote specifically for young girls/children, while Mrs Edwards's work is a short compendium. All six had their works published in the 1790s; Mrs Taylor in 1791 and the rest after 1795 with several of them seemingly relying (a few very heavily) on Murray, though, as we have seen, the latter himself was not averse to borrowing from some of his predecessors.
5 For a more detailed study of preposition stranding in the eighteenth century see especially Yañez-Bouza (2008), but also Tieken-Boon van Ostade (2011:236-41).

Bibliography

Primary sources

(a) Ancient & Medieval:

Apollonius Dyscolus. 1981. *The Syntax of Apollonius Dyscolus*, with translation and commentary by F. W. Householder. Amsterdam: John Benjamins.

Aristotle. 1984. *The Complete Works of Aristotle*, rev. Oxford translation, ed. J. Barnes. Princeton: Princeton University Press.

Bacon, Roger. 1902. *The Greek Grammar of Roger Bacon and a Fragment of his Hebrew Grammar*, eds. E. Nolan and S.A. Hirsch. Cambridge: Cambridge University Press.

Boethius of Dacia. 1980. *Godfrey of Fontaine's Abridgement of Boethius of Dacia's Modi Significandi sive Quaestiones Super Priscianum Maiorem*, with introduction and translation by A.C.S. McDermott. Amsterdam: John Benjamins.

Diogenes Laertius. 1925. *Lives of Eminent Philosophers*, 2 vols., with an English Translation by R.D. Hicks. Loeb Classical Library. London: Heinemann / New York: Putnam.

Dionysius of Halicarnassus. 1974/1985. *The Critical Essays in Two Volumes*, transl. Stephen Usher, Loeb Classical Library. Harvard: Harvard University Press / London: Heinemann.

Dionysius Thrax (pseudo?), see Kemp (1987).

Donatus, 1926. *The Ars Minor of Donatus, for 1000 years the Leading Textbook of Grammar*, with introduction and translation by W.J. Chase. *University of Wisconsin Studies in Social Sciences and History* 11. Madison, WI: University of Wisconsin. (See also Keil IV. 353-66.)

Donatus. 1864. *Ars grammatica (Ars Maior)*. See Keil (IV:367-402).

Keil, Heinrich. 1855-70. *Grammatici Latini* I-VIII. Leipzig: Teubner.

Kemp, A. 1987. 'The *Tekhnē Grammatikē* of Dionysius Thrax: English translation with Introduction and Notes'. In: Taylor (1987a:169-89).

Plato. 1964. *The Dialogues of Plato*, rev. 4th ed., Vol. III, transl. B. Jowett. Oxford: Clarendon Press.

Priscian. 1999. *Opuscula*, ed. Marina Passalacqua, Vol. II: *Institutio de nomine et pronomine et verbo* (pp. 3-41) and *Partitiones duodecimo versuum Aeneidos principalium* (pp. 43-128). Rome: Edizioni di Storia e Letteratura.

Priscian. *Institutiones grammaticae*. See Keil (1855/59:II-III).

Quintilian. 1921. *Institutio Oratoria* I, transl. H.E. Butler, Loeb Classical Library. London: Heinemann / New York: Putnam.

Siger de Courtrai. 1977. *Summa Modorum Significandi*, ed. J. Pinborg. Amsterdam: J. Benjamins.

Smaragdus. 1986. *Liber in partibus Donati*, ed. B. Löfstedt, L. Holtz and A. Kibre, *Corpus Christianorum Continuatio Mediaevalis* 68. Turnhout: Brepols.

Taylor. D.J. (ed.). 1996. *Varro – De Lingua Latina X. A new critical text and English translation with Prolegomena and Commentary*. Studies in the History of Language Sciences 85. Amsterdam/Philadelphia: Benjamins.

Thomas of Erfurt. 1972. *Grammatica Speculativa*, with translation and commentary by G.L. Bursill-Hall. London: Longman.

Varro, Marcus Terentius, 1977. *De Lingua Latina* V-X (2 vols.), transl. R.L. Kent, Loeb Classical Library 333-4. Cambridge Mass.: Harvard University Press / London: Heinemann. (See also Taylor (ed.) 1996.)

William of Conches. 1980. *Philosophia*, ed. G. Maurach. Pretoria: University of South Africa.

William of Ockham. 1951. *Summa Logicae*, ed. P. Boehner. New York: The Franciscan Institute, St. Bonaventure / Louvain (Belgium): E. Nauwelaerts.

(b) The Renaissance to 1801:

Aickin, Joseph. 1967 [1693]. *The English Grammar*. Menston: The Scolar Press.

Ash, John. 1967 [176[3?]]. *Grammatical Institutes*. Leeds: The Scolar Press.

Bayly, Anselm. 1968 [1758]. *An Introduction to Languages*. Menston: The Scolar Press.

Bayly, Anselm. 1969 [1772]. *A Plain and Complete Grammar*. Menston: The Scolar Press.
Bembo, Pietro. 1525. *Prose della Volgar Lingua*. Venice.
Bembo, Pietro. 2001. *Prose della Volgar Lingua*. L'editio princeps del 1525 riscontrata con l'autografo Vaticano latino 3210, ed. Claudio Vela. Bologna: Cooperativa Libraria Universitaria Editrice.
Buchanan, James. 1968 [1762]. *The British Grammar*. Menston: The Scolar Press.
Bullokar, William. 1977 [1586]. *Booke at Large* (1580) and *Bref Grammar for English* (1586). Scholars' Facsimiles & Reprints. New York: Delmar.
Butler, Charles. 1910 [1634]. *The English Grammar*. In: *Charles Butler's English Grammar*, ed. A. Eichler. Halle: Max Niemeyer.
Castelvetro, Lodovico. 2004 [1563]. *Giunta fatta al Ragionamento degli Articoli et de' Verbi di messer Pietro Bembo*. Rome/Padova: Editrice Antenore.
Clare, William. 1971 [1690]. *A Complete System of Grammar English and Latin*. Menston: The Scolar Press.
Collyer, John. 1968 [1735]. *The General Principles of Grammar*. Menston: The Scolar Press.
Cooper, Christopher. 1968 [1685]. *Grammatica Linguae Anglicanae*. Menston: The Scolar Press.
Dalgarno, George. 2001 [1661]. *Ars Signorum* ('The Art of Signs'). In: *George Dalgarno on Universal Language: The Art of Signs (1661), The Deaf and Dumb Man's Tutor (1680), and the Unpublished Papers*, edited with a Translation, Introduction and Commentary by David Cram and Jaap Maat. Oxford: Oxford University Press.
Dalton, John. 1801. *Elements of English Grammar*. London: W.J. and J. Richardson.
Dilworth, Thomas. 1967 [1751]. *A New Guide to the English Tongue*. Menston: The Scolar Press.
Dolce, Lodovico. 1556 [1550]. *Le Osservationi del Dolce dal Medesimo ricorrette et ampliate*, 4th ed. of *Osservationi nella Volgar Lingua*. 1550. Venice.
Duncan, Daniel. 1967 [1731]. *A New English Grammar*. Menston: The Scolar Press.
Elphinston, James. 1765. *The Principles of the English Language*

Digested: or, English Grammar reduced to Analogy, Vol. I-II. London:James Bettenham.

Estienne, Robert. 1558. *Gallicae Grammatices libellus.* Paris.

Fell, John. 1967 [1784]. *An Essay towards an English Grammar.* Menston: The Scolar Press.

Fenning, Daniel. 1967 [1771]. *A New English Grammar of the English Language.* Menston: The Scolar Press.

Fisher, A(nne). 1968 [1750]. *A New Grammar* (2nd ed.). Menston: The Scolar Press.

Fisher, A(nne). 1754. *A New Grammar* (4th ed.). Newcastle upon Tyne: I. Thompson and Comp.

Fisher, A(nne). 1762. *A Practical New Grammar* (7th ed.). Newcastle: Thomas Slack.

Giambullari, Pierfrancesco. 1551. *De la lingua che si parla e scrive in Firenze.* Firenze.

Gildon, Charles and John Brightland. 1967 [1711]. *A Grammar of the English Tongue.* Menston: The Scolar Press.

Gill, Alexander. 1968 [1621]. *Logonomia Anglica.* Menston: The Scolar Press.

Gough, James & John. 1967 [1754]. *A Practical Grammar of the English Tongue.* Menston: The Scolar Press.

Greaves, Paul. 1969 [1594]. *Grammatica Anglicana.* Menston: The Scolar Press.

Greenwood, James. 1968 [1711]. *An Essay towards a Practical English Grammar.* Menston: The Scolar Press.

Harris, James. 1968 [1751]. *Hermes.* Menston: The Scolar Press.

Hewes, John. 1972 [1624]. *A Perfect Survey of the English Tongue.* Menston: The Scolar Press.

Johnson, Samuel. 1967 [1755]. *A Dictionary of the English Language*, I-II. New York: AMS Press.

Johnson, Richard. 1969 [1706]. *Grammatical Commentaries.* Menston: The Scolar Press.

Jones, Hugh. 1967 [1724]. *An Accidence to the English Tongue.* Menston: The Scolar Press.

Jonson, Ben. 1972 [1641]. *The English Grammar.* Menston: The Scolar Press.

Kirkby, John. 1971 [1746]. *A New English Grammar.* Menston: The

Scolar Press.

Lancelot, Claude and Antoine Arnauld. 1966 [1676 (3rd ed.), 1st ed. 1660]. *Grammaire générale et raisonnée* ou *La Grammaire de Port-Royal* (ed. H.E. Brekle). Stuttgart-Bad Cannstatt: Friedrich Frommann. (First appeared anonymously)

Lancelot, Claude and Antoine Arnauld. 1968 [1753]. *A General and Rational Grammar*. (Translator unknown). Menston: The Scolar Press. (First appeared anonymously)

Lane, A. 1972 [1695]. *A Rational and Speedy Method of attaining to the Latin Tongue*. Menston: The Scolar Press.

Lane, A. 1969 [1700]. *A Key to the Art of Letters*. Menston: The Scolar Press.

Lewis, Mark. 1674. *An Essay to Facilitate the Education of Youth*. London: Thomas Parkhurst.

Lily, William and John Colet. 1970 [1549]. *A Short Introduction of Grammar*. Menston: The Scolar Press.

Locke, John. 1975 [1690]. *An Essay on Human Understanding* (The Clarendon Edition). Oxford: Oxford University Press.

Lodowyck, Francis. 1969 [1647]. *A Common Writing*. Menston: The Scolar Press.

Lodowyck, Francis. 1968 [1652]. *The Ground-work of a New Perfect Language*. Menston: The Scolar Press.

Lowth, Robert. 1967 [1762]. *A Short Introduction to English Grammar*. Menston: The Scolar Press.

Lye, Thomas. 1968 [1671]. *The Child's Delight*. Menston: The Scolar Press.

Martin, Benjamin. 1970 [1748]. *Institutions of Language*. Menston: The Scolar Press.

Mattaire, Michael. 1967 [1712]. *The English Grammar*. Menston: The Scolar Press.

Miege, Guy. 1969 [1688]. *The English Grammar*. Menston: The Scolar Press.

Murray, Lindley. 1968 [1795]. *English Grammar*. Menston: The Scolar Press.

Poole, Joshua. 1967 [1646]. *The English Accidence*. Menston: The Scolar Press.

Priestley, Joseph. 1970 [1762]. *A Course of Lectures on the Theory of*

Language and Universal Grammar. Menston: The Scolar Press.

Ramus, Petrus (aka Pierre de la Ramée). 1969 [1562]. *Gramere*, Menston: The Scolar Press.

Ramus, Petrus (aka Pierre de la Ramée). 1971a [1585; 1559 in Latin]. *The Latine Grammar of P. Ramus*, translated into English. Amsterdam/New York: Da Capo Press.

de la Ramée, Pierre (aka Petrus Ramus). 1971b [1585; 1559 in Latin]. *Latin Grammar*, translated into English. Menston: The Scolar Press.

Ruscelli, Girolamo. 1581. *De' Commentarii della lingua italiana*. Venice.

Salviati, Lionardo. 1810 [1584]. *Degli Avvertimenti della Lingua sopra'l Decamerone*, Vol. IV. Milan: Società Tipografica de' Classici Italiani.

Sanctius (Francisco Sánchez de las Brozas). 1795 [1562]. *Minerva, seu de causis linguae Latinae commentarius*. Utrecht.

Sanctius, Franciscus. 1982 [1562]. *Minerve ou les causes de la langue latine*, transl. by Geneviève Clerico. Presses Universitaires de Lille.

Sheridan, Thomas. 1714. *An Easy Introduction of Grammar in English. For the Understanding of the Latin Tongue*. Dublin: D. Thomson.

Tooke, John Horne. 1968 [1786/98]. *The Diversions of Purley*, 2nd ed., Part I. Menston: The Scolar Press.

Ussher, George Neville. 1967 [1785]. *The Elements of English Grammar*. Menston: The Scolar Press.

Walker, William. 1970 [1655]. *A Treatise of English Particles*. Menston: The Scolar Press.

Wallis, John. 1972 [1653]. *Grammar of the English Language* (6th ed.), with translation and commentary by J.A. Kemp. London: Longman.

Ward, William. 1967 [1765]. *An Essay on Grammar*. Menston: The Scolar Press.

Wharton, Jeremiah. 1970 [1654]. *The English Grammar*. Menston: The Scolar Press.

Wilkins, John. 1668. *An Essay towards a Real Character, and a Philosophical Language*. London.

Wilson, J. 1797. *Fisher's Grammar Improved*, 2nd ed. Congleton.

Secondary sources:

Aarsleff, Hans. 1975. 'The Eighteenth Century'. In: Sebeok (ed.), 383-479.

Aarsleff, Hans. 1983 [1967]. *The Study of Language in England. 1780-1860*. London: The Athlone Press.

Aitchison, Jean. 2001 [1981]. *Language change: progress or decay?* 3rd ed. Cambridge: Cambridge University Press.

Alston, R.C. 1965. *A Bibliography of the English Language from the Invention of Printing to the Year 1800*, Vol. I: *English Grammars Written in English*. Leeds: E.J. Arnold & Son.

Alston, R.C. 1967. Vol. II: *Polyglot Dictionaries and Grammars*. Bradford.

Bach, Emmon & Robert T. Harms (eds.). 1968. *Universals in Linguistic Theory*. New York: Holt, Rinehart & Winston.

Di Benedetto, Vincenzo. 1958/59. 'Dionisio Trace e la Techne a lui attribuita'. In: *Annali della Scuola Normale Superiore di Pisa*, 2nd ser., 27:169-210, 28:87-118.

Bennett, D.C. 1975. *Spatial and Temporal Uses of English Prepositions*. London: Longman.

Blank, David L. 1982. *Ancient Philosophy and Grammar. The Syntax of Apollonius Dyscolus*. Chico, California: Scholars Press.

Bloomfield, Leonard. 1914. *An Introduction to the Study of Language*. London: G. Bell / New York: Henry Holt.

Boccaccio, Giovanni. 1989 [1985]. *Decameron*, ed. Vittore Branca. Oscar Classici. Milano: Arnoldo Mondadori.

Bortone, Pietro. 2010. *Greek Prepositions. From Antiquity to the Present*. Oxford: Oxford University Press.

Brekle, Herbert E. 1975. 'The Seventeenth Century'. In: Sebeok (ed.), 277-382.

Bursill-Hall, G.L. 1972. See Thomas of Erfurt.

Bursill-Hall, G.L. 1975. 'The Middle Ages'. In: Sebeok (ed.), 179-230.

Bursill-Hall, G.L. 1976. 'Some Notes on the Grammatical Theory of Boethius of Dacia'. In: Parret (ed.), 164-88.

Cajka, Karen. 2008. 'Eighteenth-century teacher-grammarians and the education of "proper" women'. In: Tieken-Boon van Ostade (ed.). 2008:191-221.

Chomsky, Noam. 1970. 'Remarks on Nominalization'. In: R. Jacobs and P. Rosenbaum (eds.), *Readings in English Transformational Grammar*. Waltham, Mass.: Ginn, 184-221.
Constantinescu, I. 1974. 'John Wallis' (1616-1703): A reappraisal of his contribution to the study of English'. In: *Historiographia Linguistica I*, ed. E.F.K. Koerner. Amsterdam: John Benjamins, 297-311.
Covington, Michael A. 1984. *Syntactic Theory in the High Middle Ages. Modistic models of sentence structure*. Cambridge: Cambridge University Press.
Cram, David and Jaap Maat. 2001. See Dalgarno (2001).
Dickens, Charles. 1997 [1841]. *The Old Curiosity Shop*, ed. Elizabeth M. Brennan. Oxford: Clarendon Press.
Fehling, Detlev. 1956-7. 'Varro und die grammatische Lehre von der Analogie and der Flexion'. In: *Glotta* 35.214-70 and 36.48-100.
Fillmore, Charles J. 1968. 'The case for case'. In: Bach & Harms (eds.), 1-88.
Frede, Michael. 1977. 'The Origins of Traditional Grammar'. In: *Historical and Philosophical Dimensions of Logic, Methodology and Philosophy of Science*, ed. R.E. Butts & J. Hintikka, Dordrecht: Reidel, 51-79.
Göbels, Astrid. 1999. *Die Tradition der Universalgrammatik im England des 17. und 18. Jahrhunderts*. Münster: Nodus.
Hansen, Erik and Hans Frede Nielsen. 2007 [1986]. *Irregularities in Modern English*. 2nd ed., Odense: University Press of Southern Denmark.
Herskovits, Annette. 1986. *Language and Spacial Cognition. An interdisciplinary study of the prepositions in English*. Studies in Natural Language Processing. Cambridge: Cambridge University Press.
Hodson, Jane. 2008. 'Joseph Priestley's two *Rudiments of English Grammar*: 1761 and 1768'. In: Tieken-Boon van Ostade, Ingrid (ed.). 2008:177-89.
Hopper, Paul J. and Elizabeth Closs Traugott. 2003 [1993]. *Grammaticalization*, 2nd ed. Cambridge: Cambridge University Press.
Horrocks, Geoffrey. 1997. *Greek: A History of the Language and its Speakers*. London/New York: Longman
Huddleston, Rodney. 1984. *Introduction to the Grammar of English*. Cambridge: Cambridge University Press.

Huddleston, Rodney and Geoffrey Pullum. 2002. *The Cambridge Grammar of the English Language*. Cambridge: Cambridge University Press.

Jackendoff, Ray. 1973. 'The Base Rules for Prepositional Phrases'. In: Anderson, S. and P. Kiparski (eds.), *A Festschrift for Morris Halle*. New York: Holt, Reinhart and Winston, 345-56.

Jackendoff, Ray. 1977. *X-bar Syntax: A Study of Phrase Structure*. Cambridge, Mass.: MIT Press.

Jaworska, E. 1999. 'Prepositions and Prepositional Phrases'. In: Keith Brown and Jim Miller (eds.), *Concise Encyclopedia of Grammatical Categories*. Amsterdam (etc.): Elsevier, 304-11.

Jespersen, Otto. 1894. *Progress in Language: with special reference to English*. London: Swan Sonnenschein.

Jespersen, Otto. 1965 [1914]. *A Modern English Grammar on Historical Principles*. Part II. London/Copenhagen: Allen & Unwin/Munksgaard.

Jespersen, Otto. 1924. *The Philosophy of Grammar*. London: Allen & Unwin.

Jespersen, Otto. 1933(a). *Essentials of English Grammar*. London: Allen & Unwin.

Jespersen, Otto. 1933(b). *The System of Grammar*. London: Allen & Unwin / Copenhagen: Munksgaard.

Jespersen, Otto. 1933(c). *Linguistica. Selected Papers in English, French and German*. London: Allen & Unwin / Copenhagen: Munksgaard.

Kuhn, Thomas S. 1962. *The Structure of Scientific Revolutions*. Chicago: University of Chicago Press.

Kukenheim, Louis. 1932. *Contributions à l'histoire de la grammaire italienne, espagnole et française à l'époque de la Renaissance*. Amsterdam: N.V.Noord-Hollandsche Uitgevers-Maatschappij.

Law, Vivien. 1982. *The Insular Latin Grammarians*. Woodbridge: Boydell.

Law, Vivien. 1997. *Grammar and Grammarians in the Early Middle Ages*. London/New York: Longman.

Law, Vivien. 2003. *The History of Linguistics in Europe from Plato to 1600*. Cambridge: Cambridge University Press.

Law, Vivien. & Ineke Sluiter (eds.). 1998 [1995]. *Dionysius Thrax and the* Tekhnē grammatikē. Münster: Nodus.

Lepschy, Giulio (ed.). 1994/1998. *History of Linguistics*, Vols. II-III. London/New York: Longman.

Luhtala Anneli. 2005. *Grammar and Philosophy in Late Antiquity. A study of Priscian's sources*. Studies in the History of the Language Sciences 107. Amsterdam/Philadelphia: Benjamins.

Lundskær-Nielsen, Tom. 1993. *Prepositions in Old and Middle English, NOWELE* Supplement Vol. 9. Odense: Odense University Press.

Lundskær-Nielsen, Tom. 2000. *Some Views of Prepositions in 17th and 18th Century England*, Pre-Publications of the English Department of Odense University, Odense: University of Southern Denmark.

Lyons, John. 1968. *Introduction to Theoretical Linguistics*. Cambridge: Cambridge University Press.

Maat, Jaap. 2004. *Philosophical Languages in the Seventeenth Century: Dalgarno, Wilkins, Leibniz*. Dordrecht/London: Kluwer Academic.

Maat, Jaap. 2009. 'Dalgarno and Leibniz on the Particles'. In: *Language and History*, 52.2:160-70. London: Maney Publishing.

Maierù, Alfonso. 1994. 'Medieval Linguistics: The philosophy of language'. In: Lepschy (ed.), III:272-315.

Matthews, Peter. 1994. 'Greek and Latin Linguistics'. In: Lepschy (ed.), II:1-133.

Matthews, Peter. 2007. *Syntactic Relations: A Critical Survey*. Cambridge: Cambridge University Press.

Michael, Ian. 1970. *English grammatical categories and the tradition to 1800*. Cambridge: Cambridge University Press.

Miller, Jim. 1985. *Semantics and Syntax*. Cambridge: Cambridge University Press.

Moleas, Wendy. 2004 [1989]. *The Development of the Greek Language*. London: Bristol Classical Press.

Nielsen, Hans Frede. 2005. *From Dialect to Standard English in England 1154-1776*. Odense: University Press of Southern Denmark.

Padley, G.A. 1976. *Grammatical Theory in Western Europe 1500-1700: the Latin Tradition*. Cambridge: Cambridge University Press.

Padley, G.A. 1985. *Grammatical Theory in Western Europe 1500-1700. Trends in Vernacular Grammar I*. Cambridge: Cambridge University Press.

Parret, Herman (ed.). 1976. *History of Linguistic Thought and Contemporary Linguistics*. Berlin: de Gruyter.

Percival, W. Keith. 1975. 'The Grammatical Tradition and the Rise of the Vernaculars'. In: Sebeok (ed.), 231-75.

Pinborg, Jan. 1967. *Die Entwicklung der Sprachtheorie im Mittelalter*. Münster: Aschendorff.

Pinborg, Jan. 1975. 'Classical Antiquity: Greece'. In: Sebeok (ed.), 69-126.

Poldauf, Ivan. 1948. *On the History of Some Problems of English Grammar before 1800*. Prague.

Quirk, Randolph, Sidney Greenbaum, Geoffrey Leech & Jan Svartvik. 1972. *A Grammar of Contemporary English*. London: Longman.

Quirk, Randolph, Sidney Greenbaum, Geoffrey Leech & Jan Svartvik. 1985. *A Comprehensive Grammar of the English Language*. London/New York: Longman.

Robins, Robert Henry. 1976. 'Varro and the Tactics of Analogist Grammarians'. In: *Studies in Greek, Italic, and Indo-European Linguistics: Offered to Leonard R. Palmer on the occasion of his seventieth birthday*, ed. Anna Morpurgo Davies & Wolfgang Meid. Innsbruck: Institut für Sprachwissenschaft, Universität Innsbruck, 333-6.

Robins, Robert Henry. 1997 [1967]. *A Short History of Linguistics*, 4th ed. London: Longman.

Rodríguez-Gil, María. 2008. 'Ann Fisher's *A New Grammar*, or was it Daniel Fisher's work?' In: Tieken-Boon van Ostade (ed.). 2008:149-76.

Romeo, Luigi. 1975. 'Classical Antiquity: Rome'. In: Sebeok (1975:127-77).

Salmon, Vivian. 1974. 'John Wilkins' *Essay* (1668): Critics and Continuators'. In: E.F.K. Koerner (ed.), *Historiography Linguistica* I:147-63. Amsterdam: John Benjamins.

Salmon Vivian. 1979. *The Study of Language in 17th-Century England*. Amsterdam Studies in the Theory and History of Linguistic Science 17. Amsterdam: John Benjamins.

Salus, Peter H. 1976. 'Universal Grammar 1000-1850'. In: Parret (ed.), 85-101.

Sandys, John Edwin. 1921. *History of Classical Scholarship*, 3rd ed., Vol. 2. Cambridge.

Schenkeveld, Dirk Marie. 1983. 'Linguistic Theories in the Rhetorical

Works of Dionysius of Halicarnassus'. In: *Glotta* 61:67-94.

Schibsbye, Knud. 1974. *Origin and Development of the English Language II*. Copenhagen: Nordisk Sprog- og Kulturforlag.

Sebeok, Thomas A. (ed.). 1975. *Historiography of Linguistics. Current Trends in Linguistics*, 13. The Hague/Paris: Mouton.

Shakespeare, William. 1988 [1623]. *The Complete Works* (Compact Edition), eds. Stanley Wells and Gary Taylor, Oxford: Clarendon Press.

Simone, Raffaele. 1998. 'The Early Modern Period'. In: Lepschy (ed.), III:149-236.

Subbiondo, Joseph L. (ed). 1992(a). *John Wilkins and 17th-Century British Linguistics*. Amsterdam Studies in the Theory and History of Linguistic Science 67. Amsterdam: John Benjamins.

Subbiondo, Joseph L. 1992(b). 'John Wallis' *Grammatica Linguae Anglicanae* (1653): The New Science and English Grammar'. In: Anders Ahlqvist (ed.), *Diversions of Galway: Papers on the History of Linguistics from the International Conference on the History of the Language Sciences*, 1-6 September 1990. Amsterdam Studies in the Theory and History of Linguistic Science 68:183-90. Amsterdam: John Benjamins.

Tavoni, Mirko. 1998. 'Renaissance Linguistics; Western Europe'. In: Lepschy (ed.), III:1-108.

Taylor. Daniel J. (ed.). 1987a. *The History of Linguistics in the Classical Period*. Studies in the History of Language Sciences 46. Amsterdam/Philadelphia: Benjamins.

Taylor. Daniel J. 1987b. 'Rethinking the History of Language Science in Classical Antiquity'. In: Taylor (1987a:1-16).

Tieken-Boon van Ostade, Ingrid (ed.). 1996. *Two Hundred Years of Lindley Murray*. Münster: Nodus.

Tieken-Boon van Ostade, Ingrid (ed.). 2008. *Grammars, Grammarians and Grammar-Writing in Eighteenth-Century England*. Berlin/New York: Mouton de Gruyter.

Tieken-Boon van Ostade, Ingrid. 2011. *The Bishop's Grammar. Robert Lowth and the rise of prescriptivism in England*. Oxford: Oxford University Press.

Vincent, Nigel. 1980. 'Iconic and symbolic aspects of syntax: Prospects for reconstruction'. In P. Ramat (ed.), *Linguistic Reconstruc-*

tion and Indo-European Syntax, *Current Issues in Linguistic Theory* 19, 47-68. Amsterdam.

Vineis, Edoardo. 1994. 'Medieval Linguistics: Linguistics and grammar'. In: Lepschy (ed.), III:134-272.

Vorlat, Emma. 1959. 'The Sources of Lindley Murray's "The English Grammar"'. In: *Leuvense Bijdragen* 48:108-25.

Vorlat, Emma. 1975. *The Development of English Grammatical Theory 1586-1737, with special reference to the theory of parts of speech*. Leuven: Leuven University Press.

Wouters, Alfons. 1979. *The Grammatical Papyri from Graeco-Roman Egypt. Contributions to the Study of the 'Ars Grammatica' in Antiquity*, Verhandelingen van de Koninklijke Academie voor Wetenschappen, Letterenen Schone Kunsten van België, Klasse der Letteren 41, no. 92. Brussels.

Yañez-Bouza, Nuria. 2008. 'Preposition stranding in the eighteenth century: *Something to talk about*'. In: Tieken-Boon van Ostade (ed.). 2008:251-77.

Zwicky, Arnold. 1985. 'Heads'. *Journal of Linguistics* 21:1-29.

Index of Names

Aarsleff, H., 98, 252, 286
Abelard, P., 64
Addison, J., 238
Aelfric of Eynsham, 63, 100, 268
Aickin, J., 155-7, 270
Aitchison, J., 285
Albertus Magnus, 65-6
Alcuin of York, 100
Alexander the Great, 25, 28
Alston, R.C., 97, 109, 113, 145, 162, 182, 195, 204, 209, 215, 219, 282, 284-6
Anne (Queen), 164, 284, 287
Anthony (Earl of Shaftesbury), 141
Antony, M., 37
Apollonius Dyscolus, 39-47, 50, 52, 54, 267, 281
Aristarchus, 29, 31, 33, 43-4, 283
Aristotle, 27-8, 30-31, 34-5, 54, 63, 65-6, 68-9, 71, 74, 88-9, 159, 174, 186, 191, 213, 216, 246, 267, 279-80, 285
Arnauld, A, 164, 166, 200, 222
Ash, J., 219-21, 270, 285
Averroës, 69, 83-4

Bacon, F., 134, 283
Bacon, R., 66, 69, 100, 280
Bayly, A., 204-8, 273, 287
Beadon, R., 246
Beck, C., 120
Bede (The Venerable), 100
Bembo, P., 90, 282
Bennett, D.C., 139, 283
Bentley, R., 217
Blank, D.L., 35

Bloomfield, L., 279
Boccaccio, G., 92, 282
Boethius, (5th-6th C.), 63, 68-9, 280
Boethius of Dacia, 67-76, 281
Bornstein, D., 103
Bortone, P., 285
Brekle, H.E., 98
Brightland, J., 127, 163-71, 174, 177, 184, 200-201, 272, 274, 284
Buchanan, J., 162-4, 196, 212-14, 270
Bullokar, W., 97, 101, 103-5, 107, 268, 270, 277, 282
Bursill-Hall, G.L., 66, 280-81
Butler, C., 111-13, 128, 271, 273, 283
Butler, H.E., 31

Caesar, G.J., 37, 92
Cajka, K., 276
Campanella, T., 134, 283
Caramuel, J., 134, 283
Castelvetro, L., 91-2
Charisius, 37
Charlotte (Queen), 212
Chaucer, G., 106, 155
Chrysippus, 32
Cicero, M.T., 37, 60, 146, 156
Clare, W., 152-6, 159-60, 171, 270, 275, 284
Clarke, J., 202, 285
Colet, J. (see also Lily), 93, 103
Collyer, J., 163, 182-5, 271, 274
Constantinescu, I., 283
Cooper, C., 99, 127, 145-7, 149, 155, 272, 274, 277, 284
Covington, M.A., 68, 280-81
Cram, D., 119

303

Dalgarno, G., 100, 120, 130-34, 269, 271, 274-5, 283
Dalton, J., 97, 101, 251, 261-5, 268, 271, 282, 287
Dante Alighieri, 92
Demosthenes, 29
Di Benedetto, 32
Dickens, C., 255
Dilworth, T., 185, 270
Diogenes of Babylon, 32
Diogenes Laertius, 29, 32
Diomedes, 37, 50-51, 126
Dionysius of Halicarnassus, 29-31
Dionysius Thrax, 29, 32-4, 40, 279
Dobson, E.J., 145
Dolce, L., 90-91
Domitius Afer, 31
Donatus Aelius, 37, 48-57, 59, 61-2, 67, 74, 76, 93-4, 153, 267, 280-81
Douglas, J., 108
Dryden, J., 238
Duncan, D., 179-82, 270, 278
Duns Scotus, J., 281, 283
Dyche, T., 279, 285

Edward VI (King of England), 93
Edwards, M.C. (Mrs), 287
Elphinston, J., 221-8, 271, 276, 278
Erasmus of Rotterdam, 93
Erik VI Menved (King of Denmark), 281
Estienne, R., 92, 268
Eves (Mrs), 287

Fehling, D., 35
Fell, J., 238-45, 259, 270, 276-7, 287
Fenn, E. (aka Mrs Lovechild), 287
Fenning, D., 235-8, 240, 270, 286
Fillmore, C.J., 11, 285
First Grammarian, 63
Fisher, A., 143, 163, 195-9, 201, 209, 252-5, 259, 272-3, 276, 284-5
Fisher, D., 195-6

Frede, M., 35
Fridugisus of Tours, 281

Gardiner, J., 287
George (III, King), 212
George (IV, King), 206
George (Prince of Denmark and Norway), 284
Giambullari, P., 90
Gibbon, E. (father), 186
Gibbon, E. (son), 186, 188, 260
Gildon, C., 127, 163-71, 174, 177, 184, 200-201, 272, 274, 284
Gill, A., 107-9, 145, 271, 273, 277, 282
Göbels, A., 275, 283
Godfrey of Fontaine, 70, 281
Gough, J(ames), 200-202, 272-3
Gough, J(ohn), 200-202, 272-3
Greaves, P., 101, 106-7, 113-14, 127, 271, 274, 282
Greenbaum, S., 15-18, 279
Greenwood, J., 127, 170-75, 177, 184-5, 200, 249, 270, 277, 284
Guise (Lady, of Highnam Court), 243

Hansen, E.W., 113
Harris, J., 10, 162, 190-95, 209, 216-17, 228, 231, 246, 248, 251, 258, 273-6, 278, 286
Helias, P., 64-5
Herskovits, A., 285-6
Hewes, J., 109-11, 270, 277
Hickes, G., 171, 284
Hodson, J., 285
Homer, 29, 51
Hopper, P.J., 285
Horace, 60, 218, 259
Horne Tooke (see Tooke)
Horrocks, G., 279
Householder, F., 39-47, 280
Howard, C., 147
Huddleston, R.D., 18-22, 279, 286

Jackendoff, R., 11-12
James II (King), 284
Jaworska, E., 12
Jespersen, O., 12-15, 19, 100, 198, 268, 279
Johannes Aurifaber, 84
Johannes of Dacia, 70
John of Jandun, 84
Johnson, R., 143, 161-4, 168, 183, 187, 196, 213, 273
Johnson, S. (Dr), 162, 202-4, 238, 249, 256, 259, 270, 285
Jones, H., 178-9, 272-3, 276, 284, 287
Jonson, B., 113-16, 128, 164, 204, 270, 285
Joyce, J., 286

Keil, H., 51, 54-6
Kemp, A., 33, 279
Kilwardby, R., 65, 280
Kirkby, J., 186-8, 259-60, 273, 284, 287
Kuhn, T., 280
Kukenheim, L., 89, 92, 282

Lancelot, C., 164, 166, 200, 222
Lane, A., 98, 157-61, 164, 166, 169-71, 182, 201, 272-3, 275, 277, 284
Law, V., 26, 28, 37, 48, 53, 59, 71, 97, 101, 119, 279-82
Leech, G., 15-18, 279
Lewis, M., 141-5, 270, 284
Lily, W., 65, 93-5, 103, 105, 107, 109-10, 126, 128, 142-4, 161-4, 177-8, 215, 268-9, 282, 284
Locke, J., 10, 150-52, 171, 173, 185, 212, 222, 262, 273, 286-7
Lodowyck, F., 119-22, 130, 134, 271, 274-5
Lovechild (Mrs), see Fenn, E.
Lowth, R., 203, 209, 214-21, 238, 240, 242-3, 253-7, 259-60, 270, 276, 285, 287

Luhtala, A., 28, 36
Lundskær-Nielsen, T., 22, 285
Lye, T., 139-41, 270, 276

Maat, J., 119, 283
McDermott, C.S., 281
Maierù, A., 68, 280-81
Maittaire, M., 173-7, 270, 277
Martin, B., 188-90, 259, 273, 284-5
Martin of Dacia, 69, 281
Matthews, P.H., 12, 27, 32, 279
Mercy, B., 287
Michael, I., 27, 53, 62, 64-6, 69, 75, 88, 98-9, 106, 108-9, 112, 141, 146, 158, 162-3, 170, 174, 186, 199, 206, 221, 269-76, 280, 282-7
Michel of Marbais, 70, 75
Miege, G., 147-50, 154, 158, 270, 277
Miller, J., 285-6
Milton, J., 107, 217, 227
Moleas, W., 279
Molinier, G., 63
More, T., 93
Mulcaster, R., 107
Murray, L., 18, 219, 255-61, 263-5, 270, 274-6, 286-7

Newbury, J., 163
Nichols, J., 221, 285
Nielsen, H.F., 112-13

Ovid, 60
Oxford (Earl of), 215

Padley, G., 88, 97, 283
Palaemon, 31
Pardon, 279, 285
Percival, W.K., 98
Petrarch, F., 92
Pinborg, J., 65, 74, 84, 280-81
Plato, 26-7, 35, 40, 44-5, 78, 89, 213, 247, 267, 279
Poldauf, I., 97

Poole, J., 116-19, 127, 270, 276-7
Pope, A., 227, 238
Priestley, J., 208-11, 256-7, 271, 275-8
Priscian, 37, 47, 50-57, 59, 61, 64, 67-70, 76, 82, 88, 94-5, 247, 267, 281
Ptolemy, C. (Ptolemaic), 61
Pullum, G.K., 18-22, 279, 286

Quintilian, M.F., 29-31, 37, 54, 174
Quirk *et al.*, 15-18, 279

Ramus, P. (aka Pierre de la Ramée), 65, 88-9, 101, 106-7, 113-14, 268, 281
Robins, R.H., 27-8, 34-6, 88, 97, 119, 280-81, 283, 286
Rodríguez-Gil, M., 285
Romulus Augustulus, 59
Roos, H., 281
Ruscelli, G., 91

Sacerdos, 37
Salviati, L., 92
Salus, P.H., 280, 283
Sanctius, F., 65, 89, 108, 171, 268, 280
Sandys, J.E., 281
Scaliger, J.C., 134, 283
Schenkeveld, D.M., 279
Schibsbye, K., 112
Sebeok, T.A., 98
Shakespeare, W., 113, 238, 283, 286
Sharp, R., 238
Sheridan, T., 177-8, 253, 270, 276
Siger de Courtrai, 75, 82, 280
Simon of Dacia, 70
Slack, A. (see Fisher, A.)
Slack, T., 195
Sluiter, I., 279
Smaragdus, 61-2, 280
Socrates, 26, 78-9, 82
Sørensen, K., 287
Steele, R., 164
Strozzi, E., 90, 282
Subbiondo, J.L., 283

Svartvik, J., 15-18, 279
Swift, J., 208, 215, 238

Taylor, D.J., 35-6, 280
Taylor (Mrs), 287
Tempier, É., 69
Terence, 48
Theodectes, 30-31, 279
Thomas of Erfurt, 67-8, 74-84, 125, 280-81, 283
Thurot, C., 280
Tieken-Boon van Ostade, I., 98, 209, 276, 284-7
Tooke, J.H., 10, 100, 134, 191, 193-4, 245-52, 261-5, 273-5, 286
Tooke, W., 286
Traugott, E.C., 285
Tryphon, 40, 44

Ussher, G.N., 243-5, 252, 259, 270, 275

Varro, M.T., 35-9, 267
Vergil, 48, 51, 56
Vincent, N., 286
Vorlat, E., 88, 97, 287
Vossius, G., 134, 283

Walker, W., 128-30, 182, 253, 273
Wallis, J., 10, 109, 122-7, 134, 136, 145, 155, 164-5, 170-71, 200, 203-4, 271, 273, 275-7, 283-4, 287
Ward, W., 10, 162, 228-35, 247, 270, 276-8, 286
Webster, N., 215
Wharton, J., 127-8, 155, 259, 270, 276
Wilkins, J., 10, 120, 131, 134-9, 145, 171, 209, 247, 269, 272, 274-7, 283, 287
William (Duke of Gloucester), 152, 159, 284

William III (King), 284
William of Conches, 64
William of Ockham, 83-4
Wilson, J., 177, 199, 252-5, 270, 287
Wouters, A., 280

Yañez-Bouza, N., 287
Young, E., 227, 285-6

Zwicky, A., 12